NANCY BEIMAN

PREPARE TO BOARD!

THIRD EDITION

CREATING STORY AND CHARACTERS
FOR ANIMATED FEATURES AND SHORTS

CRC Press
Taylor & Francis Group
Boca Raton London New York

CRC Press is an imprint of the
Taylor & Francis Group, an **informa** business
A FOCAL PRESS BOOK

CRC Press
Taylor & Francis Group
6000 Broken Sound Parkway NW, Suite 300
Boca Raton, FL 33487-2742

© 2017 by Taylor & Francis Group, LLC
CRC Press is an imprint of Taylor & Francis Group, an Informa business

No claim to original U.S. Government works

Printed and bound in India by Replika Press Pvt. Ltd.

Printed on acid-free paper

International Standard Book Number-13: 978-1-138-07090-5 (hardback)
International Standard Book Number-13: 978-1-4987-9700-9 (paperback)

Library of Congress Cataloging-in-Publication Data

Names: Beiman, Nancy, author.
Title: Prepare to board! : creating story and characters for animated films /
Nancy Beiman.
Description: 3rd edition. | Boca Raton : CRC Press, 2017. | Includes index.
Identifiers: LCCN 2016035596 | ISBN 9781498797009 (pbk. : alk. paper)
Subjects: LCSH: Animated films--Authorship. | Animation (Cinematography) |
Cartoon characters.
Classification: LCC NC1765 .B38 2017 | DDC 791.43/34--dc23
LC record available at https://lccn.loc.gov/2016035596

Visit the Taylor & Francis Web site at
http://www.taylorandfrancis.com

and the CRC Press Web site at
http://www.crcpress.com

Dedication

This book is dedicated to A. Kendall (Ken) O'Connor—a brilliant layout man, designer, draftsman, story man, art director, and teacher who was able to explain everything from how a caterpillar's muscles move to why a 1926 trash can silhouette differs from that of a modern one. In story, these things matter! Ken was also learning about computer graphics when he was in his eighties. He was always seeking better ways to tell a story. So this is once again for you, Ken. "Circumstances alter cases!"

Contents

Section II Technique

Section III   Presentation

Acknowledgments

Jack Hannah, T. Hee, Ken O'Connor, Bill Moore, and Elmer Plummer taught at the California Institute of the Arts' Character Animation Program so that their knowledge of animation, learned from the ground up during its Golden Age, would not die with them. My notes from their classes, written between 1975 and 1979, are the backbone of this book.

A new generation of students from the Rochester Institute of Technology and the Sheridan Institute of Technology and Advanced Learning generously permitted me to print some of their class exercises and senior project materials. I thank my former RIT animation students Brittney Lee, Nathaniel Hubbell, William Robinson, Jim Downer, Sarah Kropiewnicki, Kimberly Miner, Jeremy Galante, Rui Jin, David Suroviec, Joseph Daniels, Jedidiah Mitchell, and Alycia Yee from the RIT school of Photography, for their outstanding work.

Sheridan students Bram Cayne, Yacheng Guo, Omar El-Hindi, Kyu-Bum Lee, Mincheul Park, Colin Searle, Maya Shavzin, Max Swiecki, and Melody Wang generously allowed me to use beautiful artwork from their second and fourth year projects. Professor Rafael Goldchain of the Photography Department expertly restored the still from YOUR FEET'S TOO BIG.

I owe especial thanks to Floyd Norman, Nina Paley, John Van Vliet, David Celsi, Dean Yeagle, Nina L. Haley, J. Adam Fox, Hans Bacher, John McCartney, Brian P. McEntee, and Mark Newgarden for permission to use some of their illustration work so that this did not become a one-woman show; to Chris Bailey for explaining "hybrid animation" to me in an online interview, to Gerhard Hahn of Hahnfilm AG for permission to use television storyboards from MIA AND ME, and to Elliot Cowan for drawing and describing commercial storyboards in a most entertaining fashion. Kevin Richardson and Michael Cachuela provided an invaluable guide to working on group storyboards.

I thank Margaret Adamic of Walt Disney Publishing Worldwide for permission to reprint artwork from Disney Enterprises, Inc., and Howard Green, vice president, Studio Communications, Buena Vista Pictures Marketing, for his valuable assistance.

Thanks to David Fulp for his photo of T. Hee posing in front of Ralph Eggleston's caricature portrait, to John Van Vliet for the T. Hee "ranch" portrait, and to Cyndy Bohanovsky for the Ken Anderson photo. I also thank Patricia Bernard for permission to use my illustrations from her books *Basil Bigboots the Pirate* and *Duffy and the Invisible Crocodile,* and Daniel Schechter and Globalvision Inc. for an illustration I drew for the documentary film IN DEBT WE TRUST.

Art director/author Brian P. McEntee provided terms for the Glossary and, along with Sheridan College instructor Mark Mayerson, proofread the entire manuscript for the first edition and suggested improvements to the text and illustrations. Greg Ford and Ronnie Scheib read early drafts of the book and fact-checked my Looney Tunes history. Greg also provided expert technical reviews for the new material in the second edition. My parents, Melvyn and Frances Beiman, provided "lay perspective" on the book's readability for the first and second editions. Yvette Kaplan, Tom Sito, and Tony White offered excellent suggestions for the book's format and contents at the beginning of the project, and Tony also had valuable suggestions for the third edition. Jud Hurd published my interviews with animators in *CARTOONIST PROfiles* magazine for 13 years and encouraged me to write interviews and articles on animation, some of which are excerpted in this book. I also thank my late friends and mentors Shamus Culhane, Selby Daley Kelly, T. Hee, Mary Alice O'Connor, Ken O'Connor, Frank Thomas, Ollie Johnston, and Joe Grant for their friendship and advice over the years. I extend my heartfelt thanks to the late Roy E. Disney for his love and support for the art and artists of animation.

My final thank-you is to Gizmo the cat (2001–2013), who inspired illustrations for all three editions of this book. She will always be the cover girl.

—**Nancy Beiman**
Burlington, Ontario
September 20, 2016

Author

Nancy Beiman has worked as a supervising animator, director, character designer, and storyboard artist for animation studios in the United States, England, France, Australia, and Germany including Walt Disney Feature and Television Animation, Amblin' (*now DreamWorks*), Warner Brothers Animation, Gerhard Hahn Filmproduktion, Bill Melendez Productions, and many others. She has experience in feature film, television specials, commercials, and new media. Nancy produced two independent films, YOUR FEETS TOO BIG and THE OTHER EDEN, and is working on a third, OLD TRICKS. She interviewed animation artists and wrote a column for CARTOONIST PROfiles magazine for 12 years and has conducted masterclasses in story and animation in Taiwan, Denver, and via worldwide podcasts. She earned a BFA from the CHARACTER ANIMATION PROGRAM at the California Institute of the Arts, Valencia, California and was the only female student in the first graduating class. Nancy received her MFA in design from the Rochester Institute of Technology, Rochester, New York. She has taught second year storyboard and advised on fourth year capstone projects in the BA Animation program at Sheridan College, Oakville, Canada, since 2008.

Nancy's first book, PREPARE TO BOARD! CREATING STORY AND CHARACTERS FOR ANIMATED FEATURES AND SHORTS, is the standard text on feature and short film animation storyboarding. Her second book, ANIMATED PERFORMANCE, is the only book on acting for animation written by a professional animator.

Introduction to the Third Edition

"Just be sure you don't use the words 'old-fashioned!'"

—**Roy Disney in email to author, 2005**

This book describes visual storytelling and design methods developed during the "Golden Age of Animation" and still in use today, as Roy Disney pointed out to me. But storyboard technology has changed dramatically in the ten years since the first edition of this book was published. The digital revolution makes modern television boards closely resemble those drawn for feature films. The third edition of PREPARE TO BOARD! really should have a new subheading: Creating Story and Characters for Animated FILMS. There are extensive revisions and additions to many chapters, with 51 new illustrations. New subjects, such as Action storyboards and a chapter on group projects, have been added.

No specific hardware or software is recommended in this book because technologies will change. Your imagination is the one essential tool. There is no software that will think up good situations or draw good storyboards for you. Some things, such as rough concept sketches, are still easier to produce on paper.

Some people say that story is the *only* thing that matters in animated film. I agree. Strong characters can make a weak story tolerable and a good story better, but good animation and good design never saved a bad story. Story provides motivation for the animated action. Otherwise you're just moving things around onscreen.

Basic design principles remain constant. A well-drawn character will translate into a well-designed puppet or digitally generated character. The principles described in this book's character design sections are intended for use in all media.

Although scripts are important on longer animated films, they are not necessarily written at the start of the production. Animated films may be created without any script at all. This book will concentrate on visual scriptwriting. There is a danger of concentrating solely on technique—the "how"—of storyboard (how to draw the characters and backgrounds, how to use a program) and consider story and context—the "why"—almost an afterthought. This is putting the cart before the horse.

The story drives the film. Technique is secondary.

Good stories and appealing characters will transcend their technology. Professional animators and hardcore fans will notice minor inconsistencies in a film. If the story is good, and the characters appealing, the audience will overlook these same inconsistencies. Many films are greater than the sum of their parts.

Animated characters are often able to defy the laws of gravity and physics, but animated stories won't work if they lack believability. The animated film creates its own reality. We must immediately comprehend the power of the poisoned apple, or the character weakness of a lion cub or a Beast. Boredom and frustration result if a character's properties change mid-picture solely to accommodate weak storytelling.

It is not enough to rely on the soundtrack to carry the story. Ideally, dialogue in an animated film complements the visuals and not vice versa. The very best character animation can still tell the story with the soundtrack turned off.

Good writing leaves a lot to the reader's imagination. Each reader creates their individual pictures of the settings and the characters' appearances based on information provided by the author. Author and reader collaborate to create the story. An animated film distributes a few artists' fantasies to large masses of people. We should try to make them good ones.

A good character can be developed from a story. A good character can *inspire* the story. Story is the most important thing in animation, but creating appealing characters to tell it—*animated* characters—is the *other* most important thing. Which element should the animated story develop first?

Which comes first?

Introduction to the Third Edition

Character and story reinforce one another and are created concurrently during preproduction. They will be discussed in all three parts of this book because developing one in the absence of the other is like making an omelet without eggs.

Character and story develop simultaneously!

Basic storytelling principles have not changed for thousands of years, and film language is largely the same as it has been for 100 years, but the methods of transmission have grown. New media make it possible for the storyteller to visually communicate with audiences that are distant in space and time, or speak to a global audience simultaneously. Animation is a more powerful medium today than ever before because it uses graphic and emotional communication to overcome language barriers.

Development—storyboard, character, and production design—is a marvelous creative process in which the journey is as important as the destination. This book was designed, and revised, to help you on your journey. Animation is magic. Don't settle for reality.

Thank you, and I hope that you enjoy the third edition.

—**Nancy Beiman**
Burlington, Ontario
September 20, 2016

SECTION I
Getting Started

1

First Catch Your Rabbit: Creating Concepts and Characters

There is a famous old cookbook recipe for stewed rabbit. The first sentence gets right to the point. It reads, "First, catch your rabbit."

How do you "catch the rabbit" original characters and stories? Where do ideas for original stories and characters come from?

Animation is not reality, and it is at its best when it portrays things that could *possibly* happen. Stories can be based on actual occurrences. The seed of reality provides the viewer with a point of identification and then germinates into a story that should be suitable for the medium.

Logging In: Finding an Idea

The basic idea for any film is called a *log line*. The term derives from a "ship's log" where the captain wrote the events of the day in very short, terse sentences. (*"Hit an iceberg. Didn't end well."*)

A *log line* distills the entire story into one or two sentences that describe what the film is about. It provides the foundation and framework for the film. Character relationships and events may change during the feature film's storyboard stage. The log line ensures that the main story idea does not get lost in the process.

Here are some hypothetical log lines from actual animated features:

- Surface appearance can be deceptive. People come in layers, like onions.—SHREK
- Magic comes from personal initiative and the working of conscience.—PINOCCHIO
- A callow youth learns to accept his responsibilities.—THE LION KING
- There is some good in every character.—LILO & STITCH

There is no time in a short film to explain "back story" for complicated plot points or characters. You are using a broader brush stroke than you use in a feature since you have less time. There are many ways to convey "what happened before" the film began.

In Borge Ring's ANNA AND BELLA, the pictures in a photograph album develop the changing relationship between two sisters. Here is the actual log line from the film:

- *One sister wants the other sister dead.*

ANNA AND BELLA can be viewed at https://www.youtube.com/watch?v=vuMm60nep6c

An animated film's story may grow from a grain of truth.

Inspiration for a story can be found in "human interest" stories online or actual news items. I developed my story for OLD TRICKS from a news article stating that more crimes were being committed by "elderly criminals." A quick search through several online news sites yielded the following unusual stories that could become animation "log lines":

- Robot Runs on Flies and Sewage
- Zombie Worms Found off Sweden
- Boozy Bear Plunders Camper's Beer

These actual news items already sound like log lines for animated cartoons. All of them create a picture in the mind, which the animator can translate into rough sketches for possible character designs (Figure 1.1).

Figure 1.1

Sketches based on online news reports from the BBC, the Australian Broadcasting Corporation, and Reuters News Service.

1. First Catch Your Rabbit: Creating Concepts and Characters

These headlines leave the reader wanting to know what happened next or empathizing with a character's situation. What kind of self-esteem does a fly-eating robot have? Sketch rough drawings of the characters interacting with other characters. Would these be robots or humans? Does the robot work alone? If so, then use props and location to create a conflict. Is this a fantasy film, or does it take place in the here and now? How could this story develop? Sketch some possible results, or endings, from one interaction. When you decide where the fly eating robot story takes place and who it works with, the next step is to create a *story line*—expanding the idea, usually in a sentence or two, to indicate how the story develops and especially how it ends. Does the fly eating robot find a purpose in life? Does it wind up in a better, or a worse, situation at the end of the story?

Walking the Story Line

Old-time animation story men referred to a story as the "clothesline" on which they would "hang" story and character development. The main story line was and is the backbone of the feature picture. Here is one example: *The Queen is jealous of Snow White. She wants the girl killed and eventually succeeds in doing this, but love's first kiss breaks the spell.* Snow White is the victim of a murder plot. (Note how the story was "driven" by the action of the villain!) This story line was then fleshed out with comic scenes that created relationships between the Princess, the Dwarfs, and the animals, and also developed the audience's sympathy for Snow White. You are always reminded that the girl is in danger, even in the comic scenes.

Audiences already knew the end of Snow White's story, yet they cried when she was killed. This is because the story created a personality that was not just a figure in a fairy story. The feature film is long enough to develop Show White's personality and show us her hopes and dreams for a future that is cruelly taken from her.

A short film usually develops one basic idea for its story line, and the character relationships must be well established at the start. In ANNA AND BELLA, the photograph album is literally a "framing" device for the story. Two old sisters view the pictures beginning when they are young girls. The photographs are widely separated in time. Only the most important events in their lives are animated in the film.

Whether it's for a feature or a short, the story line should be conveyed in one or two brief sentences, like a newspaper headline. If you are unable to do this, the idea needs work.

Here are some stories from existing animated films retold as newspaper-headline-style "story lines." Can you identify the films?

- Flying Elephant Rescues Mother from Jail, Saves Circus
- Missing Dalmatian Puppies, Stolen by Fur Coat Ring, Are Rescued by Parents
- Heroic Ogre Saves Princess from Dragon, Removes Tyrannical King

Exercise: Write three more "headlines" based on existing animated films. Does each headline convey a visual image of the story?

The *story line* (a brief description of the story and conflict) is the foundation of the story edifice. Walt Disney said that an animated film's story was constructed "like building a building with building blocks. Our building blocks would be 'personalities'" (Ken Anderson interviewed by Nancy Beiman, 1979.)

Story Outline and Character Explorations

The next step in story creation is to write an *outline*. This is the story, told in a few paragraphs, with character motivations and conflicts, but without dialogue or detailed descriptions of acting and settings.

This is also when you should start developing your ideas for characters. The story will influence the character's personality and appearance, and the character's personality will influence the story development. Which comes first, the chicken or the egg, character or story? Both elements are equally important and both develop simultaneously.

Characters are easier to design when placed within a story context. Figure 1.2 shows designs for (a) an ordinary dog and (b) the dog from this old nursery rhyme:

Old Mother Hubbard went to the cupboard, to get her poor dog a bone.
But when she got there, the cupboard was bare, and so the poor dog had none.

(a)   (b)

Figure 1.2

The dog in (a) is "just a mutt" without any story context. The second dog (b) shows a particular personality, age, and attitude since it is developed from a story outline (the nursery rhyme OLD MOTHER HUBBARD).

OLD MOTHER HUBBARD is a story outline. Nearly all nursery rhymes and fairy tales merely state the facts of the story without describing character personalities (and often do not offer character motivation). These old stories can become fresh again with new interpretations that develop the character relationships and situation.

The second dog is a stronger character than the first one since there is more visual information to establish the animal's personality and appearance. The words of the nursery rhyme lead to a visual interpretation where the dog, rather than Mother Hubbard, is portrayed as old and "poor."

Shopping for Story: Creating Outlines

An original story outline can be created by chance or by deliberation, or you can write a shopping list for the ingredients!

Free association can get the creative juices flowing. Use words that create visual images. Draw four columns on a sheet of lined paper and begin. It helps

1. First Catch Your Rabbit: Creating Concepts and Characters

to do this exercise with another person since you can "bounce" ideas off one another and build on each other's word associations.

The first column is a list of *characters*. Can they be animal, vegetable, or mineral? Are they organic or inorganic? You are not restricted by what exists in the real world. Put that animation magic to work. Anyone or anything is a possible animated character. Describe them in one or two words. Do not write lengthy biographies or back stories.

Should they be human or animal? Are they four-legged or two-legged? Could a character be a combination of organic and inorganic objects? Imaginary creatures are the hardest ones to do, and so if you wish to design one, make separate lists of words that describe the creature's abilities and appearance. (1) Can it fly and swim? Does it tap dance and sing opera? (2) Does it have feathers, fur, scales, or all of the above? Write down as many variations as you can think of. At this point, everything is possible. The words "no" and "can't" are not in your vocabulary.

List all of your ideas no matter how odd they may seem. Do not throw anything out at this stage. Build on earlier suggestions by free association. Be creative and have fun. But characters do not work well in isolation. They must be put into some sort of context.

Where and When Does This Story Take Place?

Write a list of possible *locations* in Column Two. These can be fanciful and vary greatly in scale. One major feature film, OSMOSIS JONES, was staged entirely on the cellular level inside a human body.

Can you place your characters inside a refrigerator, in France, on a dog's back, inside a sock drawer, under the bed, on the moon, or under the ocean? See if one location leads you to think of another, or of characters that might populate it.

The time period of your film may influence your story. A student showed me beat boards where the goddess of love, Aphrodite, is defended by an anonymous swordsman. I explained that Aphrodite, or Venus, was married to Hephaestus (or Vulcan) the god of war, who would use a hammer instead of a sword. This led to a major change in the story—and a better ending. Be sure to research "period" settings. Anachronisms (materials that postdate the time of the film) are funny if used for comic purposes. They will be distracting in a dramatic context.

Make a list of *situations and occupations* in the third column. Birthdays, weddings, funerals, jail breaks, alien abductions, trips to the dentist, preparation of a meal, a dance, a wedding, thieves, shepherds, and insurance salesmen are all fair game.

Next, list possible *conflicts and relationships* in the fourth column. What weaknesses do these characters have? Do their parents approve of what they are doing? Is one character in danger? Is it searching for something? Now, mix and match words from the character, location, situation, and conflict lists to form short sentences. See which combinations suggest images or stories. You may be inspired by a single word or may use material from all four lists. As you do this, a story may start to build itself. Draw rough sketches and *thumbnails* to illustrate ideas suggested by the word combinations. The following story outline was assembled from the four sample lists:

Characters: Vegetables (tomatoes, onions, corn, and melon).
Location: The refrigerator.
Time: Present day.
Situation: A group of vegetable criminals are in the refrigerator on Death
   Row. The cook is their executioner.

Conflict: They are on the menu and plan a daring breakout from prison.

Resolution: They escape from the fridge and get out of the house … and fall into a pig pen. The *"twist,"* or unexpected, ending develops out of the situation but provides a surprise to the audience. This is a good thing to aim for in story; predictable endings should be avoided. What other variations could be worked on this story? Try a few of your own (Figure 1.3).

Figure 1.3

Some rotten, rotten vegetables.

Getting the Treatment and Beginning Character Development

A *treatment*, or a short story version of the film story that may include dialogue but will not include scene cuts and other script formatting, may also be written by the storyboard artist. Treatments will vary in length. Feature treatments are generally a short-story style description of the acts, sequences, action, and dialogue that might be 5–10 pages long. Television treatments are much more elaborate; they break down the action and dialogue in individual scenes. I recommend Jeffrey Scott's excellent book HOW TO WRITE FOR ANIMATION to anyone interested in writing animated film scripts. Some chapters and other materials can be viewed on his blog at http://www.jeffreyscott.tv/.

Draw thumbnails of characters and situations on a lined pad while working out the story. The lines on the pad will help you maintain character volumes and create a rough size guide. Do not use an eraser and do not throw away any of the drawings. Work rough and don't worry about design details at this time. Final character design is created at a later stage. Don't just use one character

1. First Catch Your Rabbit: Creating Concepts and Characters

or explore one story avenue; we're in *blue sky* territory so anything goes, as we see in Figure 1.4. It is okay to use color when thumbnailing rough character designs, but keep the story sketches in black and white for now. You can work on self-stick notes while developing your story. This makes it easier for you to move them around and replace them.

Figure 1.4

The vegetable world in the refrigerator might have characters living on the "upper shelf" or in jail in the "vegetable keeper." At this stage of the project, no idea is too odd or weird. Lined paper helps set the proportions.

Here is a basic story rule: *Normal characters are not interesting in normal situations.* Something has to happen to get them out of their routine, in order to hold our interest and create a story.

"Normal" characters can become very interesting when placed in *unfamiliar contexts.* This time we will work with the word "wedding" from the "situation" list. What if the groom and bride are a shepherd and shepherdess? Perhaps the wedding guests could be sheep and sheepdogs as shown in Figure 1.5.

Figure 1.5

What is right with this picture? The shepherds are not as interesting as the animals. The most interesting characters should tell your stories.

A Story Should Always be Told by the Most Interesting Characters

The animals are more interesting than the shepherds in this story since they appear outside their usual context. What if the animals became the main characters? That's an improvement since humanized animal characters play to the strong points of the animation medium. Could the sheep get married instead of the shepherds? What sort of characters might interact with them? Could the wedding guests be shepherds, sheepdogs, and wolves? Do the animals behave like humans? How does this story point affect the design of the film and the characters? Can sheep and wolves be used to represent certain kinds of human personalities? Might the animals be caricatures of human relatives and character types? Recognizable human traits create sympathy for fantastic characters. It is important to make your main characters more interesting than the secondary characters. If the hero's story does not attract and maintain your interest, perhaps you are working with the wrong character. Figure 1.6 shows a more novel staging of the wedding. In this case, *extraordinary characters* (the animals) are placed in an "ordinary" situation.

Figure 1.6

Using animal characters to suggest human traits and foibles is as old as Aesop.

The wedding story may still not be working with the most interesting characters.

I call the next part of the questionnaire the "What Ifs?" What if the loving couple is from two different species? What if they are a star-crossed sheep and a wolf? What if a sheep married a sheepdog? What stories and conflicts might be created by these contrasting characters? *Extraordinary characters in extraordinary situations* are good subjects for animated films (Figure 1.7).

Figure 1.7

Extraordinary characters in extraordinary situations can make a story interesting, but some trace of "normality" must remain so that the audience identifies with them.

But in these stories, an element of "normality" should be retained so that the audience is not confused by alien rules. The hobbits in THE LORD OF THE RINGS are fantastic characters who also enjoy smoking, good food, and beer; they are something familiar that involves the audience in the fantasy adventure. They are the glue that holds the story's many subplots together.

The characters' appearances, actions, and personalities will develop from your observations and caricatures of real life.

Nothing Is Normal: Researching Action

Your most important research tool is a sketchbook. You should draw in the sketchbook every day. Visit zoos, playgrounds, basketball games, even the Laundromat. Draw *rough impressions of moving figures,* not portraits or immobile poses. Draw from a live model if one is available. Write notes next to the drawing that describe the subject's attitude and personality. Sketch quick poses that express characters in motion—avoid long, immobile poses. Then try drawing your own character designs in the same poses as the figures in the sketches. Figure 1.8 shows a page of gesture drawings that "turn into" the animated characters. ("It makes life drawing a lot more fun!" the artist said.)

Figure 1.8

A page of gesture drawings that inspired the poses of the animated characters. Sketches from THE CASEBOOK OF NIPS AND PORKINGTON © 2015 by Melody Wang.

Gesture drawings of humans and animals will help you create ideas for your stories and better action for your imaginary actors. Working from life is recommended, but dance and music videos or action films can also be used as "models" since these films portray action that is more stylized than normal. Run films in slow motion, watch the actors' progressive movements, and draw as if the model was in the room instead of onscreen. The films of Charlie Chaplin and Buster Keaton, in particular, provide good comic and dramatic action reference. Once you start observing people and animals you will see that no one and nothing is ever "ordinary." Everyone moves slightly differently from one another. People and animals also move differently when they are in different moods. These varying attitudes should be taken into account when creating model sheets and storyboards for your characters since they will influence the animation that comes afterward. You will also see that everything, even a "standard" walk, works out of a story context. Is the character happy? Sad? Carrying something heavy? Arguing with someone? All of these factors will influence every action they make. No two people will move in the same way; don't draw them as if they did.

Pets are great subjects for gesture drawing because they never stand still! Don't try to draw formal portraits. Draw them while they are playing or moving around. You will know their characteristic gestures and attitudes from experience. Work quickly and never scratch out a drawing—just draw another sketch on the same page if you are not satisfied with the first one. You'll soon be able to do it from memory (Figure 1.9).

Figure 1.9

My late cat Gizmo, drawn from memory. She moved far too fast to "pose" for any of the pictures. I drew rough sketches of her movements after she finished them. Gesture drawing is an impression of movement, not actuality.

It is a good idea to familiarize yourself with the art and mores of other times and places if you are serious about working as a story artist or character designer. Knowledge and research will help you to find the right reference materials for a film set in a particular period. This is the way to avoid *anachronisms* (items used out of their context in time) unless they are necessary for your story. Figure 1.10 is an example of an anachronism.

Figure 1.10

A computer is an anachronism in the Stone Age.

Storyboard incorporates all of the arts and a good chunk of life into its matrix. Each project presents you with an opportunity to learn about different cultures, historic eras, and characters. The storyboard (and development) artist has the enviable task of being paid to learn. Researching a film is a fascinating and educational experience.

While the Internet has made it much easier to research certain subjects, not everything of note is on the Web. Much valuable material exists in books, magazines, museums, and in your own observations from nature. An exceptional artist will use the Web combined with independent research from a variety of sources (including their own life experience) to make his or her work stand out from the crowd.

A story artist or character designer will want to learn a little bit about a lot of things, including, but not limited to dance; history (world and national); popular and high-culture music, art, film, and literature; geography; anatomy (human and animal); zoology and biology; theater; color theory; industrial and product design; astronomy; acting; sports; botany; fashion design and fashion history by decade and by country; child behavior; national customs and landmarks; fantasy in art and literature; caricature; architecture; archaeology; folktales; psychology; and any hobbies you might care to add. As we shall see in Chapter 3, it also helps to know something about yourself.

The aspiring story artist should also understand film language, learn how signature styles of filmmaking evolved over time, and be familiar with live-action and animated films from many countries and eras. Most importantly, the story artist must know the difference between feature and short animation storyboards and the boards used for television and live-action films. These differences are discussed in Chapter 2.

2

How Storyboard Took Over the Movies (and Television)

"While directing short (animated) subjects, I soon discovered that the original planning of the overall picture, where the director had complete control of the project, was where the picture was actually made good ... having OK'd the picture and taken delivery of it from the story department ... the final result was assured."

—David Hand
Director of SNOW WHITE AND THE SEVEN DWARFS

Live-Action and Animation Boards

Live-action films are now routinely storyboarded after scripts are written and before footage is shot, but live-action boards differ dramatically from animation storyboards. Live-action storyboards describe camera angles, locations (if fantastic); provide rough blocking for the actors, and the general setup for each shot. They indicate where special effects are used (*see interview with Chris Bailey in this chapter*). The figures on live-action storyboards do not represent specific actors since the casting may not yet be set. The board artist will roughly block the characters' movement in the scene without illustrating the performance. Dialogue is rarely included. One or two panels suffice for each shot unless the camera is in motion or special effects continue throughout. Live-action storyboards are used by directors, art directors, and cinematographers but never by the actors (Figure 2.1).

The animation storyboard, unlike the live-action board, *creates the characters and settings*. The storyboard *IS* the animated actors' performance. Every part of

Figure 2.1

Live-action storyboard. Staging is blocked for camera placement. The actor in panel 2 may move forward and out of the frame, but no additional storyboard drawing is required. Live-action storyboards will not contain acting or dialogue. The actors and directors create the performance from the script.

an animated film is developed in storyboard stage—character designs, acting, action, pacing, story, dialogue, effects, camera moves, direction, and editing. All actions and camera moves that will appear in the film are drawn on the boards because *an animated film is edited and performed on the storyboards and in story reel before it is actually animated or shot.*

The storyboard artist draws as many boards as it takes to convey the action and the acting in each scene (Figure 2.2).

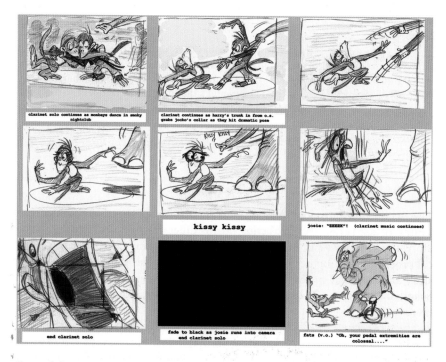

Figure 2.2

Storyboards from my theatrical short film YOUR FEET'S TOO BIG. Dialogue and brief descriptions of action are written on separate slips of paper beneath individual panels. The characters' acting is portrayed in detail.

Not all animation is based on caricature or cartoon. Some animated films may have a "realistic" design and acting style containing fantastic action and movement across landscapes that are impossible to film in live-action. Character acting will be portrayed, but may be secondary to the action. The layouts are blocked on the storyboard because they are an important part of the story. Special effects may also become a "character" in *Action Boards*. A good Action Storyboard was created by Sheridan student Colin Searle for his film OAKFIELD (Figure 2.3).

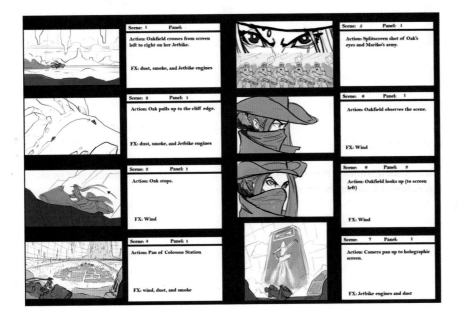

Figure 2.3

Storyboards for animated "*action boards*" bear a slight resemblance to live-action boards. They provide extensive reference for the final layouts. The action and camera movements are emphasized, but character acting is also present. Notes describe complicated movements within the scene. Storyboards from OAKFIELD © 2016 by Colin Searle.

Although animatics will be made during the storyboard process to set the timing of each shot, the final camera work for animation is not done until all of the creative work is completed. Animation camera work is a technical process recording performances and camera moves that were planned in story and layout at the beginning of production. Animation storyboard and layout artists are the equivalent of live-action cinematographers and editors (Figure 2.4).

The most obvious difference between the two media is that live-action films are directed in production and edited in postproduction. *Animation is directed and edited in preproduction, on the storyboard and in animatics.* The animation storyboard *is* the film.

Figure 2.4

The feature animation artist depicts camera moves as individual drawings on separate panels. Here is a cut from a medium close-up to an extreme close-up.

The Hybrid Film

Hybrid Animation, where animated characters appear in live-action movies, is handled a bit differently than other animation boards. The most significant variation between hybrid and fully animated feature films is that hybrid animation is composed of individual special effects shots that are edited like live-action. (Animation is considered a *special effect*; the live-action is "*practical*" or existing in reality.) Computer-generated imagery (CGI) makes it possible to create long animation takes that are edited to length, rather than pretimed. So live-action style "*cover shots*" can be used for hybrid animation. The timing of the animation is worked out when the director hands off the scene (and the rough edit of live-action footage) to the animator. The animated character's dialogue will be recorded in advance, the same way it is done in an animated film, but no animatic is created for its action.

Animation director Chris Bailey describes the type of storyboarding used for HOP and other hybrid films.

"Over the course of half a dozen movies or so and a few different directors and studios, I've evolved an amalgam (*blend*) of live-action and feature animation boards that seems to work well for me and everyone involved. First off, I like to use animation board artists because they understand acting and timing and will perform the characters. But it's important that they know film grammar and understand the camera. They need to mark their boards with 'cut' or 'cont' (*continued*) because there is no layout department to follow up after them and *workbook* their boards. They also need to understand when props need to be CGI or practical (*actual*) and the CG process in general so that they don't unintentionally make a shot more costly than it needs to be to tell the story.

(*Continued*)

2. How Storyboard Took Over the Movies (and Television)

- **"I ask that my board artists draw no more than three panels per shot"**: It's important to communicate the action and attitude of the animated characters, but I've discovered that in pitching the boards to department heads in the many prep meetings leading up to the shoot, no one has the time to flip through 12 panels of acting for one shot… *Garfield II* was the first movie where I supervised the boarding as well as the on-set and post animation work. My first (story) board review during prep was confusing to the live-action crew. The boards were feature animation style, long on acting and business but rough. It was clearly a waste of time for the various department heads to sift through pages of character business when all they needed to know what the shot was and what their potential involvement might be.

- "I quickly realized that it would be a more efficient use of everyone's time was to tell the shot in as few panels as possible; to present less acting and animation than a feature board, but more character and flow than a typical live visual effects action board. Time is precious and the simpler one can communicate the needs of a shot (are there CG or practical prop interactions? Do special effects have to be involved? etc.) the better.

- "For economy, the board artists need to think in terms of **longer shots that can be cut like live-action coverage of actors.** If there's a dinner table scene (*with intercutting between live and animated characters*), **it's better to have the animator animate two–three separate cuts as one big shot and let editorial cut it as opposed to turning over three separate shots to the animation house.**

- "When the boards were *finaled* (approved, *locked*) and to budget, I would rehearse the shots with the actors using a stuffed animal on set. When everyone was comfortable with the blocking, we would shoot a reference pass and then the plate where the actor is on their own to imagine the animated character's performance. In the (*live-action*) post process for *Hop,* the editors cut in my reference pass with the stuffed animal against the selected take of the actor. It worked better in most instances than static 2d *placeholders* I've used in the past because there was usually some timing and action to my 'stuffy pass'. The only danger was that if they hadn't all been replaced by rough animation in time for the first preview screening, they couldn't help but draw unintentional laughter."

—**Chris Bailey**
Senior animation supervisor, HOP (2011)

The trailer for HOP can be seen here: https://www.youtube.com/watch?v=9rltIeQW3Bo.

Stop-motion animation is a notable exception to the animation production chart depicted in Figure 2.5. Stop-motion characters are actual three-dimensional objects. Animators work in (very slow) real time on miniature sets. Stop-motion productions will use detailed storyboards and animatics

(Continued)

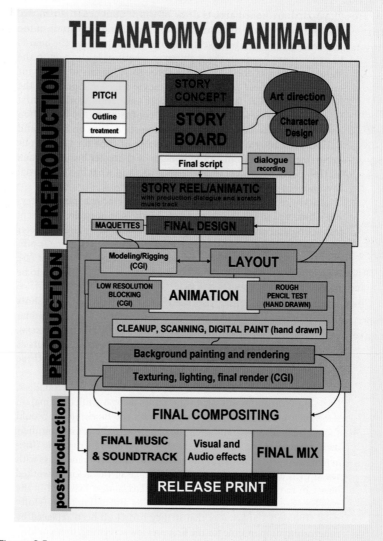

THE ANATOMY OF ANIMATION

PREPRODUCTION

PITCH

Outline

treatment

STORY CONCEPT

STORY BOARD

Art direction

Character Design

Final script

dialogue recording

STORY REEL/ANIMATIC
with production dialogue and scratch music track

MAQUETTES

FINAL DESIGN

PRODUCTION

Modeling/Rigging (CGI)

LAYOUT

LOW RESOLUTION BLOCKING (CGI)

ANIMATION

ROUGH PENCIL TEST (HAND DRAWN)

CLEANUP, SCANNING, DIGITAL PAINT (hand drawn)

Background painting and rendering

Texturing, lighting, final render (CGI)

post-production

FINAL COMPOSITING

FINAL MUSIC & SOUNDTRACK

Visual and Audio effects

FINAL MIX

RELEASE PRINT

Figure 2.5

The bulk of the creative work in animation is done in preproduction. Animation production takes longer and costs more if story or design changes are made after animation and modeling have started. Postproduction will generally take the least time, although this will vary depending on the project.

(usually done as a "pop-through" using the actual puppets) but otherwise their production resembles that of a live-action film. Puppets and sets are constructed during preproduction as the storyboard is completed. Stop-motion storyboards contain detailed backgrounds because each "location" must be constructed as an actual set. The camera work is continuous during production and the cameraman contributes creatively to the look of the film. A stop-motion film is partially edited in postproduction. Time must also be budgeted to digitally "*clean up*" or mask out the supports and rigs behind the puppets so that they do not show in the finished film.

Live-action films with elaborate special effects settings, such as the IRON MAN films, are storyboarded in the same way as action sequences in animated films. Human performers may not even carry the bulk of the action in sequences that feature fantasy characters, locations, and action designed and created by animators and special effects artists. Special effects blockbusters are also "hybrid films," but they are handled differently from films that place an animated character in a live-action world. The blockbuster special effects film may have locations, props, and characters—and, of course, effects—that are created by animators. It is easier to storyboard these very expensive films and edit them in advance, animation-style, than to shoot "cover footage" in live-action (*as Chris Bailey describes above for HOP*), create the fantasy elements without knowing whether all of them will be used, and edit the final film in postproduction. (If you used standard live-action film production methods in a special effects driven film, it would run way over budget and your studio might be out of business.)

Storyboards for special effects blockbusters are created first, as with Chris Bailey's projects. IRON MAN differs from HOP in one important aspect: an animatic was absolutely essential to edit the film and create effects and fantasy characters before the live-action was shot. Character acting on the storyboard was minimal and no dialogue was recorded for a scratch track. The actors were represented by placeholders that blocked the action in the scene. They were filmed separately against a greenscreen and their verbal and visual performances were composited with the animated characters, backgrounds, props, and special effects during postproduction.

Federico D'Alessandro, the Head Storyboard Artist/Animatics Supervisor at Marvel Studios, has posted many of his animatics for live-action films with fantastic effects (characters, action, and locations) on his Westlawn Films YouTube Channel. They share many similarities with animated film, but do not develop the actors' performances on the boards. Some of these sequences were storyboarded and created well before the live-action filming even began.

https://www.youtube.com/user/WestlawnFilms?feature=watch

Graphic Novels: Shaping the Frame

Comic and graphic novel artists have complete freedom to design the shapes of the frames and panels on the page. Panels may be vertical or irregularly shaped. Effects can be added to the panel borders, or characters can burst right through them. They may use cinematic staging, but lack the element of time that distinguishes the moving picture.

Figure 2.6 is a page from the graphic novel *David Chelsea in Love* by David Chelsea. The shattered, jagged shape, and varying size of the panels suggest the cramped conditions in the building's stairwell and the emotional attitude of some of the characters. The page is a shattered "window" that can be viewed as one work of art, but each shard is also a panel of the story. The reader determines the time spent on each panel. He or she may read them more than once, or read them out of order, and take as much time as needed to savor the detail of the illustration. The action in some panels overlaps others. **Most of the panels are vertical and none is a perfect rectangle**. A cinematic quality is conveyed by the characters' movement through numerous panels that depict progressive action and a close-up shot at the end that draws attention to one character.

Figure 2.6

A page from the graphic novel *David Chelsea in Love*. (Reproduced by permission of David Chelsea.)

Graphic novels are not cinema, even though they may use cinematic staging. There is no constraint on how long you may view each image, as there is in film, where time is edited. In addition, a graphic story need not contain movement; characters' inner thoughts can be expressed through text. In cinema, too much dialogue will make a picture "talky."

Cinema, whether live or animated, uses editing and movement of the character or the camera to show emotion and motivation. They are called moving pictures for a reason. Storyboards are closer to cinema than to graphic novels. If *David Chelsea in Love* was made into a film, we would use "jagged" or short cuts from long shot to medium shot to close-up to extreme close-up to describe the characters' emotional turmoil. A variety of framing elements in the foreground and background can suggest changes in the screen format (the actual screen format never changes!).

2. How Storyboard Took Over the Movies (and Television)

Screen Ratios: The Fixed Frame

Motion pictures have more staging restrictions than comics. *The motion picture screen or computer monitor is an unchanging horizontal " frame."* The animator creates variety in staging by moving the camera, animating the characters within the frame, editing the timing of a shot, or cutting to a new camera angle. The borders of the screen or frame are a standard size that cannot be modified by the filmmaker. All storyboard panels are actually a view of what we see on-screen. Some standard screen ratios are shown in Figure 2.7.

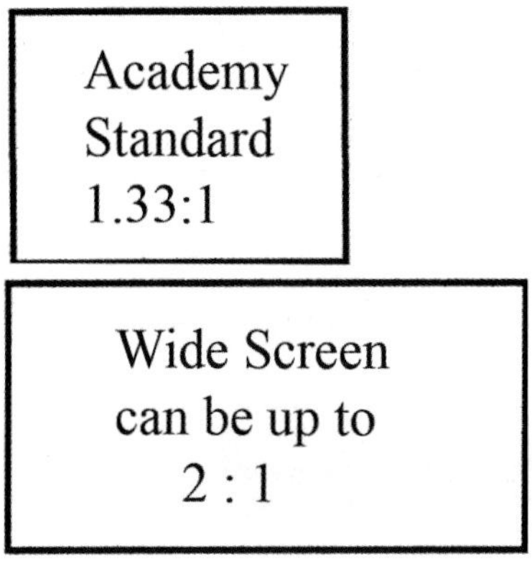

Academy
Standard
1.33:1

Wide Screen
can be up to
2 : 1

Figure 2.7

Academy Standard and Wide Screen ratios. There are many other variations, but all film and new media frames are horizontal rectangles.

The original Academy Standard screen ratio is rarely used today. Some recent examples appear in the live-action film THE ARTIST (2009) and the first scene and "inner screen" of the Disney short cartoon GET A HORSE (2013). The screen ratio will vary by production or platform. Some shows are designed to "play" on more than one (Figure 2.8).

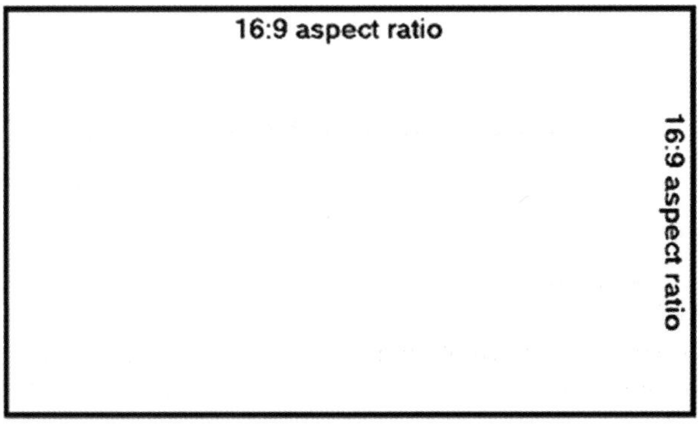

16:9 aspect ratio

16:9 aspect ratio

Figure 2.8

Many storyboards use the 16:9 screen ratio (hereafter referred to as "widescreen"). This is by no means standard—a production may be designed to be viewed in more than one format.

Television Boards and Feature Boards

The feature and short film storyboard artist's main concern is **telling the story**. Animated features and short films will have all sections of the preproduction—character, story, and production design—in development simultaneously. There can be a great deal of "wiggle room" and reworking of character designs and story points during preproduction. The final character models may not yet be set. Preproduction includes all of the artwork that does *not* appear in the finished film: character design, production design, and storyboard are all rough drafts for the final animation, editing, layouts, and backgrounds.

A television show's script is usually *"locked"* or unchangeable, and characters are frequently designed before the boards begin. Dialogue may usually not be rewritten or cut by the storyboard artist, for any reason, except in extremely rare instances (This is beginning to change, depending on the studio and the production.).

FEATURE AND SHORT FILM Storyboards Will Have

- Rough "Placeholder characters" used on storyboard, because character design may not be set. Scale and rough silhouettes are determined at the start. Final character designs will be set after storyboard is completed.
- Great flexibility with script and dialogue. Changes made by storyboard artists will be incorporated into script rewrites. A script may not exist before storyboard is completed.
- *Workbook* or *previz* that blocks the action in the scene for final layout after storyboard is finished.
- Drawings that may be very rough and sketchy, as long as they tell the story clearly.
- Camera moves that are sketched as separate panels or timed in animatics. Field guides are never drawn on the panels.

TELEVISION Storyboards Will Have

- Character designs and props that are designed before storyboard begins.
- Characters must remain on model or to scale. They do not "evolve" on the storyboard.
- Clean, finished drawings that may include detailed backgrounds. Camera moves are sometimes drawn on the panels as well.
- Scripts that are "locked" and that often cannot be changed by the storyboard artist. Some exceptions apply.
- Extensive notes under each panel describing the action and camera moves.

Television and feature storyboards now both use *animatics* to time the action before animation begins because digital programs make this affordable and practical for both. Both may use project-specific storyboard templates to maintain the correct screen ratio (these will vary by production; most television work is now done at 16:9 ratio.) But even though some preproduction methods are merging, the most important difference will always remain: Feature film stories and characters are developed as the boarding progresses. If there is a script at the start, it will be changed as storyboard artists revise and add to the story.

A television series will require the studio to produce 10 or 26 precisely timed episodes in the same amount of time it takes to make one feature film. An "assembly-line" production system is an absolute necessity in order to meet the schedules. Television air dates, whether for series shows or 30-second commercials, are *locked*, and scripts are usually unchangeable. There are no deadline extensions and no opportunities to allow the board artist to experiment with different approaches to the material. Everything has to be right the first time, or need minimal changes. Television storyboards will contain copious notes indicating the need for reused artwork and animation from earlier scenes or episodes to save time and money.

Whether television characters are old or new, a *"Bible"* of predesigned characters, props, and sets will be handed to the storyboard artist along with the script. The character and prop models must be strictly followed on the boards to keep the shows consistent (*Many ads for television storyboard stress that the applicant "must be familiar with/maintain the style of the show"*). Television storyboards for hand drawn shows contain detailed notes for camera moves and action and are very *clean* and *tight*, as shown in Figure 2.9.

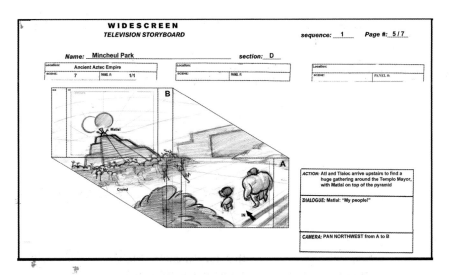

Figure 2.9

These television storyboards use 16:9 format, but also have "image safety" areas marked so that the picture may be viewed in different formats (screens, phones, or tablets). Camera moves are sometimes indicated on the storyboard panel, and are always described in notes underneath the image. (Reproduced by permission of Mincheul Park.)

Television Boards and Feature Boards

Television series boards are drawn on project-specific templates with notes for the camera moves, the dialogue, and a description of the action. The storyboard will have dialogue, descriptions of the action, and camera moves written in special panels below the drawings (*notes*). Backgrounds and correctly drawn (*on-model*) characters are required for hand drawn shows because the storyboards are sometimes enlarged and used as layouts for the animators. The character drawings on the boards may also be enlarged and used as animation keys. Acting is important, but all props, characters, and backgrounds for a hand-drawn show such as THE SIMPSONS will be *tight cleanups of on-model characters*. If a show is computer-animated, keeping the character models accurate will not be as important in storyboard and no cleanup is necessary—but keeping the characters to *scale* (consistent in size) is very important.

Backgrounds may be composited from preexisting modeled 3D "sets" and only the character "placeholders" and certain areas of the BG (a prop, an area that the character interacts with) may be drawn. The storyboards in Figure 2.10 are for a computer animated show. Finished backgrounds and camera moves were both included on the boards.

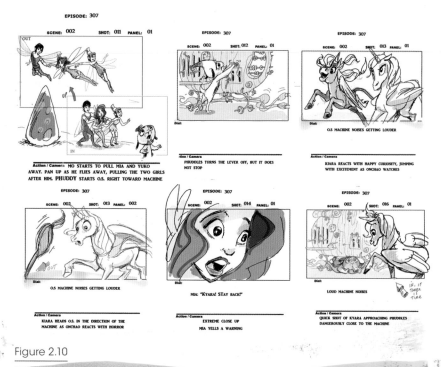

Figure 2.10

"Notes" describe action, camera moves, and dialogue in TV boards. Characters for a CGI show are drawn *to scale*. Camera moves are described in notes and may also be drawn on the boards. Storyboard test for MIA AND ME by Nancy Beiman, © 2015 Hahn & m4e Productions.

2. How Storyboard Took Over the Movies (and Television)

Animation storyboards at feature studios are still drawn as individual panels. Some television productions use this format as well. The panels for MIA AND ME were each originally drawn on individual pages.

3D animated films' storyboards are the same as those for regular feature boards except for the camera moves—which may be finalized in layout and "pre-viz". Sometimes a live-action cinematographer helps develop the dimensionality during the layout and previsualization stages of the project.

When working digitally

- You must follow specific file protocols. These will vary by studio and by production. Be sure to follow the production manager's guidelines.
- You will need to keep your files accessible and neatly organized. Back them up, too!

Television boards were not formerly "pitched" or presented for an audience—now, this is very commonly done, and there is little artistic difference between the feature and television storyboard. Keeping the panels separate makes it easy to rearrange them in different order after they are pitched, or presented, to your director or producer. They are often printed out and pinned on the wall so that all panels may be seen at once. Corrections may be roughed out on self-stick notes. This approach works equally well with short films.

Since the animated film's characters and performances are created at the storyboard stage, animation artists must be excellent actors as well as storytellers. Your acting ability is actually more important than detailed draftsmanship. Storyboards require clear, easy-to-read drawings that can be created and changed quickly. In general, you won't spend a lot of time rendering or detailing individual storyboard drawings for most productions. *Try not to spend more than five minutes drawing one panel for feature length and short animated films.* Most are done in less time than this, as will be shown in later chapters. Storyboards are never "singular"—individual panels are viewed as part of a sequence, and the entire storyboard is the means to an end (the finished film). Sometimes the end is a long time coming. Be prepared to rework and redo your boards numerous times after turnover sessions or story changes, and don't become too attached to individual images. Change is a part of life in storyboard. Do not take changes to your boards personally; by accepting suggestions for improvement and making changes where needed, you are working for what is best for the picture and saving a lot of trouble and fuss down the line. There are few sadder sights in film than good animation that winds up cut from the picture due to story changes.

Storyboard drawings are frequently used as acting and design reference for character designers who may be working on the production at the same time that the boards are created. So the animation storyboard artist is also a bit of a casting director! (Figure 2.11)

The Animated Character Casting Call involves working up a variety of character design suggestions and deciding, which ones work best in the story. Storyboard drawings are often used as reference for the designs. Some animated walk-ons become "stars" after appearing in supporting roles for other characters. (Donald Duck, Goofy, and Porky Pig are all former "bit" players!)

Television commercials are similar to feature boards in many respects. They often have short deadlines. Animatics are created using the dialogue and music that the agency has provided before the commercial is boarded and animated. Television commercial scripts are ALWAYS "Locked"!

Commercial Storyboard: An Interview with Elliot Cowan

Elliot Cowan is an accomplished animator, designer, and storyboard artist who works digitally. Here he answers a few questions about digital storyboarding for animated commercials.

Q: What process do you use to create digital boards? Do you thumbnail on paper, or work directly on screen?

ELLIOT COWAN: I work directly on screen.

If I'm working on a film project and something comes to mind over a cup of tea or eggs at the diner I'll scribble it down on paper but for the most part when I sit down to work I'm working entirely digitally. Ultimately, they're all drawings. I'm not sure it much matters how they're created as long as they're good drawings with good energy. Working digitally is simply a very convenient way of doing things.

Q: Does the new technology make it easier to create storyboards than drawing on paper?

ELLIOT COWAN: Sort of. It doesn't make drawing them exceptionally easier but it does make finishing and presenting them easier—particularly when you take it to the animatic stage. It certainly makes revisions and corrections easier, which is really the major advantage. Working digitally adds another level of fiddling about that sketching boards on paper doesn't have. Of course it does away with having to scan your boards when you're making animatics and gives you some more flexibility to create more complex ones, which is what I like to do. In the end it kind of balances out but, once again, working digitally is convenient (Figure 2.12).

Figure 2.12

A digital storyboard for a television commercial. The artist goes directly to animatic from thumbnails. There are no "finished storyboards." (Reproduced by permission of Elliot Cowan.)

Q: Do you create your animatics at the same time as the storyboard?

ELLIOT COWAN: Usually these days, yes. For most commercial jobs I tend to skip the boarding process entirely and work straight to a rough animatic. I think the client feels a little more excited about something that moves and it can be easier to sell your idea.

There is less to explain with an animatic and the less you have to explain the smoother the process is (although agencies still like to see boards). As I mentioned earlier, creating digital boards gives you the chance to add some nice movement into your animatics without a great deal of effort and I think it's worth taking the time to do so (Figure 2.13).

(simple line mouth)

Figure 2.13

This digital storyboard drawing was created in Photoshop and has separate levels for eyes, body, hands, book, head, and mouth. After the *animatic* is approved, the artist proceeds directly to layout and animation. (Reproduced by permission of Elliot Cowan.)

- Digital production methods have caused techniques to merge more and more and TV board artists now may develop the character acting, pitch boards, and create Leicas in the same manner that feature artists do. It is now not unusual for animators to transition between feature and television storyboarding.

   In conclusion: the best training for the storyboard artist is in feature animation storyboards, because you will develop storytelling, cinematic, directorial, writing, organizational, editing, and acting skills that allow you to transition from animation to television to live-action to hybrid productions with little difficulty.

Who Loves Short Shorts?

How long is a "short" film? Will the principles used in constructing a feature apply to a short film or student production? Yes, but with one difference. The budget for a student film is measured *in time*. An incomplete film may result in a failing grade. The Academy of Motion Picture Arts and Sciences defines a "short film" as having a running time of less than 27 minutes. Student filmmakers would be prudent if they kept their films' running times under 3 minutes and possibly under 2.

The computer has made animation much easier and cheaper to produce than previously. Animation postproduction takes much less time than it does in live-action unless the animation is combined with live-action or special effects. (Stop-motion animation needs time for digital "cleanup" as discussed earlier in this chapter.) Sufficient postproduction time must be budgeted for compositing and rendering the final images and mixing the sound track.

But computer graphics, 3D, special effects, or pretty visuals won't save a weak story or a poorly planned production. Errors and omissions in preproduction will snowball into major problems for all types of animation as production gets under way. It's essential to know what your film is about before you start animating since it's very hard to "fix it in the editing" at the end of the production.

So let's get started (Figure 2.14).

Figure 2.14

Improper planning in story and preproduction will result in ever increasing trouble down the line. (Reproduced by permission of Brian P. McEntee.)

3

Putting Yourself into Your Work

"Would anyone other than mother care to look at this?"

—**Frank Thomas and Ollie Johnston**
The Fourteen Points of Animation, 1975

Your experiences and adventures can be grist for an animated character or story. An experience that you *would like to have* can also provide rich material for an animated story. Did you ever fantasize about being an animal, or being able to fly? Animation makes it possible for you to do both.

Animation means "to bring to life." Life is the animator's reference book. You've met literally thousands of people in your lifetime. You have had adventures in your own home and at school, perhaps with a sister or a brother. You have had parents and real or imaginary friends. Maybe you owned a pet cat or dog. You have lived in a house, a town, or a country. A story viewed through the prism of your own life experience is far more interesting than a generic construction based on formulaic relationships. "Write what you know," the saying goes. You know yourself and your friends and family. Their personalities and qualities can be used as an inspiration to bring characters to life whether the story is contemporary or set in a distant time or place. You may not have a child of your own, but you have *been* a child, and had parents and grandparents. Animation is not about what is, but about what could be. Always take characters' emotions, thoughts, and feelings into consideration when designing them and having them act in your stories, because these will influence everything that they do.

Robert Louis Stevenson based the character of Long John Silver in *Treasure Island* on one of his friends. Stevenson gave the pirate character traits that opposed every one of the friend's virtues, but retained his energetic and ingratiating manner—and his wooden leg. Sir Arthur Conan Doyle based Sherlock Holmes on Joseph Bell, an acerbic and observant professor at the University of Edinburgh Medical School. Your characters can be based on friends, family members, or people you know. Biographical elements provide a "human touch" that enables the audience to identify with and sympathize with exotic or outlandish characters. They transform simple designs into living and breathing creatures with believable problems and aspirations. Consider Figure 3.1, which shows two penguins and an egg.

Figure 3.1

Two penguins and an egg from SNOWMEN. © 2005 Kimberly Miner.

Now let us consider the same characters within a story context. Mama Penguin has charged Big Sister Penguin with the care of her (very) little brother. Big Sister would much rather go play with her friends, as shown in Figure 3.2. Figure 3.1 shows a pair of penguins and an egg. Figure 3.2 depicts characters that relate to one another on an emotional level. The artist based the penguin children on herself and her siblings. SNOWMEN can be viewed at https://www.youtube.com/watch?v=UPon9YMvtDY.

Figure 3.2

Penguin family ties, from SNOWMEN. © 2005 Kimberly Miner.

A good story artist utilizes life experience to give a character or story a base that an audience identifies with emotionally. This is the quality in animation that communicates across time and culture. It is not necessary to literally recreate the real-life event that inspired the story. The suggestion of humanity is what creates human interest.

3. Putting Yourself into Your Work

Of course there are exceptions to this rule. You don't have to be totally faithful to reality when using it as an inspiration. You may want to leave out all human references to create a totally alien character or alienating environment. All stories, whether based on worldly or otherworldly rules, must sustain the interest of an audience. Even a monstrous character can inspire audience sympathy and, occasionally, empathy.

The Seven Dwarfs were not major characters in the Grimm Brothers' original story of SNOW WHITE AND THE SEVEN DWARFS. They were only plot motivators and did not have names. In the Disney film, the Dwarfs were each given a name that described a particular type of character. Each Dwarf reflected a different aspect of a complete human personality—not all of them good ones. Grumpy, Dopey, and Doc were more developed characters than the other four, with Grumpy being the most interesting of them all. Under the gruff exterior was a heart of gold, which he did his best to hide.

It was thought that audiences would not be able to sit for an hour to watch a feature-length cartoon. The critics would have been correct if SNOW WHITE AND THE SEVEN DWARFS had the same story construction as many short cartoons of the period. Cartoons in the 1930s frequently resolved a simple problem with music and dance in six minutes, emphasized lovely visuals over story and characterization, or were manic outpourings of creativity and "screwy" gags relying on neither plot nor logic (Figures 3.3 and 3.4).

Figure 3.3

Many early cartoons were structured around music. Some were "moving paintings" that emphasized pretty visuals over plot.

*udder removed by the Hays Office

Figure 3.4

The "screwball" humor of the 1930s produced manic cartoons with characters that were entertaining for six minutes but did not have the emotional range to carry a feature-length film.

Short films are vignettes. A feature film is a mural. Feature stories must hold the audience's interest for 10 times the length of a short film. It is necessary to pace the story well and alternate manic moments with sequences that allow the story to advance, and the audience to rest. We must care about what happens to the characters.

SNOW WHITE AND THE SEVEN DWARFS is about a murder. The villain-ous Witch/Queen wants Snow White dead and succeeds in killing her through a trick. Fortunately, a flaw in the magic enables Snow White's Prince to break the spell. This is the bare bones of the story.

SNOW WHITE AND THE SEVEN DWARFS is also a love story, but the love interest—the Prince—is offscreen for most of the picture. Originally he had a much larger role, but the more interesting Dwarfs and animals carry the bulk of the film's action. Sequences in the film are well-paced and evenly divided between comedy and drama. The famous dance party at the Dwarfs' cottage immediately follows the Witch's creation of the poisoned apple that will kill Snow White. After the dance Snow White sings *"Some Day My Prince Will Come"* as the Dwarfs and animals listen. We see and hear what the girl has to live for and know that all is about to be taken away from her. This knowledge adds poignancy to the song. The three consecutive sequences neatly encapsulate the film's entire plot and show the characters' personalities and relationships even when viewed separately from the rest of the film.

Symbolic Animals and Objects

"The Great Roe is a mythological beast with the head of a lion and the body of a lion, but not the same lion."

—Woody Allen

Animals have been used for millennia to symbolize human foibles. Most animal symbols in Western culture come from the fables of Aesop and La Fontaine and from medieval morality plays. Animal characters may be designed with human traits (Figure 3.5a). Human characters may display animal characteristics (Figure 3.5b).

(a) *A dream that will come true* (b)

Figure 3.5

(a) Grace Drayton's dreaming kitten from 1921 has babyish features common to infant humans and animals. (Nancy Beiman collection) and (b) the girl has a dis-tinctly cat-like air. (Reproduced by permission of John McCartney.)

3. Putting Yourself into Your Work

Here is a list of animals and their symbolic meanings. Some animals have been used to represent more than one human trait and opposing traits are sometimes represented by the same animal (Figure 3.6) as the following:

- Lion (Brave, dignified, the King of the Beasts)
- Rat (dishonest, dirty, and dangerous)
- Pig (greedy, selfish, inconsiderate, and thoughtless)
- Rabbit (clever and resourceful *or* timid and defenseless)
- Bear (brute strength, brawn without brain)
- Cow and sheep (unintelligent, docile, and a follower)
- Cat (sly, cruel, deceptive, and self-centered)
- Dog (loyal and brave *or* a fawning servant)

Figure 3.6

Symbolic Beasts. The viewer responds subconsciously to these cultural references, presuming that the lion is brave and the mouse is timid. What if roles were reversed so that the lion was timid and the mouse brave? The lion's outfit also displays symbolic meaning. The use of contrasting symbols creates a visual pun.

The characters in Melody Wang's THE CASEBOOK OF NIPS AND PORKINGTON were originally designed as human beings. Their clothing and expressions were based on photographs and illustrations from the 1880s (Figure 3.7). The artist found the characters more interesting and fun to draw when they were changed into a pig and a kitten. This change made them "more" human; their acting is natural and unforced. The characters' personalities work against the "symbolic animal" stereotype since Inspector Porkington is highly intelligent, caring, and professional (although he has a taste for good cooking) and Constable Nips is brave, daring, and in control of the situation despite his youthfulness. The Nasty Rat personifies the traditional symbolic role of this animal. (Can you name a film that has a rat in a positive role?).

I illustrated a children's book for Patricia Bernard, the well-known Australian author. *Basil Bigboots the Pirate* was originally about human pirates from the four corners of the earth who needed to find a "pirate shop" selling new clothes to replace their torn finery. I suggested the story might be more entertaining

NIPS AND PORKINGTON PERUSE
THE CLASSIFIEDS SECTION.

Figure 3.7

Constable Nips the kitten and Inspector Porkington the Pig were originally designed as human characters. Once they were changed into animals, their villain could literally be a Nasty Rat! Illustration from THE CASEBOOK OF NIPS AND PORKINGTON © 2015 by Melody Wang.

if we used animals instead of people to represent the different nationalities. Human characters in shredded clothing might be misinterpreted while the animals would look funny wearing human clothes, whether torn or whole. Patricia thought this was a good idea and changed her story accordingly. Basil was easy to cast as a British Bulldog. His boots and his ego were big, but the rest of him was very small (Figure 3.8).

Figure 3.8

Captain Basil Bigboots, the British Bulldog Pirate. He was originally a human, but this story point became more entertaining when illustrated by an animal. Illustration by Nancy Beiman for *Basil Bigboots the Pirate*, (Reproduced by permission of Patricia Bernard.)

3. Putting Yourself into Your Work

Which creatures would best represent pirates from South America, Africa, and China? We quickly settled on a parrot and a gorilla for the first two countries' symbolic animals. I then drew thumbnails of a Chinese dragon pirate. Patricia suggested that a panda would be a much better choice, and she was right. The panda has black circles around its eyes that suggest eye patches. This creates a *visual pun* (Figure 3.9).

Figure 3.9

Chinese pirate from *Basil Bigboots the Pirate*. I drew him in the style of a Chinese paper cutting. Illustration by Nancy Beiman, reproduced by permission of Patricia Bernard.

Patricia added an American character after I drew up this sketch of Boston Bertie, the dealer in second hand pirate ships. "Wildcat" can also mean "something unpredictable" and so this animal seemed the best choice for the role of the salesman (Figure 3.10).

Figure 3.10

Would you buy a used pirate ship from Boston Bertie? Illustration by Nancy Beiman for *Basil Bigboots the Pirate*, reproduced by permission of Patricia Bernard.

The characters in Max Swiecki's film HOOBA JOOBA also started out as human beings. They are compared to a rabbit and a house fly in the earliest sketch in Figure 3.11. Animal and insect elements were blended into the human designs and also influenced the characters' personalities. Variations in design, attitudes, and clothing were explored. The final designs eliminate clothing entirely and use a fantasy color scheme. "Blue" conveys sadness and "Orange" is the most cheerful color. These characters are neither fully human nor fully animal. The blend creates appeal and originality in the design and adds humor to the story. HOOBA JOOBA can be viewed at https://vimeo.com/63857095.

Figure 3.11

These characters started out as human beings. Animal and insect qualities were incorporated into their designs in a series of experimental sketches. The final character designs were a blend of animal and human elements that lived in a human-scaled world. HOOBA JOOBA © Max Swiecki.

These are examples of how a story became more interesting when the characters changed from human to animal or something in between. This does not mean that human characters should never be used. Use the design that you find most interesting. Always be open to alternative views when developing the characters. Experimentation in design is fun, creative, and leads to better storytelling.

"I AM A ROCK, I AM AN ISLAND."

—**Paul Simon and Art Garfunkel**
I Am a Rock

3. Putting Yourself into Your Work

See You Later, Allegory

Objects that are inanimate in the real world can come to life in your imaginary one and become symbolic or actual personalities. Some objects have symbolic meanings. For example, a rock can be used to portray strength, solidity, or immobility. It conveys a different meaning altogether when it shatters through stress or is worn down into sand by the action of wind and water.

Animation superbly conveys abstract concepts and emotions through symbolic objects and colors with the added dimension of movement over time. An "invulnerable" rock may be emotionally fragile. Water and rivers symbolize life, yet they become menacing when they flood. A cloud can be a fleecy impermanent thing or a terrifying storm. In animation, a tree is never just a tree—it may be your leading lady! An object's meaning varies depending on the story context (Figure 3.12).

Figure 3.12

The abstract concept of (a) danger and (b) humor is illustrated graphically with rocks contrasting physical permanence with emotional variability. Animation brings life to allegorical symbols and colors. ROCKS © Joseph Daniels.

The Newsman's Story Guide: Who, What, When, Where, and Why

Exercise: Design four cats.

Do not start drawing right away. Think about the assignment carefully. What information have you been given? What information is missing? A story artist or character designer will ask for more background about these cats before working on designs.

Who are they? What are they? Where do they live? When does the action take place? Why do they do, what they do, and who or what do they interact with?

If you do not ask these questions, you may still design good cats, but they will be designs, not characters (Figure 3.13).

Figure 3.13

Four cats. The designs are graphically interesting, but individual characters have not been defined. © Nina L. Haley.

Now try the assignment again, using the following information: Mama, a very proper and dignified cat, has three kittens. A story begins when you flesh out the original description of "four cats."

Now explore the characters. Are they "real" cats? Do they have human qualities or are they pure animal? Make a list of props that they could interact with. Where do they live? Which locations and props offer the best possibilities for animation? You can experiment with the scale of the mother cat to her kittens, as shown in Figure 3.14.

Figure 3.14

Kittens will have very different proportions from their mother. Body shape and agility will vary with age. © Nina L. Haley.

Now do a few small drawings (thumbnails) of the cats working with some of the props and write short sentences under the drawings describing how the situation might develop. Do not cross out any of the drawings and do not throw any of them away. At this stage, you should be open to all suggestions, no matter how crazy they may sound. You may sketch new ideas that will create a story, or take an existing story in a different direction.

How do you turn generic cats, rocks, or trees into individual characters? You could use human beings as a reference for their personalities. Start with the basics. Here's where your life experience literally comes into the picture.

Exercise: Sketch two human characters based on yourself and a friend at five years of age. Change the two humans into cats, translating the humans' attitudes and expressions to the cats' faces and bodies. Next, turn the humans into objects that portray their personality types. Experiment with the shape and scale of three different objects.

You know your own personality and that of your friend. How do you translate this quality into a character design, especially a nonhuman one? You can base the designs on caricatures, but that is not always necessary.

By just *thinking about the pets, friends, and people you have met* while you are working, you will subconsciously start to incorporate some of their mannerisms and appearances into your design and story. This will make the characters uniquely yours and not a mere imitation of a style. No two people have precisely the same experiences in life. Referring to your own memory bank will keep your designs and stories fresh. My first rough designs for Fuzz the Cat did not appeal to me at all…they seemed too derivative. Then I found an expression that reminded me of my older cat, Sam-E—a very serious fellow. The two successful head designs are highlighted in pink. Combining this head with the basic body shape from the other designs resulted in a much better looking character, as shown in the pink-nosed Fuzz at the bottom of Figure 3.15. The design will undergo further modifications in storyboard and will be finalized in the first scenes of final animation.

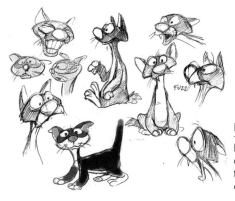

Figure 3.15

Fuzz the Cat from OLD TRICKS looked derivative at first; the more interesting face was inspired by that of my own cat, Sam-E. © 2016 Nancy Beiman.

Observe life with the artist's eye. Notice everything. Draw it in your sketchbook. You will not only have an endless source of reference for animation, you will never be bored!

Interesting drawings of human relationships and motion can be done while waiting in an airport or train station or launderette. Attend horse, cat, and dog shows and county fairs. Visit zoos and children's playgrounds. Draw in your sketchbook every day. Any situation or location becomes interesting if you observe and analyze how living creatures move and react. There is no such thing as a dull location—there is only the lack of perception of the extraordinary variety in life. Everything becomes interesting when you view it with the artist's eye.

Do not copy character designs from other animated films. It is too easy to be caught up in a style and imitate it so that the style is emphasized over the substance of your project. You will be looking through another animator's eyes and creating a pale imitation of *their* references and experiences.

Familiarize yourself with the work of artists, illustrators, and cartoonists from earlier times. Use them as inspiration for your own designs. Am I contradicting myself? No, because there have been so many more artists, cartoonists, and illustrators than there are animators. Animation is a little more than a century old. Cartoon art is 500 years old and graphic art is more than 40,000 years old. Drawing inspiration from unusual source materials will help you design characters that are graphically interesting and original. Figure 3.16 shows how I used a classic cartoonist's work as inspiration for one of my own characters. *Inspiration* builds on what has gone before. *Copying* merely dilutes it (Figure 3.17).

beach drunk and bored women

Figure 3.16

There is no such thing as an ordinary location. Interesting gesture drawings can be done at home, in a supermarket, or at a playground.

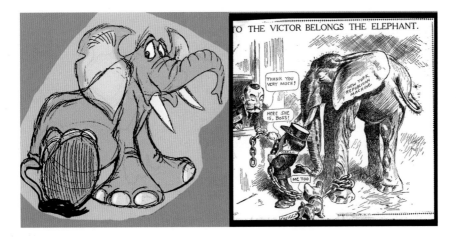

Figure 3.17

"Harry" from the film *Your Feet's Too Big* © 1983 by Nancy Beiman, and Republican Elephant by T. S. Sullivant (1904). I based my character design on Sullivant's cartoons such as the one shown here. (Nancy Beiman collection.)

Be sure to always put a bit of yourself into your work. It is true that there are no new stories. There are only stories and characters that *you* have not done before. Your interpretations of the material will make it your own. Never copy anything outright. Put your source aside after a while and use your imagination to elaborate on it. The resultant mix will lead to original creation.

Consider the character relationships from the very start of your project, because they will help you design characters that express that relationship. Emotions can develop and change over time, but the relationship remains consistent. (The penguin mama and children in Figure 3.2 will always have the same relationship to one another.)

You've now considered themes from a variety of sources and are ready to start developing situations and characters. Two approaches to story development are discussed in Chapter 4.

4

Situation and Character Driven Stories

> "Comedy and fantasy are the two most difficult things in the world to do, because your audience is not educated exactly to what, for example, a rabbit six feet high will do. You have to make him believable to yourself.... That's the basic business of the whole matter."
>
> —**Chuck Jones**

> "Your film must be ABOUT something!"
>
> —**John Hubley**

All films contain situations, or else nothing would ever happen in them. A story usually involves a character (the *hero*) that is put into a particular situation, or story context. For example, a rabbit innocently occupies a rabbit hole on the exact spot where a prospector wishes to dig for gold. The prospector attacks the rabbit. The rabbit runs away and the prospector falls into the rabbit hole. This is a *situation-driven* story because the character personalities do not influence the outcome of the story.

A character's personality can cause the situation to develop in a different manner. If I rename the rabbit hero of this story "Bugs Bunny," we instantly know how the plot will develop. Bugs Bunny reacts calmly when guns are stuck in his face, outwits the prospector, and gets to stay in his rabbit hole. Bugs' code of honor allows him to take justified revenge on the prospector because he has been attacked. The story becomes *character-driven* because the situation, and the story development, is influenced by Bugs' personality. An unknown rabbit might react differently and there would be no precedent for its behavior, as is the case with an established character (Figure 4.1).

Figure 4.1

An unknown character needs to establish its "rules of engagement" with its adversaries, whereas a well-known character's reactions may be guided by what it typically does.

Linear Stories

A *linear* story, such as the one in the previous example, develops from A (situation) to B (conflict) to C (resolution). That is to say, each section of the film develops logically from the previous one. The classic linear story explanation goes something like this: *Act One: Get your hero up a tree. Act Two: Throw rocks at him. Act Three: Get him down out of the tree.*

Some films are *situation-driven;* the universe that the characters inhabit influences their actions and personalities. Stories based on "situation" often put ordinary characters in extraordinary predicaments.

It's very important to know who or what your hero is when beginning your story. (In animation, your hero could be a talking fish or tree.) Otherwise, you might find your story wandering off in all directions. The main story line should be concerned with what happens to one or two important characters.

Character Arcs and Story Subtexts

A story with a *character arc* has heroes that overcome obstacles and character flaws to reach a clearly defined goal. At the end of the story the hero will have undergone a change of habit, personality, or even physical appearance (The Ugly Duckling literally changes into a new character.) The character develops in a similar fashion as the *story arc,* which is discussed later. Both arcs start on one level and develop through conflict to end on a different plane than the one on which they started. Happy endings leave characters in a higher, or better state than they were in at the beginning of the story. Tragic characters have the opposite fate. The story is simple and direct. *Or is it?* A film can have a deeper meaning that the hero's actions help convey to the audience. This is known as a *subtext.*

In Gene Deitch's adaptation of Jules Feiffer's MUNRO, a normal four-year-old boy is drafted into the American army through a bureaucratic oversight. The little boy "gets up a tree" when he is placed in an adult situation. The "rocks" in the story come when Munro's attempts to tell the truth about his age are ignored by the military brass. His confessions are considered unmanly. The adults refuse to see that he is just a boy. Munro attempts to adapt, but only "gets down from the tree" when he throws a tantrum and his childishness becomes obvious to everyone. At the end of the story Munro is once again a normal, unremarkable four-year old boy. He does not develop a character arc because MUNRO is really a story about foolish bureaucracy. Munro is only a catalyst that precipitates the action in this *situation-driven* story. The *subtext*—war is like a children's game; the "cause" the army fights for is childish—could easily have become formulaic and didactic if stated more obviously.

Think of the most memorable characters you have seen in an animated film. They will usually be the ones with the most interesting or dramatic character arcs. There are exceptions to this rule. The Coyote in the "Road Runner" cartoons keeps making the same mistakes, never develops a character arc, and is trapped for eternity using Acme products that never work in a story that will never resolve. He is the anti-hero in an animated form, and cannot change or escape from his situation. No wonder Chuck Jones quoted George Santayana when describing this cartoon series: *"Fanaticism consists in redoubling your effort when you have forgotten your aim."* A quote attributed to Albert Einstein is also very appropriate for the Coyote: *"Insanity is doing the same thing over and over again and expecting different results."*

Nonlinear Stories

A *nonlinear* story is relatively uncommon in animated feature films. *Waking Life* is one example. The most famous example of a nonlinear story in a feature length motion picture is probably Orson Welles' CITIZEN KANE, where the important events of a man's life are seen from three other characters' viewpoints, repeating over and over, and never from his own; the film ends where it began, with no resolution and no real understanding of who Kane really was.

Nonlinear films still have structure, or else they would be just a series of unrelated scenes. They can be pure "situation." My film YOUR FEET'S TOO BIG used the Fats Waller song as an informal structure for a series of vignettes on how an elephant does not fit into a world built to the scale of a monkey or a sheep. There are no character or story arcs; the hero's problem isn't resolved even when he meets characters closer to his own scale. He is unchanged by his experiences, and the situation will continue as before (Figure 4.2).

Figure 4.2

Harry the Elephant is out of place in a sheep-sized world in YOUR FEETS TOO BIG © 1983 by Nancy Beiman.

A nonlinear story can portray events in a particular time or place without using a story beat structure that sets a conflict and achieves a goal. It might have a documentary-style structure with dialogue providing the story context, as in Nick Park's and Aardman Animation's film CREATURE COMFORTS. This film also contains a very strong subtext about social injustice. It can be viewed at https://www.youtube.com/watch?v=pjSlB9WfpF4.

Omar El-Hindi's film SECRETS OF THE WILD: SPRING BREAK uses this documentary technique to "interview" animal students on vacation in Australia (Figure 4.3).

Figure 4.3

A "ripped" kangaroo forgets the reason why he came to show off his muscles on the beach in a scene from SECRETS OF THE WILD: SPRING BREAK © 2016 by Omar El-Hindi.

Nonlinear animation might be completely abstract. As mentioned above, these films will still contain a structure that unifies the images; music, color, and rhythmic cutting all serve to hold the audience's attention. Evelyn Lambart and Norman McLaren's BEGONE DULL CARE is a fine example of this type of filmmaking. It can be viewed on the National Film Board of Canada website at https://www.nfb.ca/film/begone_dull_care.

Formulaic Characters and Stories

There is no one way to construct a story. There is no "formula" to follow—not even in this book! The one rule that appears to be a constant is that you should not copy characters and stories that have been done, without making changes that make them yours. A successful film communicates an idea to an audience. Successful characters make us care about what happens to them. Formulaic characters never create the illusion of life because they never come to life. Their personalities and actions are completely predictable and this causes us to lose interest in their stories. Stock, or standard, heroes may overcome some obvious personal weakness or external obstacle By Working Together or Going on a Journey or By Just Being Themselves instead of *thinking* for themselves. All their problems are easy to identify and are resolved by the fadeout because the stock story formula guarantees that the audience knows exactly what to expect (Figure 4.4).

Figure 4.4

A stock story. Pick one letter from each category. "I must find the (a) ring, (b) Princess, (c) kingdom, (d) golden fleece, and rescue the (a) Princess, (b) ring, (c) golden fleece, (d) kingdom, to win the (a) kingdom, (b) golden fleece, (c) Princess, (d) ring, but first must overcome my (a) enemy, (b) lack of self-esteem, (c) father, or (d) all of the above."

Stock Characters step through the stories with no character development. There is no need to change if we know they are completely good or completely evil. There are no character arcs; only interchangeable puppets moving toward the foregone conclusion of a cardboard ballet. Perfect heroes are not appealing because they do not have any conflicts to overcome. We already know that they will win over all obstacles; there is no suspense in their story. That is why there should be a piece of Kryptonite for every Superman. Similarly, villains that are completely evil, with no redeeming qualities, can become tiresome or even unintentionally funny (Figure 4.5).

he's a

MEAN OLD MEANIE

FRIENDLESS ORPHAN

HELPLESS KITTENS

...and he wants to TAKE OVER THE WORLD!

Figure 4.5

"Stock" character types and predictable stories do not engage the audience's imagination or come to life.

"What If?" The Possible Story

Animation is at its best when it depicts something that could *possibly* exist. Duplicating reality in animation is not the best use of the medium unless you are doing special effects that must blend in with live action. If you enjoy "realism" you may want to work in this field or in live-action.

Consider things that *could* happen to the characters and the story as well as those that *can*. Remember animation is not restricted by the laws of physics or gravity! *Believability is more important to an animated film than realism.* We are able to accept an animated world where fish and rabbits talk, or where people travel to other planets without space suits. The secret is consistency. Each project has its own set of rules that guide the action of the characters and the development of the story. These are sometimes called the "What Ifs."

What if insects ran the world and exterminated people? What if fish were able to live on dry land? You can start with a normal story situation and develop it in an unusual way. Try contrasting the ordinary with the extraordinary. What if Count Dracula wanted to be a surfer dude? The idea can be the germ of a story. This is where your personal experience comes in. An appealing *character* with human desires and failings will create more interest than a standard-issue *character type* that has appeared in many other animated films. Unusual characters will solve problems in an unusual way, so that even when the story is "stock," the interpretation is not. You may put an ordinary character in extraordinary situations, as in Gene Deitch and Jules Feiffer's MUNRO; or place an extraordinary character—for example, Count Dracula—in an ordinary situation. What if Count Dracula lived in Southern California and wanted to fit in with the local culture? This contrast between character and conflict will help you to develop the story in a direction that the audience does not expect, as shown in Figure 4.6.

4. Situation and Character Driven Stories

Figure 4.6

Count Dracula, Surfer Dude. Pass the moon block!

Defining Conflict and Story Arcs

Many classic animated films have linear stories with simple conflicts where an internal or external obstacle must be overcome. The *situation* is established at the beginning of the story, the *conflict* is then developed, and *resolved* at the end of the picture. This basic structure is known as the *story arc* because the action does not proceed at an even pace, but varies in intensity. Several small obstacles may be solved along the way, building toward the climax, with the strongest emotional and story accents appearing just before the resolution. When constructing original stories, it is best to establish your main conflict first. Lesser challenges can be developed during storyboarding. You might otherwise go off on a tangent. Floyd Norman's cartoon in Figure 4.7 shows a pitch where the story man has lost sight of the whole point of his story.

Figure 4.7

A hero's goal must be clearly defined at the start. Illustration from *Son of Faster Cheaper* © Floyd Norman.

Conflicts can be summed up in a few words; some examples are given here. The stories of CINDERELLA, SNOW WHITE AND THE SEVEN DWARFS, and SLEEPING BEAUTY all contain conflicts between the heroine and jealous characters who wish to displace or kill her. This conflict may be described as: "*I want something* that you have." Some characters are victims of circumstance.

DUMBO must save his mother from jail and be accepted in the circus world. PINOCCHIO, an innocent led astray, must first deal with his own weakness in following bad advice before he can rescue his father from the whale by his own initiative. Beauty must rescue her father and also save Beast's life. Nemo's father must find his son who is lost somewhere in the Pacific Ocean. These conflicts are life-or-death situations. The characters "*must do it.*"

Simba in THE LION KING must overcome his character weakness and accept his responsibilities. This conflict may be described as "*I don't want to do it.*" Characters may prevail despite early setbacks. (This is a common device in animation storytelling.) They "*will do it.*"

Good characters make these simple conflicts interesting. It has been said that there are only a certain set number of basic plots in literature. If your characters are appealing and believable you will avoid the been-there-done-that feeling that comes when stock characters are placed in predictable situations. The character arc and story arc influence one another.

Exercise: Design and thumbnail two characters illustrating the following conflicts. You may use several sketches per example and include props.

    1. *I can't do it.*
    2. *I must do it.*
    3. *I want something that you have.*

An example is shown in Figure 4.8. This elementary conflict creates the germ of a story.

Figure 4.8

I don't want to do it. Which character displays the conflict? How might this conflict be resolved? How did it come to be? Conflict is established first, the resolution comes next...and the opening situation is developed last.

Write a few brief sentences describing your resolution to the conflict, then how it came to be. Try to write more than one and see which works best for you. You will have time to elaborate the gags and plot twists later. Thumbnail the more interesting ones. The sky is the limit at this point—this is why this phase of development is called *"blue sky."* Work with ideas that interest and intrigue you—don't create stories that you think a studio or audience *expects to see*. The best animation is made by artists who project their enthusiasm and spontaneity into their work.

Stealing the Show

The story should be told by the *most interesting* characters. Secondary characters are often used to help tell the hero's story. We often identify more with them than we do with the hero. For example, the rather ordinary Doctor Watson writes about the adventures of his extraordinary and unpredictable friend Mr. Sherlock Holmes. We see a great part of Snow White's story through the eyes of the Seven Dwarfs and the forest animals in the animated SNOW WHITE AND THE SEVEN DWARFS. These likable characters find her appealing, so we do too. We do not learn about the Seven Dwarfs' background because this material is not relevant to Snow White's story.

Subplots that distract from the main story idea should be avoided, or the film will break up into a series of disconnected threads. All subplots and secondary characters must support the main story. If the sidekick is more interesting than the hero, maybe you are telling the wrong character's story!

Heroes should have recognizable goals to achieve, obstacles to overcome, and a few flaws that make them imperfect and therefore interesting to us. If your hero easily solves every problem and never makes a mistake, they will never encounter conflict. There will be no surprise or suspense in their story because the outcome will be a foregone conclusion. Your hero will become a bore and secondary characters that *do* have obstacles to overcome will easily distract us from the main story.

Parodies and Pastiches

Parodies are mockeries of preexisting material. They will use the same plot elements and characters as the original staged as farce. Figure 4.9 shows a new staging of *Romeo and Juliet*. The characters may be taking themselves seriously, but their ludicrous appearance and the falling balcony make the scene comic. Parodies may or may not be affectionate, but you must be familiar with the original material to accurately mock it.

Parodies tend to work best in short formats. If the raucous mood continues for too long a time the mocking tone can become wearying. Parodying another movie or story essentially allows someone else to write the story for you. Your film is a reflection of another work and its success will depend on whether audiences are familiar with the original material.

A *pastiche* takes the elements of the source's style and affectionately reworks the material into something new. It can contain parody, but it is a distillation of a genre. Chuck Jones directed a brilliant series of pastiche cartoons including WHAT'S OPERA DOC? which distilled the 16-hour Wagnerian Ring cycle into a six-minute cartoon. SHREK's leads were characters from classic fairy tales, except that the roles were changed and fairy-tale clichés were turned on their heads—the "bad ogre" was the hero, the "beautiful princess" was the monster, and the "noble king" was the villain. Pastiches allow you to create original characters that have more depth and personality than a story that parodies a specific role or film.

Figure 4.9

A parody uses absurd characters and over-the-top interpretations to affectionately or sarcastically mock its source material.

When targeting a genre rather than a specific film, the animator takes cultural references that are familiar to the audience and reinterprets them to create something new. It's not what you do—it really *is* how you do it.

Beginning at the Ending: The Tex Avery "Twist"

Remember this Golden Rule of Animation Story: ALWAYS know where, and how, your picture is going to end, before you start *production*. (the creation of finished artwork that will appear on screen.)

The ending and the story conflict should be determined before you work on developing the characters and action. The middle of the story can be expanded or contracted as time and budget allows. You have to start somewhere, and your ending *must* be there.

Some films are constructed on the "moving train" pattern where the action is already under way when the story begins. Cat chases mouse, dog chases cat. Little time is needed for establishing motivation because the characters' situation is evident from the start of the film. These films typically build a series of gags, each one stronger than the other, with the most spectacular one at the finish. The Road Runner and Coyote cartoons are good examples of the "moving train" story.

Director Tex Avery delighted in creating meticulously plotted hyperbolic stories that broke all the rules of animation, but he once found himself stumped for an ending.

I interviewed Tex Avery about story construction in 1978, and we discussed this "exceptional" film (Figure 4.10).

4. Situation and Character Driven Stories

Figure 4.10

A caricature of a young Tex Avery by Nancy Beiman.

TEX AVERY: When analyzing a cartoon situation you should consider these three points: Is it a *good* situation? What can you do to develop it, and how are you going to finish it? Can you "switch" the story or do it in a new way?

Don't use dialogue unless it is absolutely necessary. You shouldn't tell what is happening on the screen.

NANCY BEIMAN: Would you have an idea of the total picture, beginning and end, from the start? Or would you build a film from a basic gag or situation and do the beginning and end last?

TEX AVERY: We'd generally start with the beginning and ending first. This leaves you room to "fill in". You should have a definite finish. A switch or surprise ending is good, a "tag." You can build up one situation to a ridiculous extent… and when the audience feels that you can't go any farther, you "top" it, thereby surprising them.

When constructing a story, you should start listing gags, not necessarily in order. Don't throw any of them out yet. "Dovetail" them until the gags become stronger and stronger. The gags don't have to be related to one another, but each should top the previous one.

One picture we didn't know how to end was BAD LUCK BLACKIE. [Author's note: This study in superstition is the story of a black cat that assists a small white kitten by repeatedly crossing a bullying bulldog's path; each time Blackie does this, ever-larger objects immediately fall in from offscreen and hit the dog on the head.] We built that picture so that it went from the bulldog getting hit by a flowerpot to the kitchen sink to a battleship. To sort of get a little humor into the thing, we had Blackie run across the dog's path differently each time—once on tiptoe, once like a Russian dancer. This was a gag within a gag. Finally we couldn't think of anything else to drop on [the bulldog]. How do you end it? Well, you're obliged to come back to the hero at the end of a cartoon. So you pull a switch—the kitten [now painted black] turns nasty and laughs like the dog did all through the picture.

NANCY BEIMAN: You didn't have that ending from the start?

TEX AVERY: No. We didn't know where we were going to end up.

Interview with Tex Avery © 1978, 2005 by Nancy Beiman

Although Tex refers to gags for short Hollywood cartoons, this manner of story development is used for plot points in feature films as well. An animation story is not an uncharted journey. Everything must be planned beforehand, but there are no formulas that you can follow to create a good story.

Tex mentions the "obligation" to show the hero at the end of a cartoon. This device is not used in all animated stories. In some cases, such as Pixar's INSIDE OUT, you may have more than one hero to consider!

Storyboards and characters develop simultaneously…so let's see about casting some characters.

5

Treat 'em Rough: Beginning Character Design and Setting Story Rules

You will need some rough character designs to put into your storyboards. Start sketching ideas for the characters as you establish your basic story line—sometimes it helps to write and draw story ideas at the same time (Figure 5.1).

Figure 5.1

These sketches were drawn on the same page as a rough outline for a personal film. Some of the text appears near the drawings. (OLD TRICKS © 2016 by Nancy Beiman.)

Try drawing more than one interpretation of each character; vary the shapes and proportions and see which ones work best for you. Consider its personality and what it has to do in the film. This will influence the design. Research clothing styles and period fashions if needed.

Work up as many variations as you can think of. The characters will *evolve* as you draw them slightly differently each time. *Evolving* means changing the design as you work with it so that the portions that you find difficult to move are simplified. There should be no problems posing the characters or having them *act* (show emotion and personality through facial and body expression) (Figure 5.2).

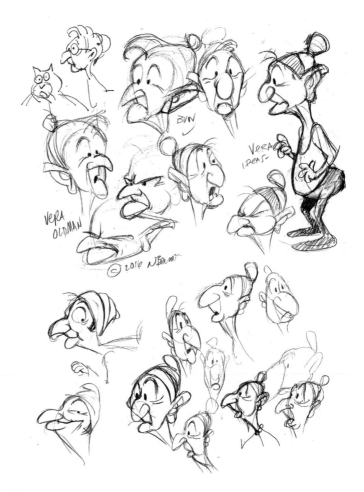

Figure 5.2

Rough character explorations for Vera, drawn over a two-day period. She is beginning to *evolve*. At this point in time, no design is thrown out. (OLD TRICKS © 2016 by Nancy Beiman.)

Do not worry if these are not the "final designs." Keep drawing until you find shapes and designs that appeal to you. The design is fully evolved when you can draw it easily. You may want to work on lined paper or an evenly lined background, because this is an easy way of determining the proportions in each design (Figure 5.3).

Once you find a design that appears to be going in the right direction, draw front, three quarter, and side views showing consistent scale, as in Figure 5.4. You might try the poses on more than one design variant. Don't worry if the different angles are not consistent at this time. The characters will continue to evolve on the storyboard, where you will be drawing them very quickly and simplification will naturally occur. The test of a good character design is whether it can perform the action and acting that the story requires.

A lined background is very helpful at this point because it allows you to compare design proportions or experiment with variations on one design. Vera's face continues to evolve as I experiment with different emotions that she'll use in the film. (OLD TRICKS © 2016 by Nancy Beiman.)

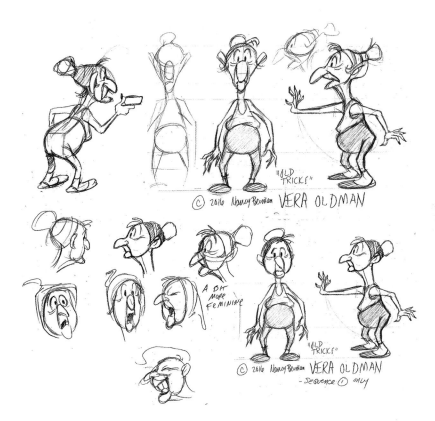

Figure 5.4

Rough sketches for two Vera-ations—at this point, I'm not sure which one I'll use. The test will come when I begin storyboard; the final design may use elements from both. (Vera from OLD TRICKS © 2016 by Nancy Beiman.)

In Figure 5.5, evolution continues as I try some more variations on Vera's design and experiment with facial expressions. I'm feeling more confident with this version of the character. The next step will be to either complete a short animated scene with Vera performing a simple action, or to storyboard the film and let the design evolve as Vera is repeatedly drawn in new poses. I will complete a lineup comparing Vera's scale with that of the other characters in the film after they are designed, and will try to keep this size relationship consistent in storyboard. The appearance of all of the characters will evolve as the boards progress, and I'll probably redo the model sheets after the storyboard is completed—with "action poses" from the boards used as reference for the animation.

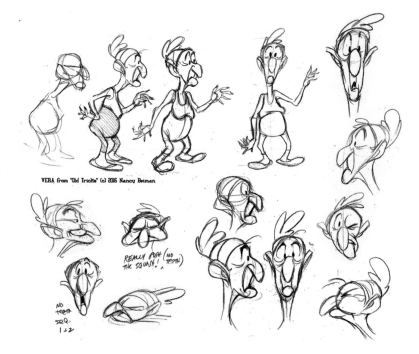

VERA from "Old Tricks" (c) 2016 Nancy Beiman

Figure 5.5

Another "Vera-ation". I try a few facial expressions, which are beginning to come more easily. Repeatedly drawing the character on the storyboard will refine the design and eliminate unnecessary details. (Vera from OLD TRICKS © 2016 by Nancy Beiman.)

I needed to design Fuzz the Cat along with Vera for my film OLD TRICKS because they appear in most scenes together. Some sketches exploring his personality appear in Figure 5.6.

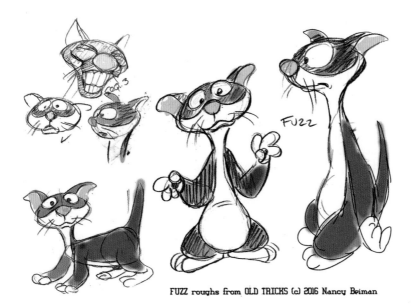

FUZZ roughs from OLD TRICKS (c) 2016 Nancy Beiman

Figure 5.6

Unlike Vera, I got a design for Fuzz the Cat that I liked almost immediately. But it evolved as the story changed—this is not the final version! (Characters from OLD TRICKS © 2016 Nancy Beiman.)

Vera and Fuzz's proportions are explored at greater length when they start to work together in Figure 5.7. Fuzz has to be small enough to fit inside a bag that Vera carries later on in the film. Simple graphic shapes are used to construct the head, body, and limbs. Legs and arms are "drawn through" the torso so that they attach on opposite sides of the body and create a feeling of volume in the design.

OLD TRICKS characters (c) 2016 Nancy Beiman

VERA   FUZZ
rough size comparison

Figure 5.7

The relationship between two characters is explored with simple props and backgrounds. (Artwork from OLD TRICKS © 2016 Nancy Beiman.)

Vera and Fuzz are shown in a simple setting with a few props that will be used in the film—like the characters, the prop design is not final at this time.

The Line of Beauty and the Line of Action

Animated characters should suggest the possibility of movement even if they are standing still. You can see how Vera's body in Figures 5.4 and 5.7 is in a slightly curved pose suggesting a thin letter S. Figure 5.8 shows an attractive girl who is constructed along an exaggerated S-curve. Both women illustrate a major animation design principle—the *line of action*.

Figure 5.8

A pretty girl that is constructed along an S-curve, or "Line of Beauty." In animation, it is called the Line of Action because it will be in motion. (Reproduced from *Scribblings 2* by permission of Dean Yeagle.)

The Line of Beauty was described by William Hogarth, but it appears in the art of many cultures. The Line, a modified S-curve, is used to create a feeling of motion and life in a still image. The cats in Figure 5.9 illustrate the line of beauty very well. Their bodies are a pleasing combination of contrasting curves and straight shapes constructed along an S-curve.

Figure 5.9

Cats display strong lines of beauty in design and in real life. © Nina L. Haley.

In animation, this line will direct the movement of the characters. It will be in a constant state of change because it appears in a long series of images. So animators refer to it as the *line of action* (Figure 5.10).

Figure 5.10

An early Vera design, showing character construction and the line of action that will change as she moves. (OLD TRICKS © 2016 Nancy Beiman.)

A good animated design will contain a line of action and use contrasting straight and curved shapes to create "fast" and "slow" areas as shown in Figure 5.11. It is possible to create movement in a still drawing because different areas are viewed at (fractionally) different times. The eye travels at slower speed and lingers longest in the more detailed areas. Faces, and particularly eyes, are viewed first.

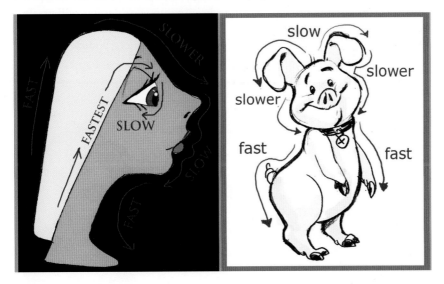

Figure 5.11

The eye travels at different speeds when viewing different sections of a design, lingering longest on detailed areas. Our attention should remain longest on the important parts of the design. "Fast" and "Slow" areas are indicated in red.

The owl in Figure 5.12 has poor silhouette value and no line of action; his pick and miner's equipment is barely visible. The toucan lady's silhouette works a bit better, but she is in a symmetrical pose with very even proportions and also lacks a line of action. The background is cluttered and poorly composed, with a chair apparently attached to the owl's back and the tree appearing to rise out of the characters' heads. This flattens the composition by creating *tangents*, which will be discussed in Chapter 10.

Figure 5.12

These characters are very *static* (stationary) because they lack a line of action. The artist has used surface detail to attempt to compensate for the lack of structure and movement. It's also very hard to see the props. In storyboard, these designs would need to evolve simpler shapes and eliminate most of the detail. (Nancy Beiman collection)

The line of action should appear in all of your character's poses, particularly when they are in motion, but also when they are at rest. The line of action will be used to determine all of the key poses for your animation. It can reverse and morph, and sometimes there will be more than one line of action working in the pose. Incorporating the line of action or beauty into your designs will create a feeling of life and movement in even a "still" drawing, as shown in Figure 5.13. The main line of action determines the pose of the characters' bodies. Secondary lines of action appear on Lali's arms and Suvali's trunk.

Figure 5.13

A character's pose might have more than one line of action. The main one will be on the body; secondary lines of action may appear on arms, legs, or other parts of the body. Goral, Lali, and Suvali from BOLLYWOOD BABY © Nancy Beiman.

5. Treat 'em Rough: Beginning Character Design and Setting Story Rules

Use a line of action in all of your character poses. Remember, these designs must be able to move. Start thinking of the animation possibilities while you develop the story's rules.

Establishing Story Rules

"I can't believe that!" said Alice.

"Can't you?" the Queen said in a pitying tone. "Try again, draw a long breath, and shut your eyes." Alice laughed. "There's no use trying," she said. "One can't believe impossible things."

"I dare say you haven't had much practice," said the queen. "When I was your age, I always did it for half an hour a day. Why, sometimes I've believed as many as six impossible things before breakfast."

—Lewis Carroll
Alice in Wonderland

The hardest assignment I have ever received was to "do whatever I liked." You can run off in all directions if you don't set the rules for your project at the start. Rules allow your new animated world and your characters to function with their own set of natural laws, which might not be those of the "real" world.

Here are some Rules created for the ROAD RUNNER cartoons by Chuck Jones and story man Mike Maltese:

1. The Road Runner never leaves the Road.
2. The action always takes place in the American Southwest.
3. The Coyote's clever traps invariably backfire on him.

It ultimately does not matter that the Coyote does not catch the Road Runner. Jones defined the Coyote's mindset and the point of the series by quoting George Santayana: "Fanaticism consists in redoubling your efforts when you have forgotten your aim."

Be sure to follow your own story's rules. If you have created a world where characters can breathe underwater without special equipment, it is disturbing to have one character suddenly find it impossible to breathe unless there is a need (and an explanation) for it in the story.

Every detail of character and setting should contribute to getting the story across as clearly as possible. If your story takes place in ancient Greece, but characters can "pop" forward to modern times, be sure to explain the rules of your new world so that we understand how and why this time shift happens. If your character must go *against* a rule—say, by befriending a character that we, and it, see as an enemy—establish your rules first before they are broken. For example, everyone knows cartoon dogs and cats hate each other. Or do they? In Chuck Jones' FEED THE KITTY, this rule is reversed when a tough bulldog falls in love with a cute kitten. At first the dog challenges the kitten, but it simply ignores the barking and makes a nest in the dog's fur. The bulldog falls in love. Conflict arises when the dog tries to hide his new friend from his mistress, who has told him that he may not have any more "things" in the house. The story ends happily when the dog is allowed to keep the kitten after rescuing it from a series of increasingly dangerous situations.

Exercise: Sketch some simple characters for the following four situations. Next, list some Rules that might affect the character relationships and the story. Illustrate each Rule with a thumbnail of the characters in a recognizable setting. Work on lined yellow pads to help you vary the proportions of each character. Keep the sketches very rough and do not cross anything out. After you have drawn a few characters sketch thumbnail drawings of possible conflicts and endings for each situation.

1. A difficult mother-in-law is visiting her daughter and son-in-law. The mother-in-law is a Witch.
2. Children on the first day of school. The characters are all single-celled organisms.
3. A small alien spacecraft lands in a suburban back yard. The alien's weapons prove to be no match against a dog and a rabbit (see Figures 5.14 and 5.15).
4. Your story takes place inside and on top of a dresser. All of your characters are made from different articles of clothing. It is laundry day.

Figure 5.14

An alien's appearance and weapons are no threat to a dog and a rabbit. How could this story resolve?

5. Treat 'em Rough: Beginning Character Design and Setting Story Rules

Keep an open mind about story and characters at this point. Experiment with different situations, let the story develop in unusual directions, and don't take the obvious way out (Figure 5.15). The rule in some story sessions is to "never say 'No'" at this point in the story's development. An idea that seems odd at first may become "right" later on. In story as with animation, it is better to go "too far" and pull back than to not act strongly enough. And with a novel interpretation, or story "twist", a familiar story can become something new and different.

You are now refining your characters' appearance and investigating how they act and interact with one another. Do your designs have appeal? We will define this essential quality in Chapter 6.

Figure 5.15

There is never only "one way" to tell a story; explore different possibilities and pick the most interesting one.

6

Appealing or Appalling? Designing Characters with Personality

Form Follows Function

"You mean somebody's actually waiting to see *this*?"

—**Director William**
*"One-Shot" Beaudine's reply when he was asked to speed up
production to meet a deadline*

You do not have to like a character to find it appealing. You need only care to know about what happens to it. Appeal in animation may be defined in the phrase, "Do I, the viewer, want to spend a few minutes or hours of my life with this character and this story? Am I willing to suspend disbelief and accept the character as a sentient being? Are its problems of interest to me?"

An appealing character is interesting to look at. Appeal does *not* mean that it is "cute," lovable, infantile, or cuddly. Monster movies contain good examples of appealing "negative" characters. We want to know about the monster *and* the victims. Victims are often disposable props who never develop as personalities. We are horrified by what happens to them, but we sometimes identify more with the monster! (Figure 6.1).

An appealing character will have a design that is interesting, but not so complex that it is unable to perform actions required by the story. The design of the character and the production must never prevent the character's actions from being clearly perceived by the audience.

Figure 6.1

Giant Ape attacks city! Do we identify with the city or the ape? We may feel empathy for the human victims and sympathy for the monster.

Form follows function in animation. The story and its action will affect your character's design. For example, if Character A has to hug Character B, it is very important to make Character A's arms long enough to fit around Character B's body! (See Figure 6.2).

Figure 6.2

Know what the character has to do *before* you model it. The design should help, not hinder, character motion.

If Character A is designed in isolation and not concurrently with Character B, such accidents can easily occur. Drawn characters can stretch their arms if necessary, but we must consider this stretchiness a conscious design on the part of the creator, not an attempt to repair a design mistake. We now are dealing with a chicken-or-egg theory. If we haven't yet set our story, but want to design an appealing character, where do we start?

Make your mistakes on paper. It is an easy matter to adjust the length of Character A's arms before you start animating, but not so easy once you have already built the puppet on a set or on the computer.

Most films contain more than one character. Before you refine designs and begin storyboarding you must first set the scale, or size relationships, of your characters to one another. You might say that...

Size Matters: The Importance of Scale

The storyboard artists should be made aware of a character's scale, strength, and physical limitations at the start of production so that they do not board actions that are impossible for the "actors" to perform. Characters without fingers and thumbs such as the penguins in Figure 6.2 would have to play piano by some other method. Dealing with a physical limitation can produce very entertaining animated solutions.

Reading the Design: Silhouette Value

A good animated character, in any medium, will have a recognizable shape. When we can identify it instantly in silhouette, we say that it *reads* well (Figure 6.3).

Figure 6.3

A famous silhouette.

Always consider silhouette value when designing a character. The standard method of testing a design is to black in the entire shape to test the readability. Create a rough silhouette for each character when you create your character lineup. Work loosely and experiment with a variety of shapes. If you have more than one character, work on them simultaneously and vary the size and shapes of the silhouettes.

Figure 6.4 shows silhouette figures of two Chinese monks that represent enthusiasm and experience. The younger character is unbalanced and top-heavy. His form was based on the shape of a long-necked vase. This character's motions are strong but ineffective, because he does not think before he acts. The Master is weightier due to his age and experience. His form is based on that of a rock; he is grounded, stable, and his moves are deliberate and decisive.

Figure 6.4

These silhouettes read well and depict typical attitudes of two characters. (Reproduced by permission of Joseph Daniels and Jedidiah Mitchell.)

The character designer will sketch the characters interacting with one another before the designs are even created, and sometimes set them into their environment as shown in Figure 6.5. Character interactions are more important than the design at this point. The scale determines everything else in the animation and staging.

Don't worry about textures and always work rough when exploring your characters' design and relationship to each other. Draw action poses at full length and also explore different facial expressions, keeping the acting *in character*. (Definition: Is it something that this character would do or feel? Does it express the character's personality?) Your story will tell you which expressions and actions are suitable for your cartoon actors. You may write a description of a character's attitudes on the page and see which of your poses and expressions

6. Appealing or Appalling? Designing Characters with Personality

Figure 6.5

Rough character exploration for Ye and Kongo. The settings are included along with experimental color schemes. (KONGO © 2014 Yacheng Guo.)

best illustrate them. If one sketch does not work, simply go on to another. Do not throw any of your sketches out! Make a paste up of the best poses and use them as rough models for storyboard or test animation (Figure 6.6). These are called *placeholders* because they are not the final design. Each character should have its own model sheet. Sometimes a scene of test animation is done and the strongest keys and breakdowns are used for an action model sheet—but storyboard drawings are also used for this purpose.

Scale is set in a character *"lineup"* possibly with a *turnaround* like the one shown in Figure 6.7. Many different scale combinations may be tried to see which ones work best. Kongo's size was greatly reduced so that Ye would read better in their scenes together. The *turnaround* shows them from different angles. Once rough size differences are agreed on, storyboard artists use the rough character sketches—sometimes only the character lineup—as *"placeholder"* or *temporary*, characters for the storyboard. The lineup may have to be redrawn after the storyboard is completed because the boards will explore the characters' design, scale, and expressiveness. In the final film, the scale may change in animation depending on the story point and staging.

Figure 6.6

The rough action model sheet of Ye is only intended as a *placeholder* for the storyboards. The final character design was not achieved until after the storyboard was finished.

Figure 6.7

Characters that work together are designed together; their scale is set in a character *lineup* that may also include important props. This lineup includes *turnarounds*, or rotations, of both characters. (KONGO © 2014 by Yacheng Guo.)

Designs will change, or *evolve*, as characters are drawn over and over on the storyboards, as discussed in Chapter 5. But additional variations may occur. The character scale may actually change at different times. Compare Ye and Kongo in the last panel of Figure 6.8 to the original sketches in Figure 6.5 and the lineup in Figure 6.7. The monster is smaller at the end of the film so that he seems to be less threatening. KONGO can be viewed at https://www.youtube.com/watch?v=dd653fppF9o.

Remember: There is no *one* way to design characters, and there is no *one* way to tell a story. All animated film is moving art, in a world that you have created. As long as your audience accepts your characters, "cheats" like the ones used in KONGO will not be noticed.

SCENE #   17   PANEL #   2

Action:
Ye breaks the surface of the water and comes out.

SFX:
Ye:haaa...

TIMING:

SCENE #   17   PANEL #   3

Action:

Ye comes out from the water, and now every thing quieted down.

TIMING:

SCENE #   18   PANEL #   1

Action:

Ye turns back his haed, and Kongo is in the water too, right now both of them feel sorry to each other.

TIMING:

PAGE :   21

Figure 6.8

The final storyboards will often "evolve" the character so that it is simpler and easier to draw. Character scale may change to make a story point. (Artwork from KONGO © 2014 by Yacheng Guo.)

Scale and Storytelling

Be sure to have your character relationships established, especially if you are modeling CGI characters. In one instance, a student designed and modeled two characters independently of one another and found that when he put them together, a rabbit was twice the size of the fox. This was not "realistic," but it was extremely funny, and fortunately for him this "mistake" worked out well in the context of his film (Figure 6.9).

Figure 6.9

A very large rabbit chased by a very small fox. The fox was originally planned to be larger than the rabbit. The mistake produced a funnier film. Most scale accidents won't end this happily.

Character scale is additionally determined by backgrounds and props. The location can cause a character's scale to vary from sequence to sequence. If you are designing "Jack and the Beanstalk," your hero will have two size relationships. The first one will be to the objects in Jack's home, and the second to objects in the Giant's castle. Scale is established by designing the props with the character, but insufficient information can cause confusion.

(a)   (b)

Figure 6.10

Jack and two chairs. The scale is ambiguous in (b).

In Figure 6.10a we can accept that Jack is a normal-sized man with a normal-sized chair because they appear to work to the same scale. Example Figure 6.10b is more ambiguous. It is not really clear in the second drawing whether Jack is a normal man with a very large chair, or a tiny man standing next to a normal-sized chair. A bit of clarity develops in Figure 6.11 with the addition of a background that shares the same scale as the chair.

Even with the background we are still not sure whether Jack is a tiny man in a normal house, or a normal-sized man in a Giant's house. The addition of a second character in Figure 6.12 that is scaled to the chair eliminates the problem. It's also very clear that not all Giants are human!

Figure 6.11

The characters' scale is set by its relationship to other characters and to background details and props. Here, the scale of the background shows that Jack is either a tiny man in a normal house, or a normal man in a Giant's house.

Figure 6.12

The new character "scales" to the furniture and makes it clear that Jack is extremely small.

Remember, large or small characters only appear that way when they contrast with other characters or background elements in the scene. The girl on the left in Figure 6.13 might just be looking for a piece of cheese. The girl on the right is offering it to a mouse, which is nearly as large, or as small, as she is.

Even "ordinary" characters can become interesting if props and appropriate costumes are designed with the figures. Tools and uniforms symbolizing specific occupations can create variety in background or crowd character designs. Never just draw "a man" or "a woman." Simple props can help define a personality (Figure 6.14).

Contrasting shapes are used in character design to create visual interest and scale portions of the character *against itself*. A very fat character's body size may be exaggerated by diminutive feet and hands. Impressions of gigantism

Figure 6.13

The girl's scale and proportion instantly changes when another character is added to the scene. Both characters in the right hand illustration are very small.

Figure 6.14

Design important props along with the characters. This will help them work well together in animation. It also helps define the characters' personalities. Shading in the silhouette tests the design's readability.

can be created by greatly distorting the scale of the head and hands relative to the body as shown in Figure 6.15. A prop building and tree aid in establishing the giant's size.

Varied proportions create interesting character designs that read well at a distance. In Figure 6.16, Character (a) is evenly proportioned with a smooth surface and no strongly defined forms. The design was drawn as an outline with no variation in the scale of the body parts. The exterior of the character was modeled first and the skeleton added later. Character (b) was designed *from the inside out*, beginning with its skeleton. The limbs and body were carefully designed to display an interesting variety of scales and textures. Although the character was very small, its silhouette read well even in long shots.

Figure 6.15

Contrasting shapes within the design, scale a character against itself. A "giant" may have large hands and a small head in proportion to the rest of its body. Background elements (a building) turn a large man into a giant. A very fat character might have hands and feet that are smaller than normal.

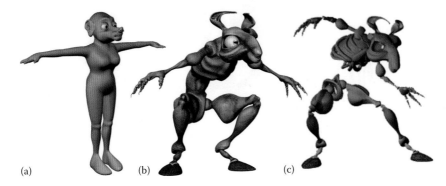

(a) (b) (c)

Figure 6.16

A symmetrical character and a second design that scales various portions of the character against itself. (Reproduced by permission of Nathaniel Hubbell.)

Study human and animal anatomy to learn how a character's external shape and range of motion are both determined by its underlying muscle and bone structure. Mammalian, avian, or reptilian skeletons can be adapted or combined to give naturally occurring or fantastic creatures a solid structure that helps you design, draw, and rig believable characters, whether real or fantastic.

Getting Into Character

Scale and proportion can indicate character relationships. Villains are sometimes larger and heavier than the heroes. Burly actors playing villains in early comedies were actually known as "heavies" because they dwarfed the comedian. This made the villain a more menacing presence and we automatically feel sympathy for the "little guy." This tradition continued in some animated cartoons. But there were comedians who turned this stereotype on its head. Laurel and Hardy, who were both tall men, often cast very small actors as their villains, as shown in Figure 6.17. These nasty little men and women made the Boys' lives miserable in countless films. The villainy was projected by their actions and attitudes, not by their physical scale, and their silhouette contrasted amusingly with that of the two comedians. It is easy to ignore the fact that Stan and Ollie are taller than these menaces because their characters' mental stature is so small.

Figure 6.17

Caricature of Laurel and Hardy with James Finlayson and Daphne Pollard, two of their small "villains."

Character models sometimes are not consistent. Tex Avery took particular delight in having small, "cute" characters react ferociously to large intruders, suddenly displaying outsized fangs or claws when annoyed. The scale of a mouth, the eyes, or the entire body would change dramatically in the famous "*Tex Avery 'take'*" and return to normal when it was over. If your characters have this ability, your lineup may contain more than one version of the same design, to show how the action changes the scale (Figure 6.18).

Figure 6.18

A cute character doing a Tex Avery "take." Different parts of the cat's body can change scale depending on its mood. Both poses should be on the lineup.

Body shapes can impart subconscious meaning to the viewer. For example, two figures in an animated story represent Youth and Old Age. I designed the younger figure in Figure 6.19 as a column of coltish long legs topped by

Figure 6.19

Characters portray their age in their silhouettes. The older figure contains some infantile features such as small extremities scaling against a larger body.

a large ellipse of a head that suggests childish inexperience. The older figure is entirely contained in a circle that symbolizes her self-sufficiency and age. The shapes tell us something about their characters before they have even begun to move.

The bony structure of the human skeleton, in particular the jaw and spine, shrinks as a person ages. This loss of bone mass and a heavier body can cause an old person's hands and feet to appear proportionately smaller than those of younger people. Babies also have large, heavy bodies that contrast with small, rounded arms, and legs. Some elderly character designs may share these infantile proportions, as shown in Figure 6.19. Young animals tend to have large feet and longer legs than adults, depending on the species. The girl in Figure 6.19 has long legs that resemble those of a young horse or deer.

Conversely, the cartilaginous tissue in the nose and ears never stops growing and joints become gnarled with arthritis as a person ages. Elderly people appear to have larger noses and ears because they really do, as illustrated by the troll family in Figure 6.20. The troll parent's hands have enlarged finger joints and her nose and ears are enormous. The young troll's skeletal definition is hidden under a layer of baby fat. Some of her body proportions resemble those of the old lady in Figure 6.19.

Figure 6.20

Youth and age exhibit significant physical differences, but there are also some similarities. The baby troll's tiny hands and large body are similar to those of the old woman in Figure 6.19. The old troll has a huge nose and ears that keep growing throughout life, as sometimes happens with older humans. Its hands are gnarled, but are relatively small in relation to its large body.

Foundation Shapes and Their Meaning

I will refer to some shapes as "foundation" shapes because they form the basis for complex designs in the art of many cultures. The three foundation shapes are *circles and ovals* (which are easiest to draw and distort), *squares*, and *triangles*. (These shapes translate into "primitives" in CGI programs.) The graphic animated symbol and the more rounded, dimensional character will both be created from the interplay of these foundation shapes. A graphically styled film may use the shapes with little modification, as shown in Figure 6.21. A dimensional character's design will seem more complex, but will still use graphic foundation shapes for its basic construction.

Figure 6.21

A simple character may consist only of foundation shapes. EM!® from *We All Die Alone* © by Mark Newgarden. (Reproduced by permission of Mark Newgarden.)

Certain shapes have taken on symbolic meaning over the centuries. Circular characters are seen as cute or nonthreatening. Squares (including rectangles) are solid and dependable. Triangles are active. This interpretation goes back to the Middle Ages, when most people in Europe were illiterate and were taught important lessons through colors and shapes used in religious art.

It is very amusing to turn these stereotypes upside down and work against type. An adorable round little character could have a nasty personality, a triangular design can be used for a reactive or passive character, and a square can be a real blockhead. Variations on the basic shapes are used in character construction in all media. The shapes have, over time, taken on specific meanings in certain contexts. Sometimes the same shape can be used to portray diametrically opposing characteristics. A circle is open and trusting or a babyish nonentity (Figure 6.22). A square is trustworthy, dependable, and centered or it can be a real blockhead (Figure 6.23).

A triangle is quick, sharp, aggressive, and insightful. Triangular characters precipitate the action and get things done. The triangle frequently appears in designs for villains and heroes. A character constructed primarily from triangular shapes will seem proactive or aggressive. Sherlock Holmes is a perfect example of this character type: he has a pointed nose, pointed fingers, wears a triangular cape, and even his name sounds "sharp." Watson, the steadfast friend who narrates the stories, sounds like a "square." Generations of illustrators have portrayed him as a square-jawed, square-bodied, and a heavyset "square" figure as a contrast to Holmes' triangular thinness (Figure 6.24).

6. Appealing or Appalling? Designing Characters with Personality

(a)   (b)

Figure 6.22

CIRCLE/OVAL: (a) Reassuring, trusting, nonaggressive, OR (b) bland, saccharine, and infantile.

(a)   (b)   (c)

Figure 6.23

SQUARE: (a) Solid, dependable, (b) strong, balanced, OR (c) unyielding, inflexible.

sherlock holmes arrests the easter bunny

Figure 6.24

Sherlock Holmes and Doctor Watson, a triangle and a square. I've accentuated Watson's "squareness" by adding a checkered pattern to his clothing.

Foundation Shapes and Their Meaning

This contrast in shape also applies to animated and live-action incarnations of Holmes and Watson. Benedict Cumberbatch's scarf and cape create an unmistakably triangular silhouette in SHERLOCK, and Martin Freeman's Watson costume turns him into a perfect "square." Mark Gatiss' face is round, which is appropriate because his Mycroft character is a "catalyst" who initiates the action in a story… as can be clearly seen in my caricature of the cast and a few extras in Figure 6.25.

Figure 6.25

The modern "Sherlock" continues the old tradition of having a thin, "triangular" actor play Sherlock Holmes and a square-jawed actor cast as Watson. Mycroft Holmes has been played by actors with round bodies—or round faces, as shown here. © 2014 Nancy Beiman

Yet a triangle, when used point uppermost as the foundation shape for a head, indicates a character of low intelligence (Figure 6.26). These stereotypical shapes can help the character's appearance convey its personality.

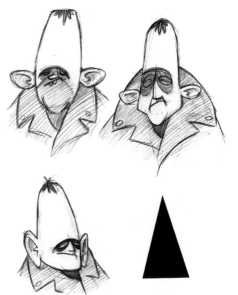

Figure 6.26

A pointy-headed gangster. (Reproduced by permission of William Robinson.)

6. Appealing or Appalling? Designing Characters with Personality

Stereotyped characters are very common: "Fat people are jolly, thin people with glasses are nerds, villains are huge and menacing." This is not true at all times, but it will be useful to you *sometimes*. Stereotypical elements may appear in the design to render characters' personalities instantly recognizable. It is more interesting to avoid using them and instead create personality through the character's body language and movement. The creation of character through movement will be discussed in Chapter 8.

You will find that you can create more variety in the design by playing forms against one another. Work for a pleasing variety of shapes, straight or flat areas flowing into curves, and good silhouette value.

Human faces are a variant on a simple pattern. Figure 6.27 shows different face shapes with the features at differing levels. One is round, one square, and two are oval. The size of the eyes, mouth, and nose vary to create even greater differences. The shape of the hair complements and emphasizes the facial design.

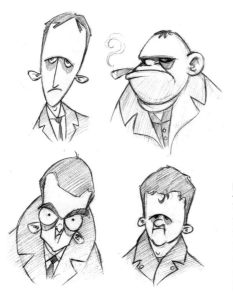

Figure 6.27

Varied proportions on basic shapes will create new characters. Faces with even proportions will often seem less lifelike than caricatures. These Gangster Studies were based on antique photographs. (Reproduced by permission of William Robinson.)

Caricatures of famous or infamous people may provide inspiration for a character design. This gives it more depth than one created from whole cloth. Figure 6.28 shows a character that I designed that was loosely based on the famous actor James Cagney, who often portrayed gangsters. Here, he is a "spider mite"—a very small, parasitic insect—but I have only drawn the design and not attempted to show its scale. The basic shape is oval, but there are a lot of square and triangular shapes in the design as well.

Figure 6.29 shows several caricatures of the same woman's face, based on an old photograph. If you use a caricature of a person as a basis for your character, determine which foundation shapes and proportions suggest their likeness. Use these shapes as a starting point for construction and vary the proportions to "push" the design so that it becomes something new. You may combine features from more than one person and even add a few animal traits to create an original character. Use sketchbook drawings as reference for typical poses and features. Vary the proportions and try several different designs where some features are

Figure 6.28

A spider mite villain in a world of insects, based on a caricature of the actor James Cagney.

Figure 6.29

Different characters are created by varying the proportions of designs based on a historic photograph. (Reproduced by permission of William Robinson.)

emphasized more than the others—but make sure that all of them work together as part of an organic whole. A good design features *repetition with variation and exaggeration*. The negative space is just as important as the positive space…check your silhouette value.

Exercise: Take drawings from your sketchbook and one photograph or illustration of a person from a specific historical era. Design a new character wearing period clothing standing in the sketchbook pose. Then "push" the proportions in several drawings as shown in Figure 6.30.

Figure 6.30

A "period style" incorporates silhouettes and colors from a particular time and place. In this case, the character was based on a rough caricature of an actual person.

Evolving the Characters

Good design is a continuing process of simplification and communication. Inanimate objects may be "organic" in the sense that animation brings them to life, but the meaning of the word differs when used in a design sense. Organic designs have shapes that flow into one another. They are not simply stuck together like a snowman. Remember that your designs describe a volume, not merely the outline of a shape. Think in the third dimension, not in line. Design the whole character, not a series of discrete components.

Identically sized foundation shapes can result in a repetitive and uninteresting design as shown in Figure 6.31. A flat and symmetrically constructed character is in danger of illustrating what I call the cookie-cutter or "Gingerbread Man" effect. This symmetry is generally avoided unless you are actually *designing* a Gingerbread Man.

Figure 6.31

Each part of the cat's form is a discrete shape with no blending. The shapes are roughly the same size, which gives the design a cookie-cutter appearance.

The cat in Figure 6.32 is slightly more organic but could use improvement. The head is roughly the same size as the body, and the length of the legs is about equal to the height of the cat's head.

Figure 6.32

Another cat, and a slightly better design. The separate parts of the body have now blended to make an organic whole.

My design for Fuzz the Cat in Figure 6.33 has more pleasing proportions; a few variations were tried, but a design based largely on triangles and circles was the one I found most appealing. The placement of joints and volumes can vary, but the character must be able to animate. My first drawing, on the left, gave me the basic construction for the hind end and the tail, but I wasn't happy with the front paws. The second drawing started to evolve the design, broadening his chest a bit, and revised his face; the flop ears were a last minute addition. There are only a few small differences in the two designs, but what a change in the personality! The final design will evolve as the storyboard progresses.

Figure 6.33

Fuzz the Cat's design at right has evolved from the original design at the left. The film's action requires him to have a long neck. A slight forehead makes him appear more intelligent. (OLD TRICKS © 2016 Nancy Beiman.)

Try experimenting with variations and combinations of shapes when designing your characters and this will make your film unique. But never consciously design characters in a style that is currently fashionable. Character designs that imitate the ones in popular animated films can often seem interchangeable…which is why I do not recommend using animated films as design reference for your projects. Use your own resources and interpretations! (Figure 6.34)

Work out basic shapes and silhouettes first, leaving details for last.

Figure 6.34

These cats are variations on a theme. Note how the leg and body proportions change in the sketches. Be creative and experiment with design based on your own interpretation of reality—don't copy other animated films.

The Shape of Things

Thus far we have only discussed organic shapes and creatures. Animation allows you to bring inorganic or inanimate objects to life. Inanimate objects have frequently been used to suggest human personality types. Their construction is similar to that used for organic characters. The only difference may be that the primary or "foundation" shapes will register more prominently in the final design, which may not permit the elastic movement commonly found in an organic character.

Use visual puns when working with inanimate objects. Silhouettes can suggest other creatures. Do a chair's proportions suggest a child or an adult character? Does a musical instrument resemble a bird? (Figure 6.35)

Figure 6.35

Three saxophones turn into goose bodies and the mouthpieces became the beaks. The silhouette creates a "visual pun," but the design resembles the musical instrument more than the bird.

Try to avoid simply slapping a face on top of the object. Work with elements in the original design. See which ones suggest facial features or limbs. A good way to work is to start with an unmodified picture of the object and do repeated drawings, each more exaggerated, to *evolve* the features from it. Think of how the object's shape can suggest other creatures. Materials can also influence character motion, as shown in Figure 6.36. This technique may also be used when turning a human character into an object or an animal.

Figure 6.36

The fluidly flexible cat's movement is caricatured in quicksilver. The inorganic and the organic blend in this visual pun.

Exercise: Blend a human or animal design with an inanimate object in three drawings. Show the human or animal character in drawing A, then draw the object that you wish to combine it with as drawing C. Blend the features in drawing B. You may add more blend drawings if necessary. An example is shown in Figure 6.37. You may find that the midpoint drawing is more interesting than the final. Each design will vary. Try changing your original character into several different objects. Then try the exercise in reverse, starting with the inanimate object and translating it into a human or animal.

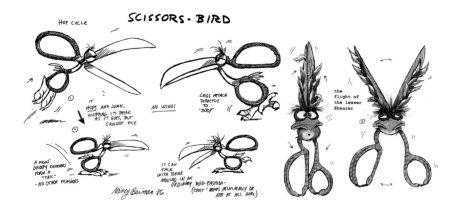

Figure 6.37

Inanimate objects can suggest human or animal characteristics and be brought to life in animation. The secret is to combine organic and inorganic elements in a way that does not completely lose the characteristics of the original object. *Evolve* the design in a series of sketches to see which features work best.

6. Appealing or Appalling? Designing Characters with Personality

Inorganic designs may have different sections appear as discrete forms (wheels and headlights on a truck body, for example). Or you may combine the organic and the inorganic in one design (a talking truck with lips in its grille). Care should be taken in this instance not to lose the quality that reads as "truck." The degree of organic input to the inorganic original will vary depending on the type of *universe* you create for your characters (Figure 6.38).

Figure 6.38

Character inspiration can come from organic or inorganic sources. These peaches from a Vancouver farmers' market resemble human faces. The farmer drew eyes on the fruit to enhance the resemblance. (Courtesy by Nancy Beiman.)

The character's personality and your story context will determine the amount of "human" and "nonhuman" influence in their design. In Figure 6.39, I have suggested an actress as a reference without actually caricaturing her, and composed the character from fruit. Her face is an orange. She has cherry lips and a leafy body. Her hair is made of pineapple slices and is topped with a pineapple leaf hat. She is drawn in an active pose because the design must be able to move. It is always a good idea to investigate how well the character "acts" (*moves in animation, expresses emotion*) before standardizing the design in a lineup or rotation of the design in one static pose (a "*turnaround*" as shown

Figure 6.39

The character's action should be drawn even in your earliest sketches. Always portray movement and expression when designing characters to see if they "act" well. "Turnarounds," character lineups, and modeling poses will come later.

in Figure 6.7). This creates a feeling of life. Remember, to animate means "*create the illusion of life.*" Your character designs should convey personality and the possibilities of motion. If your character does not move well and it's hard to get it into strong poses, it may be *overdesigned* (contain too much surface detail or lack basic structure, as we saw in Figure 5.12). If this is the case, you can do a *simplification pass*, where you keep drawing it over and over, changing the design each time to redesign, or remove parts of the design that do not work well until you are better able to turn the figure in space and make it act. The rough designs of Vera Oldman and Fuzz the Cat in Chapters 5 and 6 show how the character designs *evolve* when they are drawn in different action poses.

> "In the beginning the Universe was created. This has made a lot of people very angry and has been widely regarded as a bad move."
>
> **—Douglas Adams**
> *The Hitchhiker's Guide to the Galaxy*

Characters, backgrounds, and props that share a common context by their design are said to be from the same *universe.*

Establishing a "universe" is very important when a large crew is working on one project. Characters and backgrounds should work together and share stylistic elements that create a feeling of rightness and unity. The "universal" design principle, like all the other rules of design, can be broken if your story requires it. An alien being may literally be "from another universe" as in the film THE IRON GIANT, where the Giant was designed in a completely different style from the human characters.

The TOY STORY movies are also exceptions to the "unified-universe" theory of character design. The toys were designed in a variety of sizes and styles. A cartoon dinosaur, a troop of plastic Marines, a china piggy bank, a spaceman, and a rag-doll cowboy all fit in when they were in the "universe" of Andy's room. But when they ventured out into the "real world" outside their house, they were in a new universe where they were out of place and out of scale. (This is known as a "fish out of water" story.) Alternate universes also exist in Sid's house, where terrifyingly malformed toys are composed of elements that are wildly out of scale and context, and in the Pizza Planet dispensing machine (where the "Claw" is the only universe the alien characters know). These are exceptions that prove the rule. In most cases there will be a stylistic device—the shape of the eyes or the heads, the lightness or heaviness of the outlines, a color palette, and a common rendering style—that places a film's characters, backgrounds, and props in the same universe (Figure 6.40).

Not all animated characters have a family resemblance. How many cartoon families have children who look nothing at all like their parents? The Inappropriate Family in Figure 6.41 may be deliberately designed that way for comic purposes.

But what happens if a character's appearance changes as the story progresses? In my film OLD TRICKS, an old woman is literally transformed at the end of the picture from a poor old lady to a rich and tastelessly dressed old crone. She has a new set of teeth that changes the shape of her face; her hairdo, clothing, and her posture are all different. She's even taller than before because she's wearing high platform shoes.

When a character's appearance varies from sequence to sequence it is very important to keep some elements of the design consistent so that the audience accepts the new design as the same character. Vera's nose remains unchanged in her three incarnations in Figure 6.42. The color blue appears on her head in all

It would never work out, dear—we come from different worlds!

Figure 6.40

Characters that work together usually exist in a *universe* where their props, backgrounds, and character designs are unified by design. Characters can be from different universes if an explanation is provided in the story. Otherwise, the variation can cause confusion.

Vera Inappropriate

The *Inappropriate Family*

I.M. Inappropriate

Sue Inappropriate

Figure 6.41

Contrasting styles will call attention to themselves. Or they may make a comic point. The daughter of these two grotesques is designed in a completely different style from her parents.

Scg. 1   Seq. 2   Seq. 3

OLD TRICKS Vera First Lineup Design Variants (c) 2016 Nancy Beiman

Figure 6.42

The designs must "read" as the same character if the story calls for its appearance to change. Vera has some design elements common to all her incarnations in my film OLD TRICKS. (Artwork and characters © 2016 Nancy Beiman.)

Exercise: Design three human characters using the principles discussed in this chapter. Base one on circles, another on squares, and another on triangles. Place them on a lineup, as shown in Figure 6.42. Try rotating them in one pose, as shown in Figure 6.7.

Next, change the human designs into dogs. Keep some of the human characteristics in your new designs. Are there certain breeds whose body types suggest the personalities of the human characters?

Next, design three characters based on inanimate objects, using either the human or dog characters as reference. Use some of the same design elements in the new lineup. Will you be able to use "foundation shapes" to delineate different character types? Are these characters from the same *universe*? (Figure 6.43)

UNIVERSAL HARMONY

Figure 6.43

Unification of design creates believability in your characters and settings. Each animated film creates its own reality.

three designs. The story context also makes it very clear that it is Vera in all three sequences, because she is the only old lady character in the film.

Characters can be *over-designed*. Over-designed characters are like muscle-bound bodybuilders. They don't move with grace and suppleness. Make sure that surface details don't prevent the character from acting, or moving! Fussy surface detail is no substitute for a solid structure that allows the character to move well. Figure 5.12 shows an example of over-designed characters that have plenty of surface texture but no construction.

You may use or avoid stereotypes of scale as you use or avoid stereotypes of design. All's fair in love and animation. But what if your hero and your villain are exactly the same size? Variations on a theme will be discussed in Chapter 7.

6. Appealing or Appalling? Designing Characters with Personality

7

Working with Multiple Characters

Triple Trouble: Contrasts in Design

When you are designing multiple characters it is common to work with contrasting silhouettes, for example, tall and thin versus short and fat. We generally don't want to have all of the characters the same size. Use the foundation shapes in different proportions and construct the characters inside a silhouette, although the two pigs in Figure 7.1 are both based on circular shapes, they are constructed within a square and a rectangle.

Figure 7.1

Two recognizably different pigs. Strong silhouette values make it easy to tell characters apart. The basic construction is square, although the pigs are made up of circular shapes.

What happens when your story decrees that all characters must be of the same size and shape? They could be identical in action as well as in silhouette. This was a common practice in early animated films. An example appears in Figure 7.2.

Figure 7.2

Three pigs or one pig repeated three times?

Color can differentiate between identical designs. This was also a standard way of working in the early years of animation. Figure 7.3's pigs show distinct color variations, but they're still just the same pig design repeated three times.

Figure 7.3

Three pigs with color variations.

7. Working with Multiple Characters

A more sophisticated method of differentiating the characters varies their body language. Identically designed characters can use distinctive poses, silhouettes, and attitudes to show differing personalities. Each will move differently from the others when they are animated because their attitudes will affect everything they do. An example of varied body language on the "standard pig" is shown in Figure 7.4. Their poses are starting to show personality.

Figure 7.4

Prissy Pig, Pulchritudinous Pig, and Piggy Pig. Different body attitudes can create different characters. The middle pig now appears to be female.

You can associate certain props or costumes with each character. In Figure 7.5, props and costumes vary the pigs' silhouettes so that identical body construction can be used for different personalities. Costumes can also suggest specific locations and time periods.

Figure 7.5

Piggy Props. Prissy, Pulchritudinous, and Piggy become stronger characters and suggest their settings with the addition of props and costumes.

Show your audience what you want them to see. Avoid *telling* them about it. The environment and the props associated with a character enable the audience to *read* the story and characters without your having to resort overmuch to filmic devices like voice-overs or explanatory dialogue. Creative designs for characters, backgrounds, and props will contribute enormously to the audience's understanding of what happened before the story began.

Characters that work together should have readable silhouettes that help convey the acting and the story point. Figure 7.6 shows three animals from the

Figure 7.6

Three dog designs based on triangles, rectangles, and circles. Their outfits and attitudes suggest their ages and personalities. (© Nancy Beiman.)

same species. Their different characters are indicated through their body types and attitudes toward the cards; they deliberately suggest particular human personalities. Each dog is constructed from a combination of squares, triangles, and circles, although some shapes are more emphasized than others. When you work with multiple characters you must establish a visual rhythm that leads the viewer's eye around the composition. Characters can be designed to work in the second or third dimensions. When they are animated, they will work in the fourth dimension!

Your characters' bodies, typical expressions, actions, and emotions will become easier to draw as storyboarding progresses. Surface details will be eliminated or simplified and body shapes will change as you draw the character in different attitudes. Storyboard drawings are the most practical way to see which design elements help and which ones hinder the character's ability to act. Storyboards are a means to an end. They are not the finished art; they represent something *you want to see finished*. The scenes and characters reach fruition when they are animated. A character's appearance may change dramatically from the original rough design after a few sequences are boarded. You should wind up with an appealing design that you are comfortable working with. A character that easily conveys emotions with its face and body is known as a *good actor*.

7. Working with Multiple Characters

This process of simplifying animation design is known as *evolution*. (Figure 7.7)

Figure 7.7

Fuzz the Cat's appearance evolved to this final model during the course of the storyboarding for OLD TRICKS and will be further refined in the animation. (Fuzz © 2016 by Nancy Beiman.)

The most common mistake made by beginning designers is to assume that their first character design is also the final one. In some instances, the artist goes directly to *cleanup* without investigating the character's construction or the actions it must perform in the film. Sometimes a character has only a few poses on its model sheet. Lack of planning in character design will lead to problems down the line as surely as it does in story (Figure 7.8).

Figure 7.8

Two poses are not sufficient for a character model sheet. How does this character move? How does it open its mouth? Does it have one? This model sheet does not say.

Animated characters go through a long process of refinement and revision as a normal part of the design process. Design experimentation is particularly important in the early stages of computer animation. It is essential to eliminate design flaws before they are incorporated into the finished models. Several tools are used to accomplish this, including construction model sheets, test animation, and *maquettes,* or sculptures of the characters. Maquettes and their construction are discussed in Chapter 20.

Tying It Down: Standardizing Your Design

A storyboard artist does not need to take final character design into consideration when working on rough boards. But the character designer must be sure that the animated actors work with each other and with the backgrounds in a consistent style, so that they are all in the same *universe,* as discussed in Chapter 6.

Storyboard drawings that convey character emotions or motions particularly well will be copied onto "model suggestion" sheets. These are given to the designers along with any reference material that the directors and art directors have assembled as inspiration for the look of the picture. *Construction models* are drawn once the basic design is approved. A construction model shows the primary shapes that are used to create the character and standardizes its proportions. Figure 7.9 shows a simple construction model for Baby Bear.

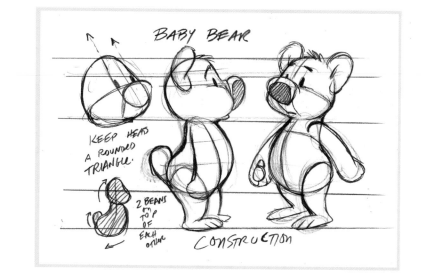

Figure 7.9

Construction models break the character's design down into *foundation shapes.*

The figures are usually first constructed in profile because it is easiest to set proportions in this view. The next step in character design is to experiment with action poses and expressions to see how good an actor your character is. Are there certain angles that work better than others? Is the character flexible? Does it have teeth at certain times? How much distortion is possible in the design? You may take good poses from the storyboard (as we will see in Chapter 15) and redraw them on an action model sheet according to your construction model. Lack or presence of teeth, and so on, are noted on the model sheet, as shown in Figure 7.10.

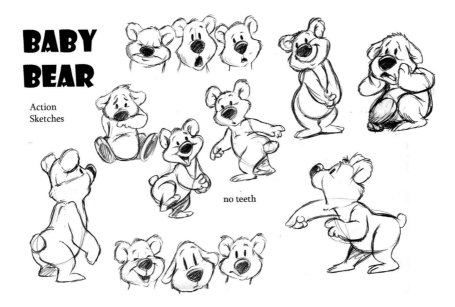

BABY BEAR

Action Sketches

no teeth

Figure 7.10

Action sketches and facial expressions may be done on the same sheet. One influences the other. Write down whether the character has teeth, pupils in eyes, and so on.

Animating a simple scene will show weak spots in the design as it moves. A walk cycle is a great way to get acquainted with your character. (I recommend doing it in three-quarter view to avoid stiffness and twinning.) Action Model sheets are usually made from copies of keys and breakdowns from an actual production scene that contains acting and dialogue. This allows you to experiment with the mouth and body shapes at the same time.

You will also find that one character's mouth shapes and attitudes will vary depending on its emotion. Does it shout often or does it whisper? Does it have teeth when it smiles? Model sheets should be a guideline to possibilities, not a restriction. Remember, your character's design is not final at this time. Be open to change. Is there too much detail? Could the hands be better constructed? Are the proportions changing as you sketch? Does it need teeth? You will modify the design during storyboard or in test animation. This is animation evolution in action. It is perfectly normal for this to happen during this stage of the process. Redo the construction model afterward if the design and proportions of the character have changed (Figure 7.11).

Body construction is done by *drawing through the design* or showing the trunk and legs through the transparent clothing level. The body may also be constructed first and the clothes added separately. In Figure 7.12 two profile drawings have been done of the same girl, one with and one without the clothing.

Draw the body through the clothes even if it never shows in the finished animation. Underlying shapes will influence external surfaces. The body shapes the clothing, unless you are designing a corseted or armored character. (Figure 7.13)

Once you are satisfied with the proportions of the face and the body, you will finalize the character model sheets by standardizing these proportions on drawings of the character in static and typical action poses. This is known as *tying down* the design. (Figure 7.14)

baby bear dialogue

--no teeth--

WHo. STOLe IT!

Figure 7.11

Animating a simple scene with dialogue helps refine mouth and body shapes at the same time. Key poses and breakdowns are assembled into an action model sheet. Dialogue is written underneath the drawings to show where mouth shapes are emphasized.

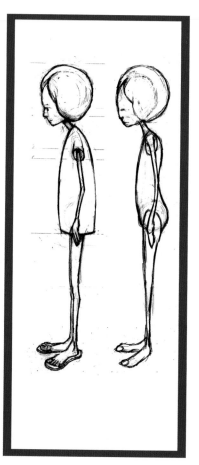

Figure 7.12

Character construction is easiest in profile. Two drawings are provided in this example. The first shows Diane's standard appearance; the other indicates the construction of the body underneath her loose dress. (Reproduced by permission of Jim Downer.)

Figure 7.13

Stiff outer garments will influence the shape and mobility of an organic character. Otherwise, the form of the body will determine the surface shapes.

Figure 7.14

Experiment with the character's proportions (a) before *tying it down* in the final design (b). The original character roughs can inspire many variants. Your final design may combine the legs from one sketch with the head and body from another. Work for proportions and design elements that please you. (Reproduced by permission of Jim Downer.)

Since the character will usually need to turn in space and work in many different angles, the next stage is to draw *turnarounds* that will show the character in the same neutral pose from front, back, and three-quarter views as if it was rotating on a turntable. Horizontal guidelines are drawn on the profile sketch to indicate the top of the head and the bottom of the feet. Additional lines are drawn at the chin, shoulder, hip, knee, and wrist line where necessary. It then becomes easier to rotate the figure from profile to front and back views, and then create a three-quarter view that will usually be the most flattering angle to the design. Diane's height is measured in whole "heads" so it is most important to standardize the distance between the crown of the head and the chin and measure body proportions by drawing "head silhouettes" alongside the figures, as shown in Figure 7.15.

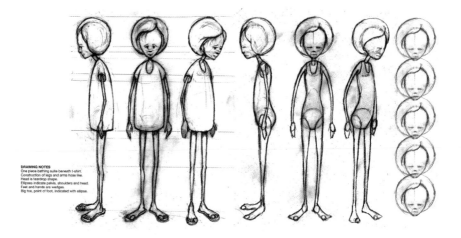

Figure 7.15

This turnaround shows Diane's volume and construction from several different angles. The new drawings are based on the proportions of the original profile drawing in Figure 7.12. Head heights are at the right side of the model sheet. (Reproduced by permission of Jim Downer.)

Character proportions are usually measured using the entire head and jaw, not just the ball of the cranium. Exceptions can be made if the head is very large or very small. Separate model sheets are drawn for facial expressions.

One dinosaur in Figure 7.16 uses its head and the other uses its body mass to measure the height and the length of their respective necks and tails. Use the simplest elements to measure proportions.

No two size guides will be the same because each one is determined by the character's design. "Fred" is 4½ heads high. He has a large jaw and small cranium so his height is measured with the entire head as shown in Figure 7.17. Fred's hair is a separate shape added after the head is constructed. Hair, hats, or long ears are indicated by a separate shape above the head after the skull is constructed underneath. Loose or flyaway hair is contained within a discrete shape, so that it may be constructed in the round.

7. Working with Multiple Characters

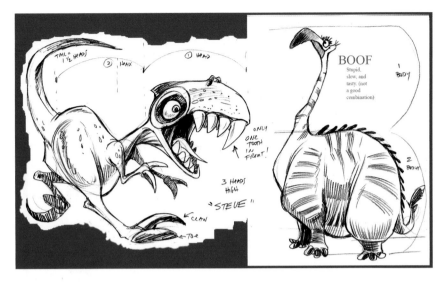

Figure 7.16

Steve the raptor's huge cranium is used to measure his face and body proportions. The Boofasaurus has a head that is too small to be used as a convenient measuring unit. Its body is used instead to measure its height and the length of its neck and tail.

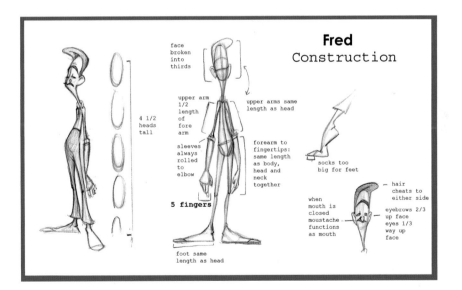

Figure 7.17

Fred's entire head and jaw are used to measure proportions for the rest of his body. Written notes and brackets are added to the model sheets. Hair shapes are added after the skull is constructed. (Reproduced by permission of Brittney Lee.)

Separate model sheets are drawn to indicate typical facial expressions. If the teeth or tongue only show in certain expressions, write a short note on the model sheet and add an explanatory sketch if necessary. And it is a good idea to know what the character's open mouth looks like, even if you don't wind up using this pose in the film. You might change your mind and the film. Leave nothing to chance (Figure 7.18).

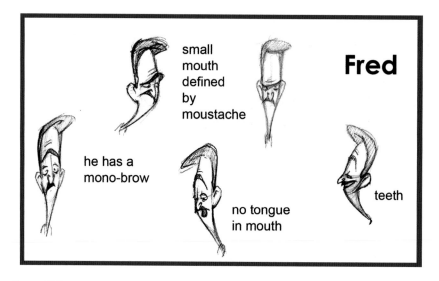

small
mouth
defined
by
moustache

Fred

he has a
mono-brow

no tongue
in mouth

teeth

Figure 7.18

Model sheets for facial expressions serve as guides for dialogue animation. Teeth and tongues are labeled along with other features. (Reproduced by permission of Brittney Lee.)

Figure 7.19 shows identical head construction for twin characters. Both characters also use the same body construction, but their proportions are very different, as shown in Figure 7.20. The expression, stance, number of teeth, and position of the ears create individual characters from the same basic design. Action poses show the range of Amma and Yuri's acting. Notes indicate the appearance of eyes and eyelids, how long the arms are, and other construction details. Amma sometimes uses extreme expressions, and this is indicated on the model sheet. Her twin brother Yuri is a more limited actor with heavier features. New drawings and new model sheets may replace the originals, once Amma and Yuri have been animated in a few scenes.

Dialogue mouth shapes for a character will vary depending on its mood and emotion. There's no standard way to animate dialogue, just as there's no one way to animate acting. Dialogue animation is conveyed by body language as well—indeed, the body attitudes are more important than the mouth shapes!

Human actors do not enunciate every word equally, as you can see if you compare the acting of Humphrey Bogart with that of Woody Allen in Figure 7.21. Even in a still drawing the two men appear to be speaking different languages. Bogart's lines are slurred and *cheated;* Allen's mouth shapes are broader. Dialogue "action

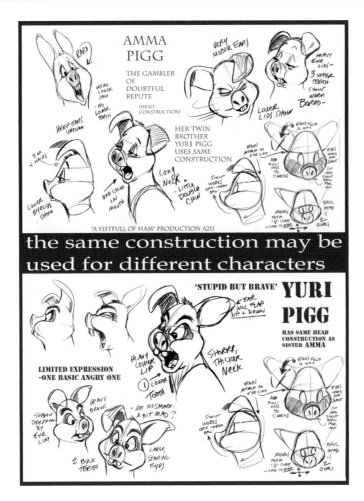

Figure 7.19

Separate model sheets for head construction and typical expressions are drawn for each character. Acting attitudes and dialogue mouth shapes may dramatically differ. Notes describe important details.

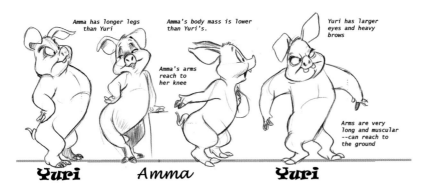

Figure 7.20

Amma and Yuri have identical body construction with variations in weight and body attitude, and this is noted on the model sheet.

Figure 7.21

No two people will say a line the same way. Dialogue is cheated in live-action just as it is in animation.

suggestion" model sheets are created after a test scene has been animated on a character, but they will always be *suggestions* not absolutes. Each character will have its own particular way of moving and talking even when two designs are nearly identical.

My Good Side: Choosing the Best Angles

Some angles will often be more "flattening" than "flattering" to most characters. A three-quarter view is usually better than seeing the character directly from the front. Rear views are also not as effective as staging characters in a ¾ back view (Figure 7.22).

Figure 7.22

Not all characters work well in all angles. A straight-on frontal view of a character will often flatten out the design. Important features may not show to best advantage. Mean Old Meanie's nose disappears in the front view.

Please refer to Chapter 10 for suggestions on how to stage your character effectively in a scene. A head may be turned into a three-quarter view, although the body is shown from the front. Avoid staging characters directly from the rear, as shown in Figure 7.23. If you are working on a scene where layout has given you an unflattering angle on your character (as occasionally happens), cheat its pose into one that shows it to better advantage.

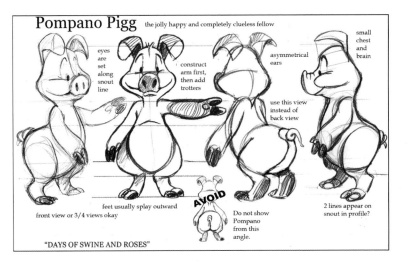

Figure 7.23

Three quarter views are more dynamic than flat staging. Flat frontal and rear views are usually avoided in animation unless the story calls for it.

Action sketches such as the ones in Figures 7.24 and 7.25 will indicate weak areas of the construction model. They are usually, but not always completed after

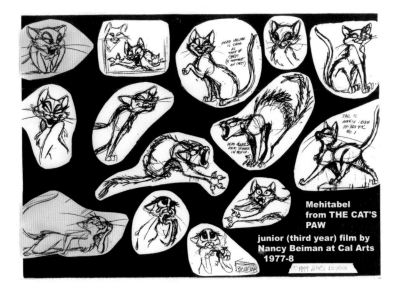

Figure 7.24

Action model sheets will show poses that may not be used in the final film. They are useful as indications of the character's range of motion and emotion. The cat's evolution is apparent in some actual animation drawings (shaded in pink) that were added after I'd completed a few scenes. (THE CAT'S PAW © Nancy Beiman.)

Figure 7.25

These action model sheets were drawn before Mozart was animated. When he was animated, the dog's head and feet grew larger than planned on the original model sheets, but since the *evolution* was not obvious, the original models were not changed. (Reproduced by permission of Brittney Lee.)

a test scene has been animated. Repeatedly drawing the character will eliminate fussy details (numerous hairs reduced to two or three, surface patterns) once you actually start turning the character in space and making it act. This simplifies and improves the design.

Action model sheets are used throughout the production to show typical character movement and attitudes. Label the sheets "Action Model Only" if the model varies from your final design. Sometimes a character's proportions and design don't change much at all.

What happens if the size differences are so dramatic that a standard lineup is not possible (say, an elephant and a flea)? Compare the small character to a portion of the larger one on a "close-up" model sheet. Figure 7.26 shows an example of a small character, and smaller props, working with Diane from Figure 7.15. The doll and its props are too small to read well when placed next to Diane in a standard lineup, so the new model sheet scales the doll and the sewing materials to Diane's knee and foot. The girl's head and hand should also be drawn on the doll's model sheet as a size guide. A small character in a big picture will have most of its action staged in close-up or medium close-up because of the scale differences between it and the other characters.

7. Working with Multiple Characters

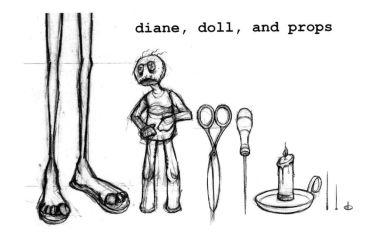

diane, doll, and props

Figure 7.26

A small character can be measured against a portion of a larger character's design on a close-up model sheet. The doll is as tall as Diane's knee. The props are scaled to the doll and Diane. (Reproduced by permission of Jim Downer.)

Exercise: When you have finalized the individual and size-comparison model sheets, draw action poses using two characters that appear together in the story. You may draw them separately or have both on the same page, whichever is easier for you. Keep the scale between the characters and silhouette value consistent with the other model sheets. Paste up the best of the combined poses on a new action model sheet. Work at your character designs until you are certain that they will work for you.

Getting Pushy with Prop Designs

Character animation developed from illustration, cartooning, and caricature. Character designs that are *pushed* or exaggerated slightly from the norm, are often more successful than those that attempt to reproduce reality. This principle also applies to backgrounds and props. A caricatured Victorian chair conveys the peculiarities of the style better than a "straight" version, as shown in Figure 7.27.

THIS CHAIR IS MUCH TOO COLD.

Oh, Jolly good, Teddy! This Chair is **HOT!**

Figure 7.27

Caricatured props work best with caricatured characters.

You might even make a character into a prop if one shape suggests another. This is known as a "visual pun." Animation frequently uses visual punning for comic effect. In Figure 7.28, a frog plays a "country fiddle" made from a worm. Both creatures appear small because we have a good idea of the scale of actual frogs and night crawlers and there is no indication that they are any different from the norm; if the scale was important to the story, (say, if the frog was actually the size of a man) more background detail would need to be included to establish the idea.

THE DUET.

Figure 7.28

A frog playing a worm as a "country fiddle" is an example of a visual pun where one shape or character suggests another.

Designing Locations with the Characters

Melody Wang's film THE CASEBOOK OF NIPS AND PORKINGTON was originally designed with human characters. The artist found animal characters more interesting and fun to work with, and so the original, human police team were redesigned as a cat and pig. Their movements were based on poses of human models drawn in her sketchbook; animal action did not influence the main characters' movements. Only one character in the film is pure "animal." The character scale is very clear even in rough sketches; the tiny kitten is dwarfed by the enormous pig and the villains (jay, raccoon, and rats) all vary in scale. Only one villain "Nasty Rat" was used in the final film—which was easier than drawing a bunch of them. One villain proved far more effective than a crowd (Figure 7.29).

Figure 7.29

The main characters in THE CASEBOOK OF NIPS AND PORKINGTON were originally human; the artist changed them to animals, and drew them in poses based on sketches from her sketchbook and life drawing classes. (© 2015 by Melody Wang.)

The props and costumes from a particular historical period (the early twentieth century) were designed at the same time as the main characters. In addition, the film took place inside the pages of an old newspaper; the characters literally "spring to life" out of the pages. The location became a character in the story (Figure 7.30).

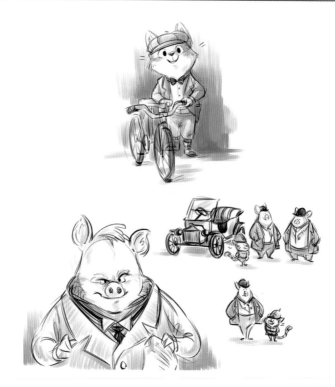

Figure 7.30

THE CASEBOOK OF NIPS AND PORKINGTON'S animal characters were designed with costumes and props that clearly set the film in the early twentieth century. (© 2015 by Melody Wang.)

In Figure 7.31 a turn of the century bicycle has three feline passengers in a publicity drawing from THE CASEBOOK OF NIPS AND PORKINGTON. The background establishes that these are normal sized cats in a human sized world. (My cats Sam-E and Louie Bear did not appear in the film!)

Figure 7.31

Louie Bear, a very large cat, and Sam-E, a normal sized cat, ride a small human-scaled bicycle with Constable Nips. (Artwork © 2015 by Melody Wang.)

The film's art direction was in muted shades of gray and brown, as if the characters were created from old newsprint. Nips and Porkington worked in the third and fourth dimensions, whereas the backgrounds remained in 2D (Figure 7.32).

Figure 7.32

The newspaper backgrounds established a flat world that worked in the second and third dimensions—the animation worked in the fourth dimension. (THE CASEBOOK OF NIPS AND PORKINGTON © 2015 by Melody Wang.)

There was no final model sheet for any of the characters; the artist determined the scale of the characters in these rough sketches and the storyboards provided the final "model." This was possible because the film did not require any 3D modelling or puppet construction. Minor variations in character design and scale occur, particularly in a scene where the rat runs through the pig's legs; this is unnoticeable when the film is screened because the staging, timing, and animation make the story point read clearly. (Animated films in any medium will modify character scale when the story requires it.)

THE CASEBOOK OF NIPS AND PORKINGTON can be viewed at https://vimeo.com/124256124 (Figure 7.33).

Figure 7.33

Character scale and design was finalized on the storyboard. This is a common occurrence in hand drawn films. (THE CASEBOOK OF NIPS AND PORKINGTON © 2015 by Melody Wang.)

7. Working with Multiple Characters

8

Beauties and Beasts: Creating Character Contrasts in Design

The most important consideration when designing several characters is *creating different body language and movement*. This consideration is not unique to animation.

Charlie Chaplin made THE GREAT DICTATOR as a rebuke to Adolf Hitler. In this film, Chaplin plays two parts. His Barber character bears an amazing physical resemblance to the Dictator. They never meet. The lives of the Barber and Dictator intersect only in the last 10 minutes of the picture when the Barber replaces the Dictator after appropriating the latter's uniform. Yet all through the film the denizens of the Ghetto and the "Tomanian" bullies who oppress them do not notice that the barber resembles the Dictator. The Barber does not see this resemblance himself. Are all the characters, friends and enemies, equally ignorant? The situation, though fantastic, is believable to us and we never notice that the comparison is never made. This is because Chaplin, as the Barber, *moves in a completely different fashion* from the Dictator. The characters' stance, silhouettes, actions, and facial expressions are as opposed as their politics. The Barber smiles often. His short and graceful movements resemble those of a small mouse or bird. The Dictator tilts his head up and back in an arrogant pose or raises his shoulders in an almost feline fashion. He usually has a scowl on his face. His movements are forceful and reminiscent of a predatory animal (Figure 8.1).

Figure 8.1

Charlie Chaplin as the Dictator.

Chaplin's performance is so skilled that it appears that a second actor plays the Dictator. When the Dictator dances with a globe we see the only occurrence of a famous gesture of Chaplin's "Little Tramp" character—a backward kick. The Tramp uses it to dispose of cigarette butts but the Dictator disposes of the world. The kick is the one gesture that the two characters have in common, but different contexts change its meaning.

At the end of the film when the Barber dresses as the Dictator, his gestures still differ from the aggressive, arrogant movements of the tyrant. We believe that one of Chaplin's characters has truly replaced the other. THE GREAT DICTATOR is a film that all animators should study (Figure 8.2).

Figure 8.2

Charlie Chaplin and the Chaplin Kick.

I Feel Pretty! Changing Standards of Beauty

"Beauty is only skin deep. Ugly goes clean to the bone."

—**Dorothy Parker**

8. Beauties and Beasts: Creating Character Contrasts in Design

It is difficult to design attractive human characters. They can easily become dull and flat. Beauty is a variable concept that is affected by time and place. What is beautiful in one era or culture may appear grotesque in another (Figure 8.3).

Figure 8.3

"Her lips were like a red, red rose; Like stars, her eyes of blue; Her neck was like the graceful swan's; I loved her. Wouldn't you?" A literal interpretation of a nineteenth-century poem produces monsters. (Nancy Beiman collection)

Films set in a particular time and place will need to be researched for details that help convey as sense of the period. These are (especially in Hollywood films) sometimes updated to more recent standards of beauty; very few films use documentary precision in recreating the period! In the late nineteenth and early twentieth century a woman was considered attractive if she wore a corset. The constricted waist and huge skirts affected how she moved; her actions were often severely restricted (Figure 8.4).

Figure 8.4

A tightly corseted waist was once the gold standard of female beauty. (Nancy Beiman collection)

The same restrictions could apply to male fashion. Men once wore clothing that showed their legs—and much more—to be considered masculine, and also sometimes wore corsets, as the Regency gentleman (circa 1822) demonstrates in Figure 8.5.

Figure 8.5

A tightly corseted waist was also once considered suitable for men!

Certain design constants may be applied when designing "beautiful" characters.

Beautiful people in Western culture often have asymmetrical faces. Take a full-face picture of a popular actor or actress; duplicate one half of it and flip it using a mirror or computer graphics program. Then try this exercise with a picture of your own face. The two resultant composites will show significant differences and may suggest two different people. Most of us have asymmetrical faces. Perfect faces are rare but not unheard of. T. Hee claimed that a 1930s actress with flawless features was the most difficult caricature assignment of his career. A small imperfection can enhance the beauty of a face. The great actresses of the 1930s—the Hepburns and Garbos and Crawfords and Dietrichs—all had slightly asymmetrical features that made their faces more interesting to T. Hee (and millions of viewers) and gave him something to caricature. A perfect face inspired a less interesting drawing (Figure 8.6).

Figure 8.6

Caricature of actors and actresses with asymmetrical faces by T. Hee. (Nancy Beiman collection)

A Face That Only a Mother Could Love?

CUTE AND NONCUTE: Other species attract us if their body and facial proportions resemble those of human infants. Puppies and kittens are *cute* because of their rounded, regular features—a design that appeals to mammalian mothers. Babyish features typically are small and delicate, occupying a smaller area of the skull than an adult's. The human baby's head and torso are huge when compared to the hands, feet, and limbs. The puppy's or kitten's body is small and the paws and head are very large. In Figure 8.7, the baby's, cat's, and puppy's eye levels are approximately one-third from the bottom of the skull. (An adult's would be situated at the halfway mark.) The eyes are large whereas other facial features are very small.

The Roswell Alien in Figure 8.7 shares the babyish proportions of the kitten, puppy, and human, but the scale is now dramatic to the point of caricature: its eyes are huge, with no whites showing; the nose is eliminated and the mouth is a lipless slit. We see this as creepy instead of cute. Human beings are also unlikely to find a young insect "cute" because their proportions are completely unlike the mammalian pattern. The caterpillar's eyes take up nearly all of its head shape and there is no clear differentiation between the head and the body. So insect babies will seem cute only to insect mothers. Animated insect characters have all been humanized to a greater or lesser degree, so that we will find them appealing rather than alien.

cute

not

Figure 8.7

Small features in a rounded face with big eyes appeal to us. We perceive most creatures whose facial and body proportions resemble those of human infants as "cute."

Gods and Monsters: Contrasting Appearance and Personality

The features of a human face are centered in an inverted triangle. Eyes are always on either side of the nose and the mouth appears underneath (unless you are Pablo Picasso). We are conditioned to find this design beautiful. Breaking this triangle can break our sense of connection to the humanity and beauty of a face's design, as shown in Figure 8.8. Some of Picasso's deconstructions of the human face are disturbing to view. People with deformed faces (for example, the Elephant Man or Quasimodo the Hunchback) can cause a great feeling of discomfort in the viewer. Designs that do not relate the facial features to each other will usually be considered "unappealing."

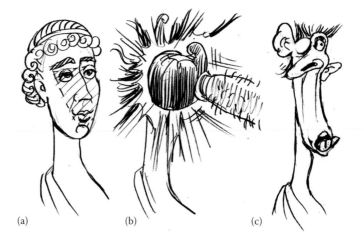

(a)   (b)   (c)

Figure 8.8

Breaking the pattern of a human face makes us feel very uncomfortable. It also makes the model feel very uncomfortable.

A slight imperfection can enhance an otherwise beautiful face. Characters with highly deformed or asymmetrical facial proportions are called MONSTERS. Humans are attracted or repelled by facial proportions and expressions. Highly irregular faces can excite fear in the viewer. Some famous monsters have partly destroyed faces or faces that lack an eye or an ear, or have too many eyes and ears. Leonardo da Vinci wrote that the "eye is the window of the soul." Shakespeare was more accurate when he had King Duncan in MACBETH state, "There's no art to find the mind's construction in the face."

A handsome man may "smile, and smile, and be a villain" and an ugly duckling may have a heart of gold. The Phantom of the Opera and the Hunchback of Notre Dame are examples of two misunderstood monsters. Erik's facial burns mirror his damaged soul; Quasimodo's spirit is noble despite his deformed face and body, because his actions are kind, brave, loving, and generous. Not that he fares any better than Erik in the end.

A character's design may announce its personality or work in contrast to it (Figure 8.9).

Figure 8.9

Monsters can frighten us even if they do nice things. There is a contrast between the horrifying exterior and the noble interior.

Both the Phantom and Quasimodo reveal human depths under the deformed face. Their actions reveal their spiritual beauty, but these characters are never considered physically beautiful. The contrast between interior and exterior makes them more appealing than the "beautiful" characters in their stories. Ugliness is easier to portray than beauty because we are more able to agree on what is ugly than on what is beautiful. Although beauty may be in the eye of the beholder, the artist is able to create it. So what makes a Princess beautiful? Her appearance will ultimately depend on the time and setting of the story. A noblewoman in Renaissance Italy will not look like a noblewoman in medieval Japan.

Though your audience is not going to be composed of historians, period character designs should contain elements that suggest the era with a touch of the modern to enable audiences to appreciate them. They should be individuals, not mannequins with period costumes. Here are some suggestions on how to get started. Look at basic clothing shapes and use the ones that best set the period and the character. Don't be literal. You can use silhouette for the look of the period without reproducing every flounce and ribbon on a dress.

1. *Research styles:* Learn something about the fashion silhouette of the period. For example, the silhouette of a man in 1860 differed radically from that of a woman. The man's and woman's silhouette are nearly the same in 1926. Use clothing and props of the period to develop the character (Figure 8.10).

2. *Use more than one source for reference:* Source materials do not have to be from the period in which the film was set. You may use an object's silhouette to suggest a character type. For example, an inflexible character might be based on a rock. A flighty human character might have some birdlike qualities. Illustrators' work is a useful source for period reference. Avoid recycling designs from other animated films because audiences are more likely to have seen them before.

3. *Draw a variety of character designs* and then combine the best features of each in the final design. Some inexperienced designers tend to draw one

Figure 8.10

Male and female silhouettes have changed over time. The silhouette of 1860 shows the greatest contrast between male and female shapes in costume history. The silhouette of 1926 shows very little difference between the two genders.

character and stay with it. Experiment with different proportions and character types and see what appeals to you. Never stick with the very first sketch unless, of course, it is the best one (as occasionally happens).

4. *Use the features of an actual person for inspiration:* This need not be a caricature and it does not apply merely to human characters. Combining the features or body type of a human with those of an animal will make the animal (or human) unique. The facial expressions of a living person can bring an historical character to life (Figure 8.11).

Figure 8.11

These caricatures of famous authors by James Montgomery Flagg were drawn from life. Incorporating the features of actual people into character designs gives them a touch of life and sparkle. What animal characteristics do some of these drawings suggest? (Nancy Beiman collection)

5. *Draw from memory as well as from life.* Since no two people have precisely the same life experience, this technique will make a design *yours.* This is why it is vitally important to keep a sketchbook, which will provide you with a unique source for character types, locations, and props. Don't just draw people standing around; capture the motion and the attitudes of poses. Draw animals and interesting architectural details as well when you see them. Keep your old sketchbooks for future reference.

6. *Avoid literalism in design.* We do not see dragons, whales, giant monsters, or lions every day or even view dogs and cats in the same way we do other humans. An animator or designer may take artistic liberties with an animal's appearance and movements—all may be forgiven if the story is working! Only when you strive for the super-realistic human design does

8. Beauties and Beasts: Creating Character Contrasts in Design

the stiff, lifeless appearance known as the *cryogenic effect* or the *uncanny valley* set in. If you design *realistic* humans, the character must move like one, hiccups, blinks, and all, so as not to appear doll-like and lifeless. Stylized design and animation of human characters will make them appear more alive than will slavish copying of real life (Figure 8.12).

Figure 8.12

These character designs for a video game set during World War I caught the martial flavor of the era without being absolutely authentic. The facial features were based on antique photographs. (Reproduced by permission of John McCartney.)

Animation design changes over time. Some design styles become clichés because of the "tributes" paid to them in other films. If you work some of your own experiences into the design and get inspirational material from a variety of sources, the resulting characters will become your original creations instead of a retread of someone else's work.

Remember: Animation is not Reality. *It's much better!*

9

Color and Design in Storytelling

The art director or production designer sets the film's period, location, prop and character design style, and color palette. Production design develops at the same time as the characters and storyboards.

The setting is an important storytelling element. Setting and props can influence a character's actions or support a story point. A film's style is an important storytelling tool. Design styles should not be used because they are popular or because some other artist worked that way. Your color palette, art direction, and character design should always support the story.

Objects that are important to the story and to the scene should be visually prominent on your storyboards and backgrounds. Less important objects can be played down and merge into shadows with very close values so that they do not compete with the center of interest. Detail should not overpower the characters. Period styles and props are there to help set the scene, not upstage it (Figure 9.1).

Figure 9.1

An example of design overkill in a background. The tonal values are close, the design is confusing, and there are many tangents where foreground elements appear to be on the same plane as the background. Although this can be used creatively, it only creates confusion here.

Evenness of tone, evenness of shape, and repetition without variation are all very well if you are designing wallpaper, but they are not helpful when you are trying to direct the viewer to a particular part of the design, or time an action. If everything is equally emphasized, there is no center of interest, and the viewer does not know where to look first.

Location, Location, Location

Atmospheric and location sketches are created in the development process to explore the story's setting; variations are created for the design, color, and lighting. A floor plan is useful if your project takes place in a specific location because it enables you to place the characters accurately in the scene. The floor plan places doors, houses, and other important objects in specific locations so that the board artist may stage the shots better. Background details and props will be drawn on the storyboard if the character interacts with them. Master backgrounds may be drawn up at the beginning of preproduction to help the storyboard artist. A master background might not appear in the finished film, but is a very useful guide for staging the action. The characters should be included to indicate scale.

Figure 9.2 is an original master background from a student film. A man sits in a house playing the piano. He plays piano with one finger. He looks tired. There are a Christmas tree and some presents in the corner of the room and a dog lying on a carpet.

Figure 9.2

Master background, House interior, and first pass. (© 2006 by Brittney Lee.)

The background is bare. It seems as if the man has just moved into the house or that he is too poor to own anything but the piano, tree, and dog. We know nothing about him or about where this film takes place. The Christmas tree gives the only hint of a time frame.

A house is never "just" a house. Objects inside a real house tell us about the inhabitants. A room is never completely empty unless the occupant is a monk who has taken a vow of poverty. People collect objects that reflect and sometimes define their personalities. A golfer might leave clubs in a corner. "Horsey" people have pictures of horses on the walls. Parents have pictures of their children on the dresser. Pet owners will have pet photos and pet toys everywhere. A child might have toys all over his or her bedroom. A poor character could have pictures cut from a newspaper tacked on the wall. Set-dressing is an important element in live-action film, but it is crucial in animation because every object in an animated film's setting and background should help tell the story and provide background information about the characters. Best of all, it does not require dialogue. The general rule in animation is: *Show, don't tell*. A pictorial introduction is far superior to voice-over narration or explanatory titles.

Animated characters depend on the audiences' suspension of disbelief to be accepted as real. A good setting can go a long way toward eliminating that disbelief and make the viewer accept animated drawings as living beings with a past.

Establishing Shots

Your opening shots are like the opening sentences of a short story. They introduce your characters and setting and establish the viewers' interest in their situation. For this reason, they are known as *establishing shots*.

Design the placement of objects in the shot in the same way you would read a sentence aloud. Emphasize some words more than others. Don't shout every word and do not mumble. Get to the point quickly, use varied inflection and pacing to keep the audience interested, and don't let irrelevant anecdotal material interrupt the story.

Let's return to the establishing shot of the piano player in Figure 9.2. We know that it is Christmas time because there is a tree in the corner. What else can be added to the background to set the stage for the story? If there is a red ribbon tied on the piano and a fireplace hung with stockings is added to the blank wall and the tree is surrounded with unwrapped presents, we get an idea of what has taken place in the room and what time of year it is. The piano is a Christmas present. Perhaps the man is still learning how to play the instrument. If the fire is lit, the time (night) and location (a cool climate) are set. Clutter in the foreground adds depth to the scene and provides a frame for the character action. The final background translates the gray tonal values into color and provides us with even more information. Warm browns and golds predominate and the cheery fire provides the main light source. The colors suggest a cold winter climate at night. We suddenly know this fellow a lot better; he's no longer just "a man." He's a wannabe piano player and dog owner who is manfully trying to master his unfamiliar Christmas present. The film's setting and characters are neatly introduced without using a single word of dialogue (Figure 9.3).

Figure 9.3

Final tonal background with overlays and a color frame from the finished film's establishing shot. The setting now tells us a lot about our characters' lives. (THE MUSICAL GENIUS OF MOZART MCFIDDLE © 2006 by Brittney Lee. With permission.)

In the last shot of the film we get a surprise. As we cut from the interior to the exterior of the house the colors shift dramatically. Warm pinks and greens and golds now dominate the scene. It seems that the Christmas story does not take place in the cool northern climate that was suggested by the design and lighting of the previous shots, but in the Southwestern United States. It isn't even nighttime! There is a radical disconnect between the style and color of the interior and exterior backgrounds. But it's still Christmas time. Snowmen (presumably made of plastic) stand on a vibrant green lawn and there are plenty of Christmas lights scattered amidst the flowers, palm trees, and sunshine. These details added an additional comic touch to the final scenes of the movie (Figure 9.4).

9. Color and Design in Storytelling

Figure 9.4

It's not nighttime, it's not cold outside, but it *is* Christmas time in the American Southwest! The art direction, color, and even the time of day in the last shot are completely different from the rest of the film. The season of the year and the characters remain consistent. (© 2006 by Brittney Lee.)

THE MUSICAL GENIUS OF MOZART MCFIDDLE can be seen at http://www.imdb.com/video/wab/vi1861354009.

Note how the color and lighting changes instantly transport us to a sunny desert in the late afternoon. Color and light are powerful tools that can create emotional resonance and add additional dimension to your storytelling.

Test your color design and art direction by changing your settings so that the color image is in gray scale. If the color is working, the gray scale will be clear; and the reverse is also true (Figure 9.5).

Figure 9.5

Good tonal values create good color contrasts, and vice versa. (© 2006 by Brittney Lee.)

Colorful Characters

Color models can go a long way toward establishing your character's personality. You should experiment with a variety of color palettes on your characters just as you experimented with the proportions and look of the original design. Never assume that your first choice will be the last or the best (Figure 9.6).

> "Walt would love it. Marc said he was like a little kid opening up Christmas presents," says Alice Davis, whose husband Marc was one of the "*Nine Old Men*" of the Walt Disney Studio and also a versatile character designer.
>
> The designers and color stylists had to appeal to a very demanding audience. Alice Davis explained how Marc Davis and designer Mary Blair would pitch concept art to Walt Disney.
>
> "You had better have something to have Walt going on when he finished with all the drawings, because he would want more. Mary would have lots of drawings taking one idea and showing different ways [it] could be used.... Where a lot of guys would do two or three drawings, Marc and Mary would do twelve or more, giving Walt a variety to choose from. Marc said one day a young man came to [Walt] with one drawing and said, 'What do you think of this, Walt?' Walt looked at it and then turned and looked at him and smiled and said [sweetly], 'It's *very* difficult to choose between *one*.'"
>
> **Alice Davis**
> *Interview with Nancy Beiman, August 2000*

Figure 9.6

"It's *very* difficult to choose between *one*."—Walt Disney. Experiment with different color combinations on characters; your first attempt may not be the last.

Color models will change depending on the story and the mood of the character. It's customary to have different color models for each character showing standard hues by day and night. Costume changes will call for an additional series of models. Or character color can have an emotional context; a character's appearance may indicate how they are perceived by others (Figure 9.7).

Figure 9.7

Emotion can also influence the character color model; it may not be consistent from sequence to sequence, or even from scene to scene. (OLD TRICKS © 2016 Nancy Beiman.)

Figure 9.8 shows the Three Bears in color. In this extreme case, each bear's color now indicates its species. Papa is a polar bear, Mama is a black bear, and Baby is a honey bear! A character's final colors will often "bear" no resemblance to the tonal values used for it on rough storyboard drawings.

Figure 9.8

The Three Bears display colorful variants indicating their different origins. Dramatic character coloration will affect art direction for the entire film.

The character's color and design may change depending on location or time of day. In Figure 9.9, Vera Oldman's character has a different color model for each sequence. Sequence 1 takes place in daylight and Sequence 2 is a nighttime scene, so the Sequence 1 color scheme is grayed down to indicate changing light. Sequence 3's character and color model are dramatically different because this is what the story requires. These are the first versions of the character's color models; other variations will be tried as project development continues.

OLD TRICKS Vera First Lineup Color Models   (c) 2016 Nancy Beiman

Figure 9.9

Color can be used to indicate the time of day or the time of life. Vera Oldman's first two models are "day" and "night" versions of the same design with a costume variant. Sequence 3's model shows a dramatic change in color and design that illustrates a story point. (OLD TRICKS © 2016 Nancy Beiman.)

Character and background palettes are typically designed at the same time. This integrates dramatic palettes like the ones in Figure 9.10 into the film's *universe*.

Figure 9.10

Character colors are designed along with the backgrounds. (Frame from SITA SINGS THE BLUES reproduced by permission of Nina Paley.)

The characters will read well on their backgrounds because they were designed to work together. Color models are placed on the backgrounds to test readability and each is modified as needed.

Color has a natural vocabulary because so much of our color inspiration is derived from nature. We have named colors after flowers (Rose Red), fruit (Orange and Lemon Yellow), plants (Grass Green), and birds (Peacock Blue). These are all natural, realistic colors.

Animated characters need *not* be rendered with natural colors! Maurice Noble said that it's desirable to *have fun* with the graphic potential of your characters, and that reality in design and color was optional. Animated characters may fly, change shape, or morph into something else at will. Why settle for conventional coloring? (Figure 9.11)

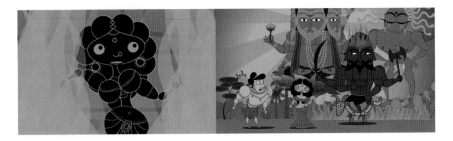

Figure 9.11

SITA SINGS THE BLUES uses bright colors based on the art of India. The illusion of a burning figure is created with a silhouette. (Reproduced by permission of Nina Paley.)

In Figure 9.12, the entire palette changes along with the story context. One character is viewed differently by two other characters. The "color" of their thoughts literally appears on screen. Can emotional qualities only be conveyed by dramatic color changes? As it turns out, we don't have to throw out the purple baby with the green bathwater.

Figure 9.12

A character's thoughts and emotions can be projected onscreen through the use of color. Color does not need to be realistic.

Colorful Characters

Symbolic Colors

Color has different meanings in different cultures. In Eastern cultures, red is the color of joy and life. In Western culture, it symbolizes life, but it is also the color of rage, lust, and danger. I will be speaking of color from the Western perspective for simplicity's sake.

Following are some emotional associations that we typically assign to color. These perceptions are so strong that they read well even if the color appears outside of a story context:

> *Red*: Life, love, rage, passion, danger, warning, speed, male sexuality, and strength
>
> *Orange*: Warmth, enthusiasm, optimism, and happiness
>
> *Pink*: Female sexuality, life, good health, youth, sentimentality, innocence, and childishness
>
> *Blue*: Peace, water, unity, spirituality, happiness, and stability; *also* coldness, depression. A *bluenose* is one definition of a prude. Male babies may wear blue clothing. A *blue-collar worker* is someone who works with their hands.
>
> *Black*: Power, fashion, sexuality, sensuality, and mystery; *also* evil, fear, death, unhappiness, and the unknown
>
> *Green*: Luck, nature, and vigor; *also* lack of experience, illness, envy, and bad fortune
>
> *Yellow*: Sunshine, joy, gold, inspiration, royalty, youth, and hope; *also* dishonesty, cowardice, and illness
>
> *Purple*: Royalty, wisdom, richness, age, and luxury; *also* arrogance, mourning, and cruelty
>
> *White*: Purity, innocence, perfection, and cleanliness; *also* coldness and death
>
> *Gray*: Boredom, blandness, sadness, and illness; *also* simplicity and mystery

Color may be used against type. THE CORPSE BRIDE, a stop-motion film, used a funereal, monochromatic color scheme of grays, blacks, and purples for the living characters and a bright, fully saturated riot of color for the ghosts in the Afterlife.

Let us observe how a color variation on a *portion* of a character's design changes our perception of that character.

Figure 9.13 shows a simple character. The eye color is within the normal color range for this species. The eye and pupil create a nice, readable color combination that would work well for a project with "realistic" art direction.

Figure 9.13

The starting point of "realistic color."

Figure 9.14 shows several different color variations in Figure 9.13. The first figure does not convey any emotional quality. But see how the remaining eye color combinations create the feeling of different emotions—and possibly different species—when the rest of the design does not differ in any other respect from the realistic original.

Figure 9.14

Here are three color variants on the *eyes only* of the character in Figure 9.13. The skin and hair colors are unchanged. Strange or unusual eye colors appear to convey different emotional meanings based on our cultural perceptions.

Exercise: Create a simple human or animal character. Design him or her so that the eyes are prominent. Color the figure using hues that are found in nature. Now change only the *eye* and *pupil* color of this character, leaving all other colors consistent with your original. Create several examples because "it's difficult to choose between one." You need not use naturalistic color, but may try any combination that takes your fancy.

The changing eye color of the characters in Figure 9.14 creates an emotional context when there is no other variation between the figures. Will changing the color of other portions of a character's anatomy have the same effect? Many parts of the human body have symbolic meaning. We know that the eyes are "the windows of the soul." Here are some popular cultural associations for other body parts:

HANDS: *Open hand*: creativity, generosity, peace and friendship, supplication, and prayer. *Fist:* Violence or strength. The *right* hand symbolizes good qualities whereas the *left* hand and left side of the body generally conveys a negative meaning. Gloves can also be symbolic (Figure 9.15).

Figure 9.15

The hand's covering can also convey a symbolic meaning.

FEET: Life path, activity, and agility. If *large*, they convey comedy or clumsiness. Caricatured characters are sometimes described as being designed in a *Bigfoot* style. Shoes are important indications of character. *Boots* symbolize violence, militarism, and fear. If the feet are *barefoot*, they may symbolize either poverty or freedom (Figure 9.16).

Figure 9.16

Feet and footwear can help establish a character; like everything else in the film, they need not be "normal."

Other parts of the body signify different emotions (Figures 9.17 and 9.18).

Figure 9.17

HEART: Spirituality, love, the soul, sincerity, and trust. Or it can be broken.

Figure 9.18

STOMACH: Vulgarity, greed.

HAIR: Sensuality or vanity. If a man's hairline is *receding*, it can make him seem ineffectual (especially if it is combined with a comb-over). If hair is very *abundant*, it can convey a free or untamed personality. When *bound*, it signifies emotional restraint (Figure 9.19).

Figure 9.19

Hair has great symbolism in many cultures.

Color accents are also useful in storytelling. In Figure 9.20, the color Red is applied first to the character's nose. The next version changes the color of its entire face. Red is then applied to one of its hands, and finally to one of its feet. The color's meaning changes depending on the body part it's applied to. No other changes have been made to the figure.

Figure 9.20

A color variant will create an emotional impact if applied to individual body parts. You do not have to change the entire palette to convey meaning. The symbolism of the body part complements the color symbolism and helps refine the context. A different interpretation will arise with each change of hue and limb.

Red is the most emotional color and conveys many meanings. A red nose can signify illness or drunkenness; a red face, anger, or embarrassment; the third character has been caught red-handed; and a red foot may have been recently injured or simply be wearing mismatched socks! These are some stereotypical interpretations that come to mind when viewing character color variations outside of a story context.

Exercise: Place three copies of one of your character model's poses on a white background. On the first pose, add the color purple to one of your character's hands. Add purple to one of its feet on the second pose, and over its entire face in the third. Repeat the exercise with red and green variants and see how your perception of the character changes.

If a prop is added to each of the drawings in Figure 9.20, our perception of the red accents will dramatically change. A red hand may signify an accident with a paint can or the aftermath of an axe murder. A red nose may result from inebriation or a simple head cold, depending on whether the character is associated with a bottle or a box of tissues (Figure 9.21).

Figure 9.21

The addition of props changes the meaning of the characters in Figure 9.20. In some cases the emotion conveyed is now the opposite of that provided by the original image.

Here is another example of how prop designs can tell part of the story. An ordinary five-year-old girl is having a tea party with stuffed toys in her ordinary bedroom. The extraordinary element in this story is the odd bird that literally crashes her tea party and tries to eat one of the toys.

The original atmospheric drawing had two or three toys in the room and nothing at all on the walls. Additional objects were added to create scale. We are now absolutely certain that we are in a child's bedroom, and that the child is very fond of stuffed toys (Figure 9.22). Pools of light with slight shadows isolate the figures in the tonal sketch and direct our attention precisely where the filmmaker wants it. Pastel-candy colors on the characters and the final backgrounds accentuated the childlike and vaguely laughable quality of the intrusive bird. A soft spotlight effect highlighted the area where the action took place.

9. Color and Design in Storytelling

Figure 9.22

A child's tea party with a guest. The final CGI staging is very close to that of the original design. (Reproduced by permission of David Suroviec.)

I Can See Clearly Now: Reference and Atmosphere

Animator Milt Kahl once said, "There ain't nothin' harder to do than *nothin*'!"

A house is never just a house! Don't leave rooms bare. Find items, textures, and colors that help set the period and tell us something about the occupants (Figure 9.23).

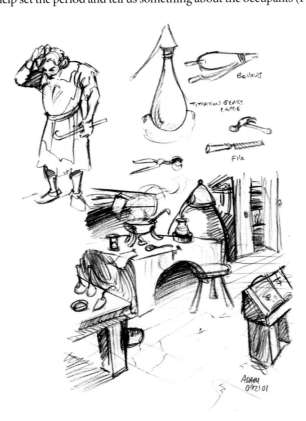

Figure 9.23

These conceptual sketches were drawn for a film set in the medieval period. The artist researched props that might be found in an alchemist's lair. (Reproduced by permission of Adam Fox.)

When considering a setting for your film, ask yourself the following questions:

1. Is this time period appropriate for the story? What year is it? What season? What time of day? Could this story take place in an unusual geographical location?
2. Is this a visually interesting time period or style? Some periods have better design elements to work with than others. (There is a reason why very few films are set in the 1970s.)
3. What shapes and colors suggest the period? Faded earth tones suggest different time periods than bright, plastic colors. Perpendicular architecture with strong verticals suggests the Gothic Middle Ages. Strong horizontal lines are reminiscent of late twentieth-century architecture. These details can be used as visual patterns throughout the film.
4. What materials are everyday objects made of? Are they handmade or mass-produced? Are they made of wood or metal or plastic? Textures and colors taken from everyday objects can be used on the characters to help maintain visual continuity.
5. If the setting is a natural one, is it a jungle or a forest, outback or desert? What colors dominate each of these locations? (Colors can, of course, be changed for artistic reasons, but you should know where you are starting from.)
6. Does the story take place on this planet or in this dimension?
7. If not, establish the rules of the fantasy world at the start of the story. What design elements can suggest that we are not in the real world?
8. What is the tone of the story? Is it whimsical, crazy, or serious? This will affect the treatment of the backgrounds.
9. Will your colors be sunny or dark? Are pastel colors more suitable for the story than saturated colors? Would the story still work if it were set in a different period?
10. Do the characters fit into this setting or does the story make use of *anachronisms* to create conflict or interest in the story?

Anachronisms are scenic elements or characters that postdate the time period of the movie. They are usually unintentional mistakes (such as Roman legionnaires wearing wristwatches). Anachronisms can also be used intentionally as shown in Figure 9.24. In SITA SINGS THE BLUES, 1920s pop tune lyrics provide humorous commentary on a story from ancient India. The art direction

Figure 9.24

Ancient Hindu deities sing and dance to American popular songs from the 1920s in Nina Paley's SITA SINGS THE BLUES. The design blends stylistic elements from both eras. (Reproduced by permission of Nina Paley.)

combines Indian and Art Deco designs. It is perfectly logical to show Hanuman the Monkey King playing jazz trumpet in this film's *universe*.

Remember that reality in animation is whatever you want it to be. It's not necessary to remain slavishly faithful to one design or historic period in your art direction as long as the mixture of styles is believable and the story point is conveyed clearly.

If the story takes place in "a typical house in modern times," can the backgrounds contain details that suggest the personalities and tastes of the characters? Do they have hobbies or interests that might tell us something about them? For example, if your character is a teenage girl, would she have posters on her wall? What sorts of books might she have in her room? Does she play a musical instrument? Does she collect anything? Would these books, instruments, and collections look different if the girl was a Goth? And how do you define "typical"? A "typical house" will not look the same in Lesotho or Lapland. "Typical" houses also vary between New York and Los Angeles, Beijing and Tokyo, London, and Paris.

How do you research a fantasy setting? *Think like the character* and analyze the story points, then repurpose familiar objects in a new context. If your story is set in the King of the Cats' court, would the characters own human-style chairs and tables? What would they be made of? It's very unlikely that the King of the Cats would sit on a hard wooden chair. Cushions or beds might be more appropriate for a cat. Use your imagination and be creative with your art direction. Investigate shape and color from your film's time period and setting.

Incorporate some familiar elements into the art direction for contrast with the more fantastic elements. Assemble reference materials for color and design from magazines, photographs, paintings, Internet sites, and books. Research different periods and locations and keep the reference materials in front of you as you construct your setting. Then you may use a period style or work with a combination of designs. You might use a modern color palette in a period film. Use gray or blue tonal values on master backgrounds to establish the lighting and keep the color contrasts the same intensity as the tonal values (Ken O'Connor stated that if you did this, "any color combination would work"). Be sure; place the characters in the shot for scale. You may work at full size or paint over copies of storyboards or layouts. Experiment with color variations. Digital media makes this easy, but adds some difficulties, as Hans Bacher explains below (Figure 9.25 and 9.26).

"(The) size (of the artwork) is unimportant and you can work 10 times as fast as with traditional techniques... (but) with all of its advantages, technology today can give you some headaches as well... there are so many little tricks, so many filters, nice gradients, and easy changes of color that you could actually work on the same piece of art forever.... It is a good decision to stick with that idea and not get lost and sidetracked with the temptations of technology.... Look at the artwork the next day. If it still looks good, then you can live with it."

—**Hans Bacher**
Dream Worlds (*Focal Press, 2008*)

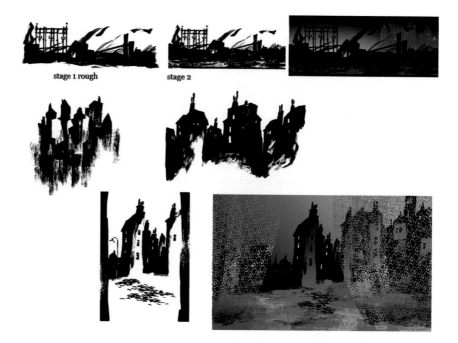

stage 1 rough   stage 2

Figure 9.25

The production designer experiments with texture and lighting first, then adds color to set the time of day. (Artwork from AFTER MIDNIGHT © Hans Bacher.)

Figure 9.26

The character is added on a different level for scale after the master background is completed. Preliminary thumbnails will include both character and background. (AFTER MIDNIGHT © Hans Bacher.)

Don't leave a house's interiors and exteriors bare. Find items, textures, and colors that help set the period and tell us something about the characters (Figure 9.27).

Figure 9.27

Vera and Fuzz eat breakfast in a kitchen that was last redecorated sometime around 1960. The storyboard is a rough color sketch for the final art direction. (OLD TRICKS © 2016 Nancy Beiman.)

Exercise: We are in a country town near the seashore on a late summer day in the historical period of your choice. There are two houses visible. One has a barbecue out back, a surfboard on the front lawn, and flowers in the windows. The next-door house is made of gingerbread. The front yard features a deep hole with a chain leading into it and a sign marked "Beware." The trees are very oddly shaped. Creatures fly in and out of the attic. The surrounding fence is made of lollipops and candy canes. Now do some rough thumbnails for the scene. Also design the characters that live in these houses. Work on paper or in digital media if you are comfortable with it. Draw thumbnails and then proceed to a finished master background in gray tonal values and textures. What is the scale of the scene? Are the characters human? Work for contrasts between the houses and their occupants. Even conventional-looking characters will seem less normal if they live in the second house. Add the characters to the master background with appropriate props. After you have finished the tonal version, add color to set the mood and time of day.

Do this exercise a second time with different settings and colors, but use the same character. You might try varying the scale of the houses, props, and characters. If you boarded the same story twice using the different locations, you'd end up with radically different results even if you never changed another thing.

Remember to apply the same principles and experiment with design, color, and scale when creating your own characters and settings.

Chuck Jones said, "I don't want realism. I want *believability*." Animated film creates its own reality in animation and design. Design your characters with the setting and develop both in the context of the story. Don't be overly literal; use creative license to interpret and redesign your reference materials—don't copy them. The audience will accept your alternative reality if you communicate well. In animation, normality is whatever you want it to be. Like Alice, you might find Wonderland down a rabbit hole.

You are now ready to begin storyboarding your film.

SECTION II
Technique

"THE FOUR HORSEMEN OF THE APIGCALYPSO."

10

Starting Story Sketch: Thumbnails and Tonal Sketches

At this point you have a rough story idea and rough character designs to act it out.

The verbal blueprint for your project must now be translated into visuals. A character *lineup* (such as the one in Figure 6.7) or an atmospheric sketch sets the characters' scale to each other to the background, and to important props. *Placeholders* such as the ones in Figure 10.1 are used to stage the action and acting on the boards if character designs have not yet been finalized.

Figure 10.1

Very rough drawings will read as the same character if the silhouette values are good. This woman's headdress, oval face, and silhouette make her easy to identify when an artist draw her in different styles. The main concern at this point is to tell the story with recognizable characters.

Rough drawings will read as the same character as long as the character silhouette makes them identifiable when drawn in different styles. This system saves time since storyboards for one production may be drawn by several different artists. Sometimes boards are redrawn when final character models are set. If a character's final design is dramatically changed (younger, older, taller, and shorter) the original eyelines will no longer work. The staging will be changed on the boards before layout (the first stage of *production*) can proceed.

All Thumbs: Quick Sketches and Thumbnails

Character designs and storyboards both start out as rough and simple *thumbnails*.

Thumbnails are drawn thoughts. These small sketches, combined with brief notes, capture ideas for a story or character so that the memory is not lost. Thumbnails can be worked up into a finished drawing at a later time.

Since your animated actors are imaginary, thumbnails allow you to work out details of the performance and "rehearse" the acting quickly and simply before going to final animation. They should be spontaneous—capturing your thoughts as quickly as you can draw them down. Thumbnails are used for all types of animation because they reduce the number of retakes and keep the animator's mind focused on the performance.

How and Why Do You Thumbnail a Sequence for a Storyboard?

Animation and live-action storyboard artists both block the cutting and composition of scenes. Where they differ is in the acting. As discussed in Chapter 1, live-action storyboards block camera moves and plan special effects; they never show the character acting. Animation storyboards must portray the acting that is required in the scene, and are thumbnailed roughly to explore different interpretations before the final boards are drawn. The animator then interprets the storyboard "script" to create the performance.

In storyboard, you are ultimately thinking of the entire project, not individual scenes or sequences. Storyboard must work within the story line and contribute to our understanding of the characters and their situation. Art direction, layout, and background are also determined by the story requirements.

Storyboard is the blueprint for everything that comes afterward.

Always work *rough* at first in storyboard. Do not use detailed rendering or modeling on your drawings. Use tone and color (if required) to make it read well, but don't spend too much time on it. Draw several versions of the scene in thumbnails if you think you can stage something better. Keep all your sketches—there is no "wrong" at the beginning of a project, only possibilities. Something that might not appear to work now may work later on. Thumbnails allow you to change the story and your mind before the production gets too far along to allow changes without tears. Storyboards may be thumbnailed on self-stick notes so that they can be easily changed and rearranged as shown in Figure 10.2; they are in effect, miniature storyboards. Compare them with Figure 10.3 where the acting is developed by the animator in thumbnails that block key poses for the same scene.

Figure 10.2

A storyboard's rough thumbnails are the dress rehearsal for the final presentation storyboard. They may contain notation because the storyboard is still being developed. Panels 4–6 (highlighted in blue) are rough drawings on self-stick notes that show staging and a brief indication of the acting in the scene.

(a)   just mailing a letter   (b)   once more, with feeling!

Figure 10.3

Frank Thomas' example: (a) A man mails a letter, or (b) A man mails a letter to someone he loves. The emotional state of the character affects every move he makes. These *Thumbnail* drawings portray different stages of the animated action in Scene 2 of Figure 10.2 (represented by blue panels).

Figure 10.3 shows two versions of a simple animated scene originally described by animator Frank Thomas. The first sketch (a) only shows the basic action, but (b) is a series of *thumbnails* that convey the character's attitude and personality along with the action. The thumbnails develop the acting that was only hinted at on the storyboard.

Reality Is Overrated

Use reality as an inspiration when creating animated characters and stories but adapt it, don't copy it. Real life provides basic reference material. Animation improves on it.

Animated characters should be believable, not realistic. The laws of gravity and physics may change in animation. A character can float on a cushion of emotional bliss as shown in Figure 10.3 or change its physical shape, color, or size when its mood varies. Visual hyperbole, caricature, and stylized action are much more interesting than literal renditions of natural motion. Animation combines caricatured action with artistic, graphic, and cartoon symbolism to create a new form of acting. This is the reason why "*rotoscoped*" or "*mocapped*" animation is not as interesting as character animation created from the imagination. These techniques imitate, and are restricted to, what is possible in reality, although subtly caricatured character animation in any medium routinely surpasses it.

The most important considerations in story sketch and character design are *selection, simplification,* and *emphasis.* You *select* what you want the viewer to see, *simplify* the staging so that there is a defined center of interest, and *emphasize* important elements in the scene.

The following elements are used to create a story sketch:

- Line, value (light and shadow)
- Silhouettes and shapes (consider both positive and negative space)
- Texture
- Color (occasionally)
- *Each board drawing should read from a minimum distance of 15 feet.* Storyboards must read from a distance because they are commonly pitched to a large audience in a large story room. This applies to all media. Tonal modeling enables the drawing to read from a far greater distance than boards done only in line. The two boards in Figure 10.4 demonstrate greater and lesser degrees of readability. Try viewing this illustration from the other side of the room. If you wear glasses, view the boards without them.

Figure 10.4

Storyboard (a) will be visible from the other side of the room. Storyboard (b) will not read unless the viewer is very close to the boards.

- *The optical center of the screen is higher than the actual geometric center of the screen.* The optical center is where your "optic"—the viewer's eye—goes first. It is located slightly above the actual center of the screen. Objects placed at the optical center will automatically draw the viewer's attention. Staging and design can be utilized to counter the natural tendency to look at the optical center. Optical and actual screen centers are depicted in Figure 10.5.

Figure 10.5

The optical center of the screen is higher than the actual center. It is a frame's focal point that is recognized first by the human eye. Wide screens will have two optical centers; smaller compositions will use one, above the center of the screen.

Exercise: Create a simple palette of basic tonal ranges by dividing a rectangle into four sections as shown in Figure 10.6. The rectangle need not be very large.

a. Put your darkest value in the top panel. It does not have to be a "solid black." Label this "a."

b. The lightest value is determined next. It will be at the bottom of your chart. If your lightest value is white, leave the bottom panel blank. If you are boarding a shadowy or foggy scene, the lightest value could be gray and not pure white. Whichever way you go, put your lightest tone at the bottom of the diagram and label it "b."

c. Next, take a value that is roughly halfway between the darkest and lightest. Put that tone on the second panel from the top and label it "c."

d. Take a tone halfway between your middle value "C" and lightest value "B," put it in the third panel, and label it "d."

Refer to these values when completing the storyboard exercises.

NOTE: Digital tone reads darker than pencil because it is a solid, rather than a variable tone. It's best not to use a pure black panel as your darkest digital value; use a dark gray panel instead, as shown in Figure 10.6.

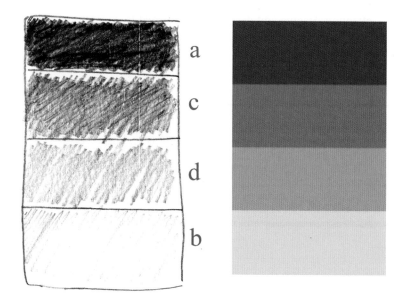

Figure 10.6

A progression of tonal values. Four values should give you enough range to emphasize areas of the frame that you want the viewer to see first. You must be able to create the tones quickly on hundreds of boards. Contrast between these values can create a wide variety of moods and lighting effects.

10. Starting Story Sketch: Thumbnails and Tonal Sketches

Why use only four values? Why not use a dozen? Storyboards are revised so frequently that it would be a shame to spend hours creating full *presentation boards* with fully rendered backgrounds and beautifully drawn characters only to see most of them "go by the boards" when the story changes (as it assuredly will). Simple tonal values add depth and readability to the boards with a minimum of tears. The number "four" is merely the smallest number of values I recommend that you use. It is permissible to use five. You should not spend all your time working on fussy tonal details in the drawings at this stage. Your object should be to work quickly, concentrate on depicting important story points, and make the boards read well using simple line and a few distinct tonal values.

Tonal values set the mood of the sequence and direct the eye to the most important areas of the frame. Use tonal values to maximize readability. Line drawings are the least effective communicators. Figure 10.7 is a busy composition with no real emphasis on any particular area.

Figure 10.7

This linear composition is confusing and we don't know where we are supposed to look.

Poorly applied tonal values can *misdirect* the eye. In Figure 10.8, the coat on the wall appears to be the center of interest because it contains stronger tonal contrasts than the main character. We are supposed to be looking at the office guy at the desk. The strongest tonal contrast should appear on the areas of greatest importance.

Figure 10.8

Our office guy is at his desk. His coat should not have a strong tonal accent unless it is the focal point of the scene. Use your strongest tonal contrasts on the most important things in the scene. Don't misdirect the audience's eye by emphasizing unimportant details.

Good tonal values will create a feeling of depth in the scene, enable a drawing to read for the requisite 10–15 feet, and direct the eye to the center of interest. In Figure 10.9, the background has been "knocked down" (had its contrast reduced) by making it a single value. Different values indicate depth of field in the scene. The character is isolated by a pool of light that helps set the mood and improve the drawing's readability.

Figure 10.9

In this version tone places different elements at varying distances from the camera. Foreground silhouettes frame the shot and direct the eye toward the character. Background elements can be simple suggestions because they are not as important.

Figure 10.10's pastoral scene contains strong tonal values and good silhouette value on the characters, but the three trees in the background trees have extremely dark tone that distracts us from the characters. The pigs and the trees share a common picture plane. The staging is flat and uninteresting.

Figure 10.10

Everything in the frame is drawn to the same scale and appears to be on the same picture plane. The background has the heaviest tonal values and distracts us from the characters.

10. Starting Story Sketch: Thumbnails and Tonal Sketches

The composition is improved when the trees and pigs are rescaled so that some of them are closer to the camera and some farther away. Figure 10.11 reads better than Figure 10.10 because the strongest contrasts are now on the characters rather than the trees and background. There is a feeling of depth to the scene.

Figure 10.11

Varying the scale of the characters and background items creates a feeling of depth and interest in the scene.

Exercise: Draw a storyboard panel in line similar to the one shown in Figure 10.7. Pin it on the wall and view it from the other side of the room. Does the image read clearly? Next, shade the central figure with your darkest tonal value (A). Use the lightest value (B) on the background and the two medium values (C, D) for prop or background detail. Pin the second drawing on the wall and view it from the other side of the room. The second drawing should read more clearly.

Graphic Images Ahead!

Indications of light and shadow should be kept simple. Four values are commonly used: light, dark, and two medium values, as described in Figure 10.6.

Line defines *contour*. The contour is the *shape* or silhouette of the object or character (Figure 10.12).

Figure 10.12

Line defines the contours of an object. Size relationships can create an illusion of depth, but the third dimension is easier to indicate with tone than with mere line.

Tone defines the *volume* of the objects and characters. Volume indicates the third dimension. Tone also serves to define the depth of field in the shot. Certain objects will seem closer or farther away with the aid of tone (Figure 10.13).

Figure 10.13

One pig recedes into the background when darker tone is applied; the other pig appears to advance toward the camera because it has the strongest tonal contrast. The illustration is identical with Figure 10.12; only the tonal accents have changed.

If the characters are in a dark or night scene, you must be sure that we can still see them on the storyboard. A dark gray background ensures that the characters still read well, even if they only appear in line. Very dark compositions will not be legible (Figure 10.14).

Figure 10.14

The action in a night scene must be shown on the storyboard. You can leave the characters in line and use tone to shade the entire frame, leaving the characters visible. This creates a nighttime effect without losing the story point.

Basic lighting is used on the storyboard. These are quick sketches, not finished layouts. Remember that the darkest part of a shadow appears nearest the light but, as with night scenes, avoid using your darkest values on shadows. They will distract from the center of interest. Reflected light creates a lighter value on the side of the object that opposes the light source, as shown in Figure 10.15.

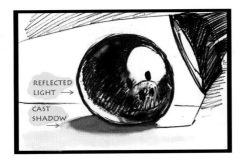

Figure 10.15

Direct lighting creates strong shadows. The farther away the light is from the subject, the more diffuse the shadow. Cast shadows are strongest of all. Avoid making your cast shadows the darkest element in the scene unless that is where you want the audience to look. The eye is drawn to the area of strongest contrast.

Objects at the optical center of the frame will normally be noticed first, but strong tonal contrast and directional elements can direct the eye elsewhere, as shown in Figure 10.16. Remember that the optical center of the frame is higher than the actual center.

(a)   (b)

Figure 10.16

(a) Elements within the frame can direct the eye away from the optical center. The pink girl's arm provides the strongest "pointer" leading to the plate of cookies and (b) shows the visual pattern of the composition.

Tonal values are used to highlight important areas of the storyboard frame. Some common techniques used in graphic illustration and animation are shown in Figure 10.17.

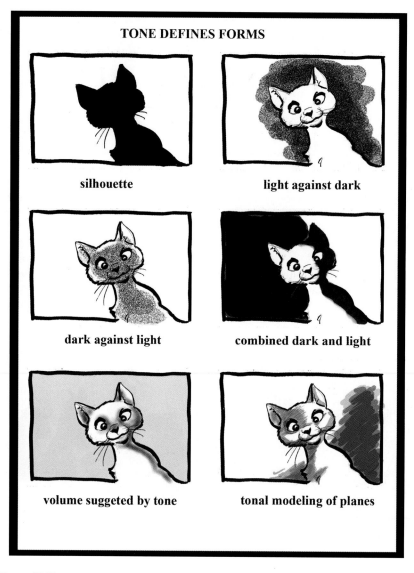

TONE DEFINES FORMS

silhouette

light against dark

dark against light

combined dark and light

volume suggested by tone

tonal modeling of planes

Figure 10.17

There is more than one way to skin a cat, or draw one! Tone can be applied in many ways to change the character's mood, the time of day, and the emotional context of the scene.

Negative and positive space must both be considered when designing storyboards.

A figure may be isolated while in the mid of a crowd. Figure 10.18(a) shows a crowd scene with one pig at the optical center of the panel. The frame has been carefully designed to draw the eye toward the central character: (1) The central pig contains the greatest value contrast; (2) Dark negative space on the background forms a letter "V" creating a pointer that isolates and leads to the center of interest; (3) The foreground pigs are rendered with close tonal values so they do not distract from the center of interest. Their animation will be underplayed; and (4) Background characters are handled as one unit that isolates the main characters and frames the action.

Tonal values can be used to direct our attention to different areas of the scene at different times. In Figure 10.18(b), a pig at screen left now contains the greatest tonal contrast. The eye views this pig first, but the central pig is still differentiated from the crowd (though to a lesser extent) by the same design elements described in Figure 10.18(a). The eye travels from the character with greatest contrast to the character isolated by directional elements in the frame. This example is only a still frame. Tonal values, positive and negative shapes, directional elements, and spatial relationships between characters are constantly changing in an animated motion picture. These elements must read well at all times. The viewer's attention must be directed to the center of interest even when it is in rapid motion.

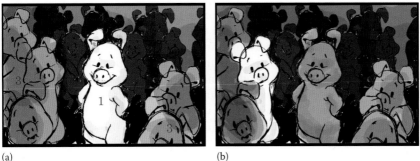

(a)   (b)

Figure 10.18

Negative space and tonal contrast can vary in one scene over time. Tonal values are used to direct our attention to (a) one figure in the middle of a crowd and (b) a secondary figure interacting with the main character.

It is not necessary to render elaborate backgrounds in every frame of a storyboard. *Establishing shots* introducing new locations or sequences will have the most detailed backgrounds and tonal values. Figure 10.19 shows an example. Most panels won't have elaborate backgrounds like this, although it is possible to duplicate the first panel's background digitally and insert it in all panels in the scene. Television boards can use this method; feature boards usually don't.

Goldilocks: "Wow, this is sure a change from the fairytale woods...I've always wanted to visit Noodle Beach!"

Goldie: "Papa Bear's money sure buys a lot for honey! And this little drink is a whole lot tastier than that old porridge!"

Figure 10.19

The first scene in a new sequence is called an Establishing Shot. A detailed background is required whenever we are introduced to a new location. Floor planes, horizon lines, and sketches of important props will usually be sufficient background for the remaining panels in the scene.

You can create and duplicate backgrounds in every frame, thanks to digital tools. Since they must not distract from the characters, areas of the background may be erased as the characters move through the scene.

The first panel of every new scene in a sequence will contain background detail, but they will not be as fully rendered as the establishing shot. Scenes in the same location may have only partial backgrounds, a horizon line, or a simple floor plane that appears in line only. The audience will accept that the characters are working in the same setting throughout the sequence. Provide them with enough material to visualize the setting and their imagination will "fill in" the missing materials. If a character interacts with something on the background, that item will be drawn in greater detail, and contain a tonal or perhaps a color accent. If the scene pans to a new location, you will draw in the background during the camera move and continue as before, showing relevant background details only where needed. Horizon lines and ground planes are always important and should be present even if your character is flying or swimming. This will make it appear to move through three-dimensional space. Without a background indication it may not appear to be moving at all, as you can see in Figure 10.26. Remember, storyboards are done quickly and are frequently changed.

Layout man Ken O'Connor always stressed that you "should not paint the Sistine Chapel ceiling for a three-second shot." In other words, it is a waste of time and effort to put extensive detail onto your backgrounds if the scene is too short and the action too fast for the audience to see it. Background patterns can interfere with the character action. Figure 10.20 shows some problem backgrounds and their solutions. Elaborate backgrounds are better suited for long and medium shots. Simple tonal backgrounds work best for closer shots.

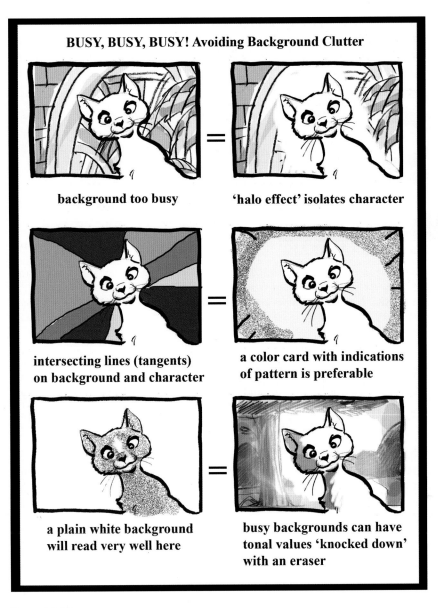

BUSY, BUSY, BUSY! Avoiding Background Clutter

background too busy

'halo effect' isolates character

intersecting lines (tangents) on background and character

a color card with indications of pattern is preferable

a plain white background will read very well here

busy backgrounds can have tonal values 'knocked down' with an eraser

Figure 10.20

The character performance must read clearly. Background detail should support it, not interfere with it.

The Drama in the Drawings: Using Contrast to Direct the Eye

The human eye is drawn to the area of greatest contrast just as it is naturally drawn to the optical center of the frame. The greatest contrast is between black and white as shown in Figure 10.20. (No, this isn't a contradiction. Pure black and white boards can create a feeling of drama or horror—just remember that the characters and action must read clearly on the background!) This principle applies even if your tonal values are relatively close, as Figures 10.21 and 10.22 demonstrates. No matter how close the values, the characters must stand out from the backgrounds.

Helpless Girl: "AAAAAAAAAAAH!"

Punk Gull: 'AAAAAAH!"

Figure 10.21 and 10.22

A screaming gal in a monster movie and a screaming gull in a beach picture. The eye immediately goes to the areas of greatest tonal contrast even when the values are close, as shown in Figure 10.22.

The strongest tones should be applied to the most important part of the composition. Do not emphasize backgrounds at the expense of the characters. Do not eliminate backgrounds entirely and have characters acting in empty frames. Let's look at a few examples of "what **not** to do" in storyboard.

MISTAKEN IDENTITIES: Your storyboards should be staged *as clearly and simply as possible*. Overly complex staging can obscure the meaning of the sequence and make the boards harder to read. The basic rules of good composition apply to storyboards just as they do in any visual medium: don't jam things into the corners of the frame, don't misdirect the viewer's eye, and make sure that your meaning is clearly conveyed through silhouette value, composition, tone, value, and (if necessary) color.

Here are some common mistakes from beginners' storyboards. **Panel 1** of Figure 10.23 is poorly staged and has no clearly defined center of interest—are we supposed to look at the characters, or at the view outside the window? The silhouette value on the houses is very good; this draws our eye to the background. Unless your scene is about the houses, this is misdirection. There are strong vertical and horizontal lines leading us AWAY from the intended center of interest (the bowl), which is poorly situated at the very bottom of the frame. The characters are stuck in the corners whereas the houses are framed by the window. If they are not important, you should not direct the eye toward them. One of the characters appears to be part of the window and curtain. *Anything at the bottom, or edge, of the frame will be lost to screen cut-ins. Never put anything important there.* **Panel 2** is an extreme close-up of... *whose* eye? It is not possible to tell here. Extreme close-ups are like chili pepper... they should be used as a garnish, and not too much. Cutting from long shots to extreme close-ups is bad film grammar and should be avoided. **Panels 3 and 4** stage the same action clearly. The emphasis is on the character acting; there is just enough background to tell us where we are, and the close-up works logically out of the previous scene.

Panels 5 and 6 of Figure 10.23 both show poor silhouette value. Silhouette value does not mean that the character MUST be a black or white shape surrounded by light or dark backgrounds! Remember to always put the strongest contrasts on the most important aspect of the frame. **Panel 7** is "just right."

Figure 10.23

The panels on the right are better than the ones on the left. Do not emphasize the wrong areas of the frame with inappropriate detail or tone; the most important areas should have the greatest contrast. Good composition is also important.

Test your tonal values to be sure that they are reading well. If the values are too close, they may run together and make it difficult to see the action; if they are too far apart, you may have a variety of centers of interest on the same board that makes it difficult to establish where the eye is supposed to look first.

View the boards upside down, in reverse, and through half-shut eyes. (This last trick lowers the contrast and enables you to see if the values are reading separately or running together.)

The characters' appearance and personality will develop as they act and react on the storyboards. Storyboard drawings are frequently pasted up into "*action only*" model sheets to help determine the final character design because they show actions and expressions that the character needs to be able to perform in the film. An action model sheet appears in Figure 10.24.

Figure 10.24

This action model sheet of Papa Bear is a paste-up of rough storyboard drawings that capture his personality and typical actions. Not all of the designs are alike. An action model sheet is used by the animator for acting tips and by the designer as reference for the character's final appearance.

The Best-Laid Floor Plans

For the sake of argument let us assume that your story and characters work with props and visual landmarks in a recognizable location. Drawing a simple floor plan will help you stage major scenic elements, such as doors and windows, along with furniture and other inanimate objects. If your picture is set outdoors, you can place landmarks such as rocks, paths, streams, and trees into the floor plan. "Wild" forests are always meticulously planned in animation!

Floor plans are usually shown from a three-quarter angle or a top-down view. I prefer the top-down view because it shows all portions of the location equally well and lets you block your character's action with little effort. The three-quarter view is useful for establishing character scale to props or other elements in the shot. A three-quarter floor plan is necessary for CGI projects that literally create the background in the third dimension, as shown in Figure 10.25.

floorplan: Master, Gondola

master tonal background

3D Master Floorplan

Figure 10.25

The artist creates a floor plan viewed from overhead and the tonal background based on it. A three-quarter view floor plan is a more accurate indication of scale. This technique is used for 2D and 3D animation. (Reproduced by permission of William Robinson.)

At this stage, you may work up a tonal Master Background based on your floor plan, but this is not always necessary. I have worked on productions that were handled both ways. In some instances the art director provided a master background with tonals for the board artists to work with. This was a useful tool because the action involved multiple characters in a busy kitchen with several work tables on the floor, a huge fireplace along one wall, prop-laden shelves, and doors at opposite ends of the room. An example of a master background and an elaborate floor plan of this type are shown in Figure 10.26. Master backgrounds typically include the characters to indicate relative sizes and scales.

Figure 10.26

This floor plan locates the windows and every dish on the table. The master background includes the characters for scale. (Reproduced by permission of Adam Fox.)

Some locations may not need a floor plan. Figure 10.27 shows characters on a color card or *"limbo" background* (a) and (b) on a background in deep space. Some graphically-designed films deliberately eliminate backgrounds and have the action playing out on color cards. Cutting and the screen direction of the animation will provide continuity of movement in these films.

Figure 10.27

The same characters appear to be (a) motionless on a featureless background or (b) moving through outer space.

The kangaroo and koala appear to be stationary when placed on the color card. There is nothing in the panel to indicate that they are in motion. The star field background suggests that they are flying and gives a better feeling of movement (literally) through space than the color card does. Both approaches are correct, depending on what your film's style is, and what your characters have to do. If the characters on the color card were moving across the screen we would believe that they were animating in space (perhaps in two dimensions). But you must keep your screen directions consistent either way, to avoid confusing your audience.

So... if your characters are working in a defined location—be SURE to draw a floor plan for the scene or sequence along with the character lineup for scale as a guide for beat boards and storyboard. This will give you an idea of the "stage" that your characters are working on and help prevent embarrassing continuity errors. If there are enough scenes between two "changed" backgrounds, and the screen direction is consistent, no one except a professional will notice that a table is now on the other side of the room, or a picture is not in the same location as in earlier scenes. But in the end, your audience must believe that the location that you are using is reasonably consistent, or they may lose the story point. Floor plans will help you plan your action and acting.

In Chapter 11, we will find the beat that sets the rhythm of every film. It's called a Story Beat for a reason.

11

Boarding Time: Getting with the Story Beat

A sculptor was once asked how he carved an elephant from a block of wood. He replied, "I take this knife and carve away anything that does not look like an elephant" (Figure 11.1).

Figure 11.1

The Elephant in the Room or removing the inessentials.

Like sculpture, animation develops complex forms from simple beginnings. A basic idea is modified and developed, but instead of working with a block of marble animation is a bit more similar to a patchwork quilt; the whole is made up of many smaller pieces that viewed together create the finished artwork. In both cases, you must have some rough idea of how the finished artwork will look before you start working on it.

A sculpture can be viewed from many different angles. A motion picture's viewpoint is *locked*. The director "directs" your attention to specific areas of the frame and the editor sets the viewing time for each shot, exercising total control over the production. Storyboard artists function as a combination of director and editor. They create the blueprint for the remainder of the film.

Storyboard drawings describe an idea. They are not a series of individual drawings. They may be lovely works of art in their own right, but if a story point does not *communicate instantly* the boards are not working. When an idea or a design is clearly communicated we say that it *reads* well.

Like the sculptor of the elephant, animation storyboard artists start with a rough object and gradually develop it into a more elaborate form. If major story points and character relationships are not planned well at the beginning of the project, they will have to be reworked later on. Weaknesses tend to become more obvious as the production advances, and changes become more expensive in proportion. This is why animation is edited first, in storyboard form, before the animation begins.

Working to the Beat

Story beats are major turning points in the plot of the picture. A new beat can indicate the introduction of a new character, a sudden internal or external crisis, a fantasy, a dream, or a change of location or time. Live-action screenwriters will indicate the story beats in an outline before writing the script. Animation storyboards will use *beat boards* to illustrate the major story points before the rest of the storyboard is completed. Beat Boards (they are always plural) are drawn after you have a rough idea of your character designs, log line, setting, and story outline. They are very similar to storybook illustrations. Figure 11.2 is an illustration I did for a children's book. The "invisible crocodile" is tearing up the house. The little dog and cat react with surprise. It might be possible to stage all of this action in one scene of an animated film. Simon Tofield stages all of the action in his SIMON'S CAT cartoons this way.

Figure 11.2

Beat boards and book illustrations both portray multiple actions in a single drawing. They can be very elaborate because they are not timed. (Illustration from *Duffy and the Invisible Crocodile* by Nancy Beiman, reproduced by permission of Patricia Bernard.)

Illustrations and beat boards do not have to work out of the previous scene, as a storyboard does. They are not timed. They may show events that take place minutes or years apart. Figure 11.3 illustrates the next story beat of *Duffy and the Invisible Crocodile*. It's very fast action—poor Duffy is being tossed out of the house because she is blamed for the damage that was actually caused by the Crocodile. We first see the broom and Duffy, and only afterward see the Crocodile and the Cat watching the scene from behind the fence. We can take as long as we like to view the scene, including the details of the floor tiles, Duffy's fur, and the fence. If this was turned into an animated storyboard, the action would probably not all play out in one scene. Very short scenes and a variety of camera angles would be used to better convey the furious action. There might first be an *establishing shot* of the exterior of the house to show us where we are. Cut to a closer shot of the crocodile running out of the doorway carrying something in its mouth. Cut to the fence as the crocodile pops up behind it with the piece of rug in its mouth. The cat pops up right next to the Crocodile. Cut to a close-up showing the cat's reaction to something happening offscreen. A new angle from their point of view lets us see Duffy unceremoniously tossed out of the house by the woman with the broom. The various actions in the scene are now happening at different times and the pacing will vary to increase the feeling of excitement. The view shown in Figure 11.3 would never appear in the storyboard or the film.

Figure 11.3

Beat boards and book illustrations can contain several actions occurring simultaneously because we have no time limit for viewing them. (Illustration from *Duffy and the Invisible Crocodile* by Nancy Beiman, reproduced by permission of Patricia Bernard.)

Story beats are NOT scenes in the film, but summaries of many scenes. As a result they are never done in close-up, but are usually staged in medium to long shot.

There may be a dozen or more story beats in a feature film. Features often develop subplots and additional storylines to complement the main character's story. It is always a good idea to keep the main storyline simple and focused without too many complications. Subplots, additional characters, flashbacks, and fantasy sequences can be added later on to flesh out a longer film, but you must never lose sight of the main story line.

Short films will usually have three or four story beats depending on the length; and they may not have subplots. The characters and situations are introduced in the first beat; complications or conflicts develop in the middle section, and the story resolves in the last beat. Fairy tales often follow this structure, so let's break down the story beats for one of them. Figure 11.4 shows all the story beats for LITTLE RED RIDING HOOD except the finale.

Beat (1) Little Red Riding Hood starts out for Grandma's house.
Beat (2) She meets the Wolf.
Beat (3) The Wolf goes to Grandma's house and puts on Grandma's clothes.
Beat (4) Little Red Riding Hood meets the Wolf in the house.

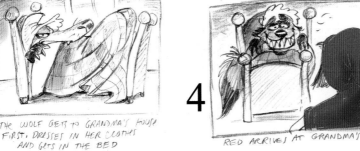

Figure 11.4

Story Beats for LITTLE RED RIDING HOOD. A final beat will describe the resolution of the story. Color accents help Red Riding Hood *read* better. Written captions clarify the action. Draw a final beat board describing how you might end this story.

As you can see there are more than three beats in LITTLE RED RIDING HOOD. Since the locations and characters change during the story, the four story beats shown in Figure 11.4 take place in more than one *sequence*. A sequence is a series of consecutive scenes that are related by story point (not background or setting!) You may use two beat boards to illustrate a story beat (but no more than two.) In this story, each pair of beat boards illustrates one sequence. Panels 1 and 2 are the beat boards for Sequence 1 where Red and the Wolf meet in the woods. Panel 3 and 4 are the beat boards for Sequence 2 where the Wolf dresses as Grandma and Red meets him again, this time in the house. If The Huntsman enters the house to rescue Red, he's still in Sequence 2. If you cut to a new location to show the

Huntsman hearing Red's screams and preparing for battle, it would be a new sequence (3); Red's rescue by the Hunter would be Sequence 4. We will discuss sequences at greater length in Chapter 13.

Exercise: Draw a panel for the final story beat (resolution) of LITTLE RED RIDING HOOD. You may use the original ending or make up one of your own.

Sizing Things Up

As we learned in Chapter 6, character lineups are drawn before the beat boards are created to show the main characters' scale to each other and to important props. These lineups will usually not contain final designs—only "placeholders"—and no cleanups are required at this stage. Unlike television animation projects, which design the final characters and environments before scripts and boards are created, feature and short animated films often set final character models AFTER the storyboard is finished. This is because the character design may change as the story is revised. Sometimes the scale of the characters will change from that of the lineup when you start boarding. In Figure 11.5 we see that Harold is much larger on the beat board than he is in the lineup. The new scale would cause a problem during storyboard because it would affect the layout, acting, and camera angles. The student corrected Harold's scale in the final storyboards. If a character grows or shrinks or changes its appearance during the course of the story, character lineups will include the variations. Nothing is left "to chance!"

Character Lineup

Harold   Sally   Benjamin

Beat one: Sally needs to feed Harold.

Beat two: Benjamin wants to play with Sally's dog.

Beat three: Sally introduces Benjamin to Harold.

Figure 11.5

Character lineups are a rough scale guide created before the story beats and boards. If you find the characters' size relationships changing in the story beats or boards, simply revise the scale model or the storyboards, so that they are consistent. This story has three beats and takes place in two sequences. (Reproduced by permission of Bram Cayne.)

Remember that *beat boards do not illustrate individual scenes in the movie, but ONLY summarize the story.* Beat board drawings *will never appear on the final storyboards* because each one represents a series of scenes or even an entire sequence. As a result, beat boards are rarely close-ups, but are usually staged in medium to long shots.

The next illustrations show how a beat board is developed into a storyboard for a short animated film. In Figure 11.6, Mincheul Park develops a story from a simple *conflict* determined in a classroom exercise—*"Something is in the Way"*—and used three beats to convey the situation, the conflict, and the resolution in one sequence.

- A man is talking on his cell phone while driving when a deer appears in the headlights. He doesn't hit it, but it falls over anyway.
- The man is heartbroken when he thinks he's killed the deer. He's even more upset when he sees that the deer has a family.
- While the man is crying, the deer and its fawn steal his car and run him over.

Although one character appears in close-up in two of the boards, the story point is carried by background action that is staged in medium long shot.

Never use extreme or "tight" close-ups on beat boards.

Beat 1: A driver, distracted by his cellular phone, does not see a deer in his car's headlights. He stops the car...

Beat 2: ... too late. The deer appears to be dead; the driver tries to revive it.

Beat 2: The driver is very upset as he realizes the deer has a family.

Beat 3: While the man is crying, the deer steal his car.

Figure 11.6

There are three story beats but all the action takes place in one sequence. Beat boards are never staged in extreme close-up, though some characters may be closer to the picture plane than others. (Reproduced by permission of Mincheul Park.)

Beat Board to Storyboard

Figure 11.7 shows how the story beats for *Something is in the Way* were expanded into storyboards. The beat boards were the outline or foundation for the story. The storyboard develops the action and the acting, and uses creative camera angles, sometimes showing us the action from the man's point of view. The boards are sketched roughly before final boards and color accents are completed. These boards were pitched twice: once during the rough stage, once during final. Some changes were made and panels added for the final version.

Why use Beat Boards at all? Why not start at Scene One, Panel One, and continue straight ahead to the end of the story? If you start with Panel One and keep going to the end, you may never reach it. There is a danger, when working in a straight-ahead manner, of losing sight of the main theme. This is a particular problem on longer films where each story artist will work on a different story beat or sequence. The story crew must see how their section of the project fits into the bigger picture so that they do not go off on a tangent. Entire sequences may be edited out of the film if communication is not established between the directors and the crew. A short film that loses sight of its story line may become so long that it is not possible to complete the project in the allotted time period. Story beats are like signposts on the production roadmap. Beat boards are a visual representation of the story's beginning, major plot twists, and—most importantly—ending. They divide your film into clearly defined sequences and simplify production. Beat boards tell you where you are going and make sure you stay on the road.

Note how none of the beat board drawings appear on the final storyboards (Figures 11.7 through 11.9). The storyboards "flesh out" the acting and action with cutting and a variety of camera angles. Starting with beat boards and using them as a guide ensures that the story never wanders off topic. Thanks to the beat boards the artist, unlike the driver of the car, knows exactly where he is going.

Figure 11.7

Beat One is expanded into storyboards that use a series of scenes to develop acting and action that was only summarized in the story beat drawing. Using more than one panel for an action or scene also provides an indication of timing for the Leica reel. Panel 7.5 was added after the pitch. (Reproduced by permission of Mincheul Park.)

Figure 11.8

Beat Two develops the man's personality as he reacts to what he thinks he has done. (Reproduced by permission of Mincheul Park.)

Beat Two (Figure 11.9) now has some amusing action and acting between the man, the fawn, and the adult deer that develop their personalities. It is easy to add bits of "business" at this stage and revise the boards as necessary. A close-up of the man was inserted between panel 20 and 21 after the boards were pitched and labeled "20.5."

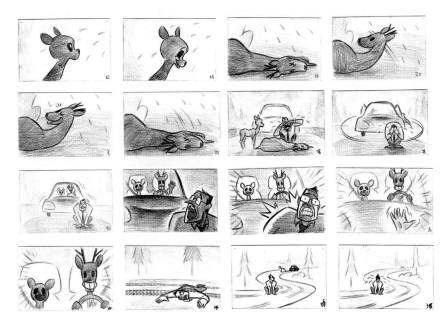

Figure 11.9

Beat Three resolves the story with a little black comedy. (Reproduced by permission of Mincheul Park.)

The final beat now contains a bit of black humor as the fawn and the deer reveal their trickery before stealing the man's car.

Figure 11.10 shows another well-known story broken down into beats (with a twist ending).

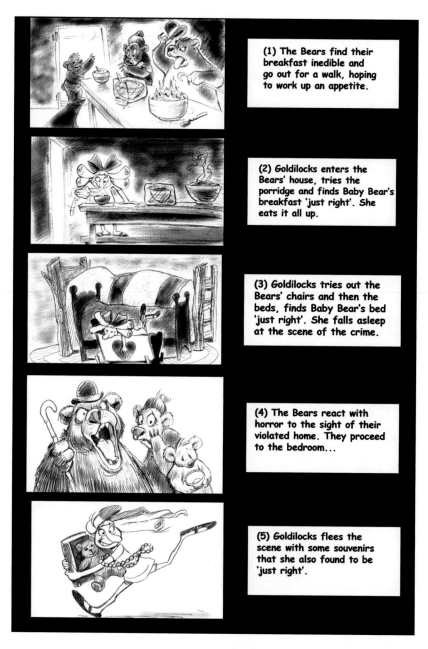

(1) The Bears find their breakfast inedible and go out for a walk, hoping to work up an appetite.

(2) Goldilocks enters the Bears' house, tries the porridge and finds Baby Bear's breakfast 'just right'. She eats it all up.

(3) Goldilocks tries out the Bears' chairs and then the beds, finds Baby Bear's bed 'just right'. She falls asleep at the scene of the crime.

(4) The Bears react with horror to the sight of their violated home. They proceed to the bedroom...

(5) Goldilocks flees the scene with some souvenirs that she also found to be 'just right'.

Figure 11.10

Each panel illustrates one story beat for GOLDILOCKS AND THE THREE BEARS. (1) The Bears find their breakfast inedible and go out for a walk. (2) Goldilocks breaks, enters, and eats Baby Bear's porridge. (3) She remains at the scene of the crime in Baby Bear's bed. (4) The bears return and discover the intruder. (5) Goldilocks makes her getaway.

11. Boarding Time: Getting with the Story Beat

If *Goldilocks and the Three Bears* was a feature film, we could develop subplots and additional character bits that would not be practical in a shorter film. There could be a "twist" in the story that changes the relationships between the characters, as we will see in Chapter 13. Embellishments of personality animation, art direction, and timing are developed in storyboard.

How Many Panels in a Story Beat?

It is okay to use two panels for each beat if the story point reads better as a result. No more than two panels should illustrate each beat. Story beats are *illustrations* that represent several minutes of screen time; always remember that they are not scenes in the film. Figure 11.11 expands the fourth beat in Figure 11.10. The additional panel shows that Baby Bear is being specifically targeted by the unknown robber, and amplifies the Bear family's rage.

Figure 11.11

One or two beat boards may represent an entire sequence. *Beat boards are not scenes in the film.* They illustrate and encapsulate the main story points. Camera angles, cuts, acting, and timing will be determined as storyboards are developed out of the beat boards.

Nursery rhymes provide excellent examples of story beats because they are the bare bones of story with no extraneous material. Generally each line of a rhyme will describe one story beat. Here is an example of a couplet with three distinct story beats:

> *Yesterday upon the stair, I met a man who wasn't there.* (Beat 1)
> *He wasn't there again today.* (Beat 2)
> *I wish, I wish he'd go away!* (Beat 3)

We receive the following information about the characters and settings:

- The action takes place in one location over a period of two days.
- The "man who wasn't there" disturbs the narrator in some way.
- One character is a man.

No other information is given. We do not know the time period, who or what the narrator is, or what type of building the "stair" appears in.

The beats for this story are already worked out for you. Experiment with ways to illustrate them. Your first step will be to decide who or what the characters are and how the story ends. Next determine where the story takes place—interior stair, exterior stair? Staging the action on an exterior stair rather than an interior one would completely change the story.

Lighting can indicate the passage of time more than the two days. Do we begin the story at daybreak or at night? Setting the story at night might make this a horror picture. Is the narrator onscreen? Is the "man" ever visible? Sketch some of the most interesting results. The simplest staging is usually the best.

You should now be able to find the major developments in your own stories and create beat boards to illustrate them. You can base a story on a simple conflict (example: "*I don't like you.*") Your *first beat* will introduce the setting and characters. Your *second beat* can introduce a problem or obstacle that the characters must deal with. Your *third beat* might show a twist that develops when they try to deal with the problem. The *final beat* will be the resolution of the problem or the end of the story. Keep the story simple. Remember, acting and characterizations are developed in storyboard. Beat boards are a visual synopsis of the story.

The ending is the most important beat, so I usually recommend getting to it first, so that you do not wind up having the picture simply come to a stop.

Once you have created beat boards for your story, you are ready for your first *pitch,* or presentation before an audience. A beat board enables you to show and tell the basic story (*pitch it*) to an audience in a compact form and receive immediate feedback on whether your storytelling is working.

Use a pointer to indicate each board as you *pitch* it to friends and colleagues. (A ruler or wooden dowel works well. Laser pointers can be distracting and are not recommended.) Describe the actions in the scene and act out the character parts as you point to each panel. You may embellish your descriptions if you feel that this will help your presentation. Acting is important! "Perform" the different parts and vary your vocal intonation to bring the characters to life. (Storyboard pitches are discussed in more detail in Chapter 18.)

Note the reactions of your auditors during and after the pitch. Did they understand everything in the story? Were they able to follow your story? You may find that everything is reading well, in which case I congratulate you. More typically, you will have to redraw some panels to improve or clarify the story. Don't worry if some drawings need to be changed at this point. It is better to nip potential story problems in the bud so that you won't have to rework the boards later on after hundreds of drawings have been done.

Beat boards are your first story checkpoint. The story beats build the framework of your film and create the story's setting and conflicts. They tell us who the characters are, what they want, and what happens to them. Story beats are like the foundation of a house. You can't build a lasting structure on a bad foundation. Get a strong story now, so as to prevent collapse later on.

12

Roughing It: Basic Staging

The visual elements and spatial relationships of the animated picture are constantly changing in fourth-dimensional space. Each scene must read instantly whether their time onscreen is long or short. Here are some tips that will help your boards read clearly and well.

Made You Look: Directing the Eye

Different eye levels or horizon lines indicate that we are viewing the scene through the eyes of particular characters. Figure 12.1 shows two different characters'

(a) (b)

Figure 12.1

(a) This dramatic upshot shows the door viewed from the eye level of a small dog.
(b) This is the same door viewed from the eye level of his owner. *The Musical Genius of Mozart McFiddle* © by Brittney Lee.

subjective views of the same background. The perspective and camera angle are more caricatured in the dog's-eye view.

In Western culture we read text from left to right. We read film frames the same way. A character will *read* "first" when it is on the left side of the frame as shown in Figure 12.2. The eye goes to the figure at screen left and moves to the group at screen right a millisecond later.

Figure 12.2

One figure appears to dominate the crowd as well as the scene because it is standing at screen left, where our eye naturally enters the frame. The character is also isolated by tone and by the positive and negative space in the frame. The other pigs read as a group rather than as individuals.

If this figure's composition is reversed, the group at the left is seen before the isolated figure. *Flopping* or digitally reversing the panel dramatically changes the meaning of the scene. In Figure 12.2, our point of view is that of the elegant pig. In Figure 12.3, we have a pig's eye view of elegance—direct from the pen.

These two shots would not work if they appeared consecutively on an actual storyboard, because the artist has *crossed the line.*

Figure 12.3

The crowd is now the center of interest. Nothing has changed except for the orientation of the storyboard panel. It has been "*flopped,*" or reversed.

Care must be taken to avoid *crossing the line,* or breaking the compositional 180° arc when staging scenes. The picture plane is divided in half to establish the viewer's perspective. The "Line" also bisects the characters, which must always have the same left-right directional relationship to one another. Consecutive shots staged from opposite sides of the 180° axis as shown in Figures 12.2 and 12.3 would be disorienting to the viewer if they were in an actual film because the characters appear to have suddenly changed places. A simple diagram of the 180° line appears in Figure 12.4. The closer the camera is to the central axis, the more dramatic the staging of the shot. The Line runs through the center of interacting characters in a scene. The storyboards for scenes following a *"flopped"* panel must usually also be flopped to maintain the continuity.

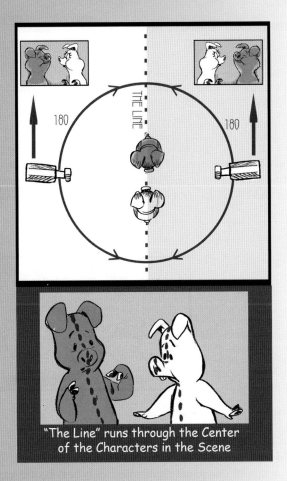

"The Line" runs through the Center
of the Characters in the Scene

Figure 12.4

The camera will usually remain on one side of a 180° axis to prevent confusing reversals of directional elements. The dramatic content of a scene is enhanced when the camera is staged very close to "the line."

A *neutral shot* has a character heading either toward or away from the camera, as shown in Figure 12.5. It may be intercut with shots that contain strong directional elements without fear of breaking the 180° staging rule. You may cut from a Neutral Shot to a shot staged on the other side of the Line.

Figure 12.5

Characters moving toward or away from the camera are staged neutrally. You may cut from a neutral shot to any other angle and maintain directional continuity. Overhead views can also function as neutral shots.

Arrows can be used to establish the direction of the incoming motion when characters enter the frame from offscreen. The arrow determines the direction of action *outside* the frame. Speed lines (borrowed from the comics) are used to indicate the direction of action *inside* a frame. Figure 12.6 shows Papa Bear entering from offscreen as Goldilocks "speedily" exits.

Figure 12.6

Papa Bear enters from offscreen with the help of a directional arrow. Goldilocks makes a break for the door, trailing speed lines.

Do not use arrows to point out the center of interest within the frame. Your staging should read well without them. A common error is to try to stage the entire scene's action in one panel. Remember, only beat boards can do that. . . your storyboards are working in the fourth dimension and must show the progression of the action! Use additional panels to continue action within the scene. *New storyboard panels should be drawn for every change of ACTION, ACTING, and LOCATION.*

This applies to television boards as well as to features and shorts (Figure 12.7).

Figure 12.7

Do not use arrows to indicate the progression of action in a scene. New panels are added for changes of acting and action within a scene, not just for cuts to a new location. *The Musical Genius of Mozart McFiddle* © by Brittney Lee.

The storyboard blocks the action and "rehearses" animated characters' performances.

Animators use these visual guidelines to tailor their acting to the needs of the story. A skimpily boarded sequence will not convey the character's thoughts or motivation to anyone but yourself.

Since anything is possible in an animated world, characters and objects may appear in several places at the same time. Multiple drawings in a panel represent *separate phases of one action occurring in a short period of time.* Speed lines can show us the progression of the movement. Two panels are used to show the action in Figure 12.8 to prevent confusing overlaps in the bouncing ball's flight paths.

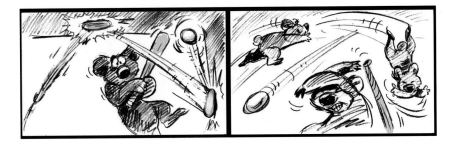

Figure 12.8

An animated object may appear simultaneously in several locations. Multiple drawings and speed lines on the same panel indicate rapid movement taking place in a short time period. Additional panels are used for longer actions.

One panel is not sufficient illustration for a scene unless the scene is very short. Figure 12.9 is an example of a poorly conceived storyboard panel. Arrows and multiple limbs substitute for acting. Each panel should contain one idea; this panel has three. Which one should we notice first?

Figure 12.9

One panel is not sufficient to illustrate complex actions taking place over time. This type of action is best illustrated on multiple storyboards.

Each storyboard should contain one idea. The number of boards per scene varies with the complexity of the idea. Papa Bear's moral dilemma is displayed in two scenes, the first of which is illustrated on one panel. In the second scene, we pull back (*truck out*) from a close-up of Papa Bear to reveal Mama's horrified reaction to his dastardly villainy (Figure 12.10).

Figure 12.10

The action in the previous figure has been expanded into three scenes on three storyboards. The acting is emphasized and the staging helps pace the action.

12. Roughing It: Basic Staging

It's always better to have too many boards than too few. Too few boards will make it very difficult to explain the progression of the scene's action—you should show us, not tell us, what is going on in the scene.

You will also find it difficult to time the action and edit your scenes when shooting your Leica/animatic. Use as many panels as you feel you need to get the story point across. This will be discussed further in Chapter 14.

I'm Ready for My Close-Up: Storyboard Cinematography

Characters have the best silhouette value when seen in straight profile, although action staged exclusively in profile can create confusing cuts. A profile shot of a character heading from screen left to screen right (Figure 12.11a) followed by one of another character heading from screen right to screen left (b) leads us to assume that they meet (c) because both characters are traveling (in profile) on the same plane. A cutaway shot can be inserted between them to correct the misapprehension. A better solution would be to use different camera angles and perspectives to show that the characters are moving in three-dimensional spaces (Figure 12.12).

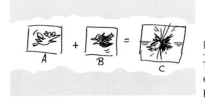

Figure 12.11

The two birds collide because they are traveling in opposite directions on the same plane.

Figure 12.12

Varying the angles creates a feeling of three-dimensional spaces and eliminates the collision course.

A three-quarter view of a character is usually more interesting than a frontal or profile shot because it creates a feeling of depth and the third dimension. Both pigs in Figure 12.13 read well, but the three-quarter view allows for more depth in the staging and acting than the profile shot.

Figure 12.13

A three-quarter view is more interesting than a straight profile because it adds the illusion of depth and dimension to the character.

Characters staged in the center of the frame should be in dynamic poses so that the negative space isn't divided evenly. Avoid the "gingerbread man" look by putting some torque on the body so that the pose is not completely symmetrical. Examples of the "gingerbread man" and more dimensional staging of the same pose are shown in Figure 12.14.

Figure 12.14

"Frontal views" read better if the character is placed slightly off center in the frame and turned slightly into three-quarter view. Most animated characters look best from a three-quarter angle. A straight frontal view often falls flat.

The eye may be led around the frame by contrasting tonal values or colors, variations in positive and negative space, directional elements in character and background designs, and the amount of detail that appears in specific areas of the frame.

Detail varies with scale. Important scenic elements should contain more detail than secondary items and distant objects should be rendered with fewer details as they recede from the picture plane. The Close-up Bear in Figure 12.15a is rendered in a sketchy style commonly used for more distant objects and so appears more remote than Far-away Bear, who is the center of interest in (a), but recedes into the background when the detailed areas are reversed in (b).

Figure 12.15

A close object that contains no interior detail will appear more remote than an elaborately rendered background area, and vice versa.

Structure: The Mind's Eye

Whose viewpoint is the action seen from? Do we see it as a "fly on the wall" or from the perspective of one of the characters? Staging will affect the mood of the scene. It can reveal subliminal meanings or subtexts for the scene that are not indicated in the dialogue.

Figure 12.16 (1) illustrates a very old joke, "A kangaroo walks into a bar." Example (1) is a literal representation of this. But a kangaroo can move in a more interesting manner. So example (2) has the kangaroo hopping into the bar. A second panel is needed to complete the action in Scene 1 as the animal lands on the barstool and orders a beer. Versions 1 and 2 both then cut to a *neutral* close-up of the bartender (Scene 2) where he says his line. (*A neutral angle lacking a strong indication of camera direction allows us to cut to either one of the over the shoulder shots in Scene 3 without "crossing the line.*")

Figure 12.16

The staging is more interesting when the kangaroo hops in and lands on the stool.

Figure 12.17 shows two versions of the kangaroo's reaction in Scene 3. The camera angle changes the story point. A *downshot* over the bartender's shoulder in example A makes the kangaroo appear smaller, and more desperate for a drink. The bartender dominates the composition. A *"Dutch Angle"* or tilted camera, adds a feeling of unease or menace to the scene. An *upshot*, as shown in example B, makes the kangaroo appear powerful and dominant. Showing the ceiling in an upshot can indicate "confinement" even if the location is a large room. The kangaroo and bartender always have the same size relationship, although the camera angle determines which one dominates the scene.

Note that it is possible to cut to both of these angles from the *neutral shot* in scene 2. Either one will be correct.

Production: Shaggy Dog Story   **Scene:** 3

Kangaroo: "And at these prices, mate, you won't see many more."

Production: **Scene:** 3

Kangaroo: "And at these prices, mate, you won't see many more."

Figure 12.17

Changing camera angles can change character relationships. You may cut from a "neutral shot" (Scene 2, close-up of bartender) to either one of these angles— both will work.

Work for an interesting variety of shots. Each shot must contribute to the story. Don't use extreme cuts because you *can; use the best staging for the action.* Medium shots and long shots distance us emotionally as well as physically from the characters. Close-ups are more intimate and can show us their reactions and inner thoughts. Successful animated films have been created in one scene, as in Simon Tofield's SIMON'S CAT series, but every film is different. Use film grammar correctly. Thumbnail a scene from different angles to see which one works best for your story. An example of this technique is shown in Figure 12.18.

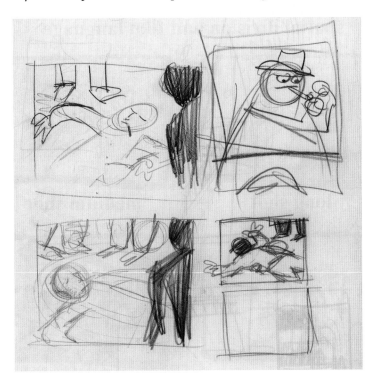

Figure 12.18

Thumbnail drawings by T. Hee showing three possible angles for the same storyboard panel. (Nancy Beiman collection)

Ken O'Connor recommended drawing a floor plan with cameras blocked in at different angles, as shown in Figure 12.19.

Figure 12.19

Ken O'Connor suggested adding camera indications to a simple floor plan. This helps the artist choose the best angle for the shot.

Here are some guidelines to follow when creating storyboards (Figure 12.20):

- Work for clarity of staging.
- Simple staging is always the best.
- Make sure that your shots work into one another.
- Use good film grammar.

Figure 12.20

Use the language of film to tell your story. A close-up is more intimate than a long shot. Don't jam characters against the frame line.

The storyboard artist also uses the character's *"eye-line"* in *point of view* shots. Tiny Goldilocks would see more things in an upshot whereas tall Papa Bear might see things in downshots (camera angles from his viewpoint would be high above most of the scene's other characters and elements). Characters in a two-shot will make or avoid eye contact depending on the situation. Use a variety of shots to avoid errors like the ones in the next illustration. Figure 12.21a shows what happens when you match horizons on cuts and do not consider character eye-lines when composing your storyboards. Who are Goldilocks and Papa Bear talking to, what are they looking at, what is their size relationship, and where are they standing? The background is identical in all three frames and we view the characters from the same angle even though one is much shorter than the other. Matching horizon lines make the two characters appear to be popping on and off the screen in the same location, or turning into one another, rather than standing in different areas of the room. Goldilocks appears to be larger than Papa in the last panel. Since they never make eye contact we cannot tell who they are talking to even though they are the only characters in the scene. This is an example of bad *film grammar*. A character lineup to determine scale (described in Chapter 7) and the use of varied camera angles eliminates this problem in Figure 12.21b.

(a) matching horizon lines + poor eye lines = error

(b) varied angles + good eye lines = correct

Figure 12.21

Characters' eye-lines should make us believe that they are looking at one another. Matching horizon lines on a cut give the impression that the characters are popping on and off the same background. Always consider your characters' scale (size relationship) to one another and to important props in the scene.

Cutaways to reaction shots of another character can cover small continuity goofs. A bad cut can be eliminated in this fashion, as shown in Figure 12.21b. Make sure that your characters' eye-lines are in the correct direction, so that they appear to be looking at one another.

Do not animate the camera. Work out action thoroughly for story points before determining cuts and camera moves. Concentrate on the best staging of the action. Use the moving camera to help tell the story, not distract from it.

Design your frames. All elements in the frame should have a purpose and help tell the story. In Colin Searle's film OAKFIELD, a faceless robot barman appears to show fright when it realizes the identity of the woman seated at the bar, as shown in Figure 12.22. The staging is clear and the angles are well chosen. The character movement is extremely underplayed, and the robot's agitation is shown by scenes that get shorter and shorter as the tension builds. The "whip pans" are from the robot's point of view as its head turns rapidly to the wanted poster and then back to Oakley at the bar. As the truth dawns on it, the robot drops the glass it is polishing. Although she is seen in downshot from the robot's point of view, we first see Oakfield in tight close-up and slight upshots—indicating that she is very much in control of the situation. Tonal values appear in areas where the filmmaker is directing your eye. The robot has no face, so their "eyes meet" as Oakfield stares directly into the camera, which represent its and our point of view.

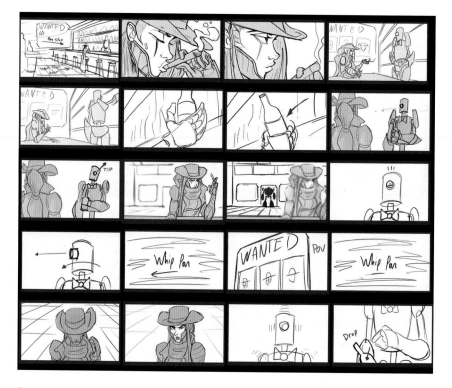

Figure 12.22

The increasing terror of the bar-bot as it realizes that its customer is a dangerous criminal is shown by rapid cuts including a "whip" pan of the camera away to a wanted poster and back to the seated Oakfield. She looks into the camera, meeting the robot's and the audience's gaze. (OAKFIELD © 2016 by Colin Searle.)

Tangents are intersecting lines that direct the viewer's attention to a specific point. It is commonly used in design and graphics, but is generally avoided in animation because it flattens the composition and destroys the illusion of depth in the frame. Figure 12.23 shows two frames with numerous tangential absurdities such as a tree that appears to grow from a little girl's head. The tangents are corrected in Figure 12.24.

12. Roughing It: Basic Staging

Figure 12.23

Tangential lines flatten perspective and eliminate differentiation between the characters and the backgrounds. They can also direct the eye to an important part of the composition, but too often the tangent distracts from the center of interest. Tangential areas are highlighted in red.

(a)   (b)

Figure 12.24

Panel (a) moves the background and (b) moves the character. Tangents disappear and the illusion of the third dimension is restored.

Use tonal values, not pure line. Storyboards work best in tone. Linear ones do not read as well from a distance and they won't show moods or time of day. There is also a danger of losing the characters against a busy background. Tonal values can be applied and modified to direct the eye precisely where you want it to go as shown in Figure 12.25.

Figure 12.25

Close tonal values help knock the patterns in the background down and focus our attention on the characters. A section of the tonal background can be rubbed out for a "halo effect" around the center of interest. (Reproduced by permission of William Robinson.)

The Wonderful World of Color Accents and Color Keys

Since storyboards are done quickly and are constantly being changed, animation boards are usually not done in full color. The use of *color accents* on black-and-white boards will help put over a story point faster than mere black-and-white boards.

Figure 12.26 shows panels from a storyboard that uses color accents as an important part of the story. Color, especially the color of the symbols on the

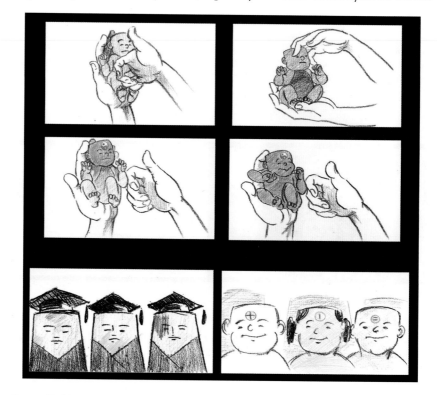

Figure 12.26

The hero and heroine of this story were brought to life through color and bore brightly colored life-symbols on their foreheads. Gray tonal values were used for the backgrounds and a symbolic death-figure. A character died when its color faded to gray. In this instance, color accents on the storyboards were an important part of the storytelling. (Reproduced by permission of Rui Jin.)

characters' heads, signified life. Gray values symbolized death and sadness. Color gave individuality to characters with nearly identical silhouettes. These boards could have been done in grayscale, but were far more effective in color.

In Figure 12.27a color accent shows an enraged tomato turning "red" with emotion. The color is used (in lieu of arms and legs) to show character acting and emotion. Color, like tone, can direct the audience's eye to specific areas of the scene. It is not necessary to use color in the rest of the panel; simple tonal values allow the background to read well.

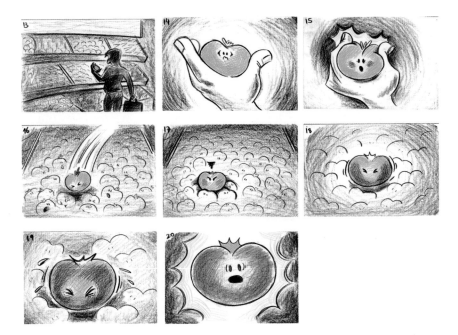

Figure 12.27

These storyboards use color accents to show a tomato's embarrassment at being squeezed through its "unripe" and "ripe/blushing" color. The color accents convey the story point more clearly than mere gray scale would. (Reproduced by permission of Maya Shavzin.)

Sometimes it is necessary to use a full color frame in a storyboard to make a story point. In Figure 12.28 innocent vegetables are boiled in a soup. The camera follows the steam upward as we *cross dissolve* to a new scene that reveals the little winged vegetable angels frolicking in Vegetable Heaven. A quick swish pan (synonymous with *whip—pan*) south transitions to a new scene of a lone tomato being grilled in Vegetable Hell. The original panels only use color accents. "Vegetable heaven" and "vegetable hell" read much better with the addition of two full color panels, also known as *color keys*. Note how the focus of the final scene shifts from the color-accented tomato in the original version to the torture chamber/grill in the color key. Color keys will also be used to create a *color script* that shows the changing moods and locations for the entire film. Each film will have unique color keys determined by the story points and emotional points that the filmmaker wishes to emphasize. Many additional examples of color keys appear in later chapters. Color scripts will be discussed in Chapter 17.

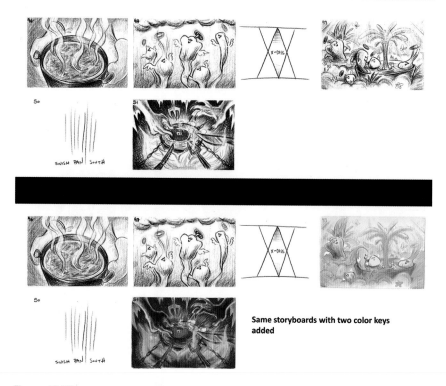

Figure 12.28

Vegetable Heaven and Vegetable Hell. The black-and-white version has a color accent that directs the eye to the tomato character. Full color in specific panels (color keys) emphasizes the changing emotional and physical environments. *Transitions* (cross dissolve and *swish, or whip* pan) indicate changes of location and the timing of a camera move. (Reproduced by permission of Maya Shavzin.)

Avoid placing the character directly against or on the frame line. This creates a tangent and it is also weak staging. A portion of the aperture is lost when the film is projected (depending on the medium, the "safety" area can be up to 15% of the picture area even on flat computer monitors). Portions of your character may be cut off by the frame. All lettering must be created inside this "safety zone" or else it may be cut off when the film is projected, as shown in Figure 12.29. Figure 12.30 corrects the problem. Note that the man's arm is no longer parallel to the frame line.

Figure 12.29

Characters and lettering must fall within the letter-safe area. Modern monitors have larger safety areas than older ones, but a portion of the frame is invariably lost. Characters' heads and bodies should not intersect the frame. The portion of the image that is in the white area will be cut off when the film is screened. Red tones indicate the lettering safety area.

Figure 12.30

The action and text now appear well within the letter-safe area. The man's arm is staged at a diagonal to eliminate parallels with the frame.

And finally…avoid cutting off the characters' heads, especially when we first see them. Figure 12.31a is terrible staging. This does not mean that you can never show only a portion of the character's body. The story may require that you stage a scene without seeing the character's face. Or their heads might actually be cut off for a reason, as shown in Figure 12.31b. But don't get too precious with the camera angles. You should stage the action in the most effective (usually simplest) way and avoid using fake widescreen, or cutting characters' heads off, because you saw this in another film. The camera is not the star of your film. It represents the director's and the viewer's eye. Offbeat staging can be a useful storytelling tool. It should not be a gimmick that calls attention to itself. Technique should never upstage content.

(a)

(b)

Figure 12.31

(a,b) Cutting off a character's head should be avoided, unless that is the point of the scene.

Exercise: Analyze one sequence of a classic live-action film by stopping the DVD or video during each scene and drawing simple thumbnails of each shot's composition. Observe how the camera is used, how the action is staged, and when and why cuts are made. Next, repeat the exercise with one sequence from a feature animated film (you might also analyze one sequence from a short film). What are the similarities and differences between the two films?

12. Roughing It: Basic Staging

13

The Big Picture: Creating Story Sequences

It's now time to start refining your story by breaking it down into *sequences*. Chapters in books indicate a new location or story point. Sequences are like chapters in a film. They break the narrative into manageable sections or modules, making it easier to construct and pace a longer story. It also makes it easier for a group of artists to work on portions of a longer project while other portions are being revised, as frequently happens in feature animation. Sequential structure makes it easier for solo artists to complete a film as well, as we will see in this chapter.

Types of Sequences

Sequences are *sometimes* defined by location. The "balcony scene" in *Romeo and Juliet*, if filmed, would be regarded as a sequence since all the scenes take place in the same location. But you can't define all sequences by their location because:

- An *action sequence* (for example, a chase) may take place in many different locations, as shown in Figure 13.1.

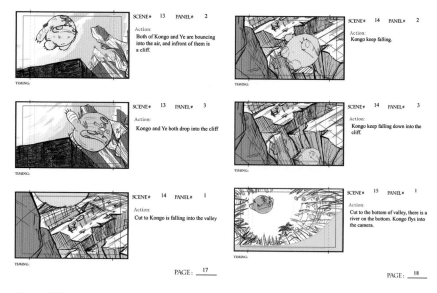

Figure 13.1

Characters may pass through many different locations during a chase sequence; the storyboards include detailed backgrounds that resemble small layouts. (KONGO © 2014 by Yacheng Guo.)

- A *dream or fantasy sequence* might take place in more than one location or time period, or even in a character's imagination, as shown in Figure 13.2.

  Figure 13.2 is an example of a *flashback* in which Papa Bear remembers the first time he ever met Goldilocks. The action in the flashback takes place in Papa Bear's mind and introduces a location and character from his past. At the end of the flashback, we return to the present time and the original location. Sequences may change order as the film's story

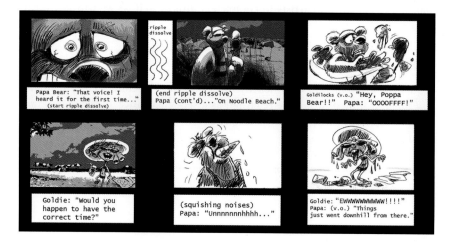

Figure 13.2

Sequence 1.5 is a flashback that takes place partly in a character's mind, but one story point is illustrated.

13. The Big Picture: Creating Story Sequences

is revised. The decimal point indicates that this sequence was added to the story after the main sequences were boarded and its "old" sequence number (4.1) tells us that it formerly appeared later in the film. Old numbers are retained since the sequence may be shifted back to its original position. This routinely happens in feature film production.

- A *flashback* or *flash forward* in time may greatly change the characters' relationships. The character designs will need to have some common visual element (a character might wear the same item of clothing at a younger or older age), so that the story can be followed.

A good example of a *flash forward* appears in Pixar's film UP, which takes place over a 70-year time period. Carl Fredricksen and Ellie meet as children in an early sequence that also introduces Charles Muntz, the explorer whom they admire. The couple marry, and their forty-odd years together are summed up in a six-minute long *montage sequence*. A montage is a series of scenes not necessarily related by time and location that illustrate the same story point. In this montage, Ellie's entire adult life passes before your eyes. The Pixar Wiki entry about Ellie's life takes longer to read than the sequence, which illustrates the same story points, takes to view (http://pixar.wikia.com/wiki/Ellie_Fredricksen).

Karl and Ellie's appearance changes greatly during this montage sequence, but a portion of their design remains constant so that we may always identity them. Karl is introduced wearing glasses as a child and while the frame styles change along with his design as he grows into youth and old age, he is always shown wearing them.

- Sequences are developed from the main story beats as subsets within the picture. Each sequence will contribute to the main story but may introduce new elements such as plot complications or new characters.

In Figure 13.3, Goldilocks enters the story just as the Three Bears leave their house. She goes into the house and some of the same locations will appear in two sequences: the introduction of the Bears in Sequence 1 and the introduction of Goldilocks in Sequence 2. Different story points are made, so action in the same location is broken up into separate sequences like chapters in a book.

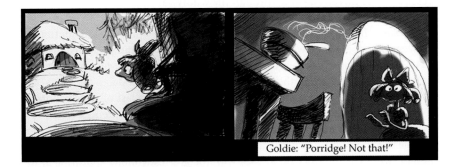

Goldie: "Porridge! Not that!"

Figure 13.3

Sequence 2 introducing Goldilocks takes place at the Bears' house, as did Sequence 1 which introduced the Three Bears. The same backgrounds and props will be used for both sequences, although lighting and camera angles will change.

- Story artists give their sequences *names that summarize the story point rather than the setting*, even if they take place in the same location. So, Sequence 1 of the Three Bears' story is titled *"The Bears' Bad Breakfast,"* and Sequence 2 is *"Goldie Breaks the Locks."*
- Whether real or "fantastic," all scenes within a sequence will illustrate the same story point.
- So the definition of "sequence" is: *A series of consecutive scenes in a motion picture that are related by story point.*

Beat boards in short films usually give you the *plot* or *story line* of the film in one to three sequences. Longer films allow filmmakers to vary the pace of the storytelling, develop the characters' personalities, add *subplots* or secondary story lines, and explore the film's *universe*. If you consider sequences as "chapters" in your film, you will have little difficulty identifying where they begin and end. You will also see which sequences develop the story arc and which distract from it.

Story and Character Arcs in Longer Films

Films with longer stories will usually have a three-act structure that is then broken down into separate sequences. There may be subplots and secondary characters' stories in a longer picture, but the main character's story line will be the backbone of the picture.

> *Act One*: Introduction of the characters and their conflict.
> *Act Two*: Complication of the situation, possible subplots, and a setback for the hero.
> *Act Three*: Resolution of the conflict in the main story and the subplot(s).

Sequential Construction in Dickens' A CHRISTMAS CAROL

Charles Dickens' 1843 novel *A Christmas Carol* is constructed very like a motion picture. The story moves backward and forward through space and time. Each chapter introduces a new story idea and new characters. Three chapters contain dream sequences-within-the-sequence that resemble film montages. Scrooge's presence is the thread running through the wildly varying time frame and locations. He's the glue that holds the story together.

The *story line* (plot) of *A Christmas Carol* is the spiritual redemption of Ebenezer Scrooge, a man who loves money more than human relationships.

A Christmas Carol's chapters can be divided into three feature-film style acts and five sequences, as we see in the next example. Act One introduces the characters and the setting; Act Two has three Dream Sequences, the last of which contains a Nightmare and an Epiphany for the hero; and Act Three is the Resolution and Epilogue. Character and story are developed more in a three-act structure than is possible in a short film. The hero may encounter a few small setbacks in the first act and larger ones as the story progresses with the greatest conflict appearing at the climax of the story. These setbacks and the response to them develop the *character arc*. Each sequence develops the main story with Scrooge and a secondary story line with Bob Cratchit's family. The main *story arc*—the events in the story that deal with Scrooge's redemption—progresses from A to B to C in a direct manner that might be predictable in a lesser writer's hands. It is Scrooge's character development

13. The Big Picture: Creating Story Sequences

that makes *A Christmas Carol* interesting. Scrooge's attitude changes from confrontational to sentimental during a series of flashbacks, then—after a horrific *flash forward* (sudden jump-cut to future events) and *epiphany* (realization of a great truth) at the climax of the second act—he is first repentant, then jubilant.

Each ghost represents a portion of Scrooge's life. Their revelations build the story arc and influence Scrooge to change his character arc after a grand epiphany in Act Two, Sequence 5. The story emphasis is always on Scrooge and while secondary characters and the subplot with the Cratchit family show the consequences of his actions; they never distract from his story.

Act One

Sequence 1: Introduction of Scrooge and Bob Cratchit
Sequence 2: Marley's Ghost

Act Two

Sequence 3: The Ghost of Christmas Past (Flashback: Sentimental Dream)
Sequence 4: The Ghost of Christmas Present (Flashback and Flash Forward: Revelatory Dream)
Sequence 5: The Ghost of Christmas Yet to Come (Flash Forward: Nightmare)

Act Three (Epilogue)

Sequence 6: Scrooge Awakens (Epiphany)
Sequence 7: Scrooge's Transformation (Christmas Day)
Sequence 8: Scrooge Confronts Bob Cratchit

I have named the three dream sequences in Act Two to show their different moods, described the use of flashback and flash forward, and given the Epilogue its own Act with three sequences. Dickens sums up Scrooge's redemption at the end of the story in a few short paragraphs, leaving most of the action to our imagination. Film must illustrate the action and show the resolution (Figure 13.4).

Figure 13.4

All the characters and subplots in Dickens' *A Christmas Carol* contribute to the main *story line* of Scrooge's redemption. Each ghost appears in a new sequence of Scrooge's *story arc*. He is then motivated to change his *character arc*.

In the first act of *A Christmas Carol*, Marley's Ghost warns Scrooge of his probable fate and announces the three ghostly visitors to come. This is Scrooge's first setback. He will not be allowed to continue living as he has been. The Ghosts show Scrooge his current *story arc* from his childhood to his death.

A second setback—a doomed romance—appears in a flashback sequence in Act Two, Sequence 3, and prompts Scrooge to actually end the sequence. When he is shown a flash forward to his own death and burial at the end of Act Two, a repentant Scrooge is motivated to change this *story arc*. He cannot change the past, but he can reshape the future by changing his relationships with the other characters in the story.

Scrooge has an *epiphany* (realizes a great truth) after the vision of the future and is then given a chance to change the ending of his own story. Scrooge's new character arc also changes the story arc of the subplot with the Cratchit family. He is literally a different character in a different story when the book ends (Figure 13.5).

Figure 13.5

Ebenezer Scrooge is literally a new man in a new story at the end of A CHRISTMAS CAROL. His transformation is completed in a dramatic *epiphany* at the end of the second act, where he sees his future state—the only one he can influence—and receives one last chance to give his story a new ending.

Subplots and Secondary Storylines

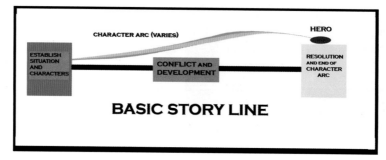

Figure 13.6

The main *story line* (plot) will introduce the characters and their situation, describe a conflict that may come from within the character or from without, and show its resolution.

13. The Big Picture: Creating Story Sequences

A simple main story line, as in Scrooge's redemption, appears in Figure 13.6. His story arc is very straightforward: Scrooge is the hero, villain, and point of conflict of his own story. He overcomes his evil nature and leads a different life. Secondary characters' stories can develop in *subplots,* as shown in Figure 13.7. These subplots can show another aspect of the hero or the situation. In *A Christmas Carol,* Bob Cratchit and his family are in a subplot that mirrors Scrooge's story; Tiny Tim, the crippled boy is the complement to Scrooge's crippled soul. Plot and subplot are linked by Scrooge's presence or influence; both of them end with the death of a main character at the end of Act Two and their redemption in the epilogue. In *A Christmas Carol* much of the action in the Cratchit subplot takes place "offscreen." Only incidents that directly affect Scrooge are described in detail. His is the main story, and Dickens never loses sight of it. We could become distracted if the stories of Tiny Tim and the other Cratchit children were given equal time with Scrooge's.

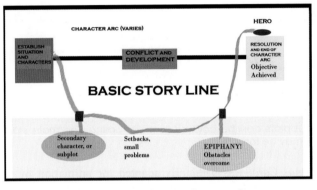

**Subplot and additional story beats
can be added to develop the story
and characters**

Figure 13.7

A *subplot* with secondary characters can add depth to the main characters' story arc. An *epiphany* is a sudden realization of truth.

   Always remember that the subplot is never as important as the main story line! Your film should not spend more time with the secondary characters than the hero, or spin off so many subplots that the main story line is completely forgotten. If your secondary character is more interesting than your hero, the film might be about the wrong character! Some animated films lose sight of the main story and run off in all directions (Figure 13.8).

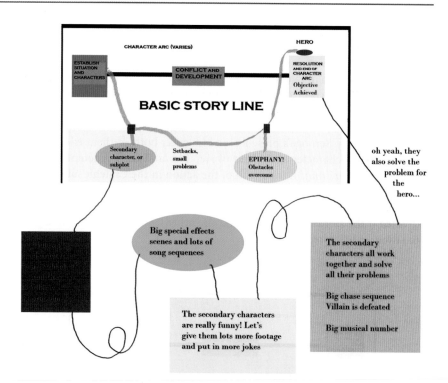

BASIC STORY LINE

CHARACTER ARC (VARIES)

HERO

ESTABLISH SITUATION AND CHARACTERS

CONFLICT AND DEVELOPMENT

RESOLUTION AND END OF CHARACTER ARC
Objective Achieved

Secondary character, or subplot

Setbacks, small problems

EPIPHANY! Obstacles overcome

oh yeah, they also solve the problem for the hero...

Big special effects scenes and lots of song sequences

The secondary characters all work together and solve all their problems

Big chase sequence Villain is defeated

Big musical number

The secondary characters are really funny! Let's give them lots more footage and put in more jokes

Figure 13.8

Too many subplots can be confusing or distracting. The main story line (and characters) may be forgotten.

A *Christmas Carol* was brilliantly adapted for animation by the Richard Williams Studio in 1971 using a sequential structure similar to the one described here. Some sequences such as the nephew's party on Christmas Day were edited from the original novel, but the story was beautifully translated into animated visuals, and the abridgment did not dilute the power of the story. It can be seen here: https://www.youtube.com/watch?v=ZTzyC9CZuOA.

> "But where is the ambiguity? Over there, in a box!"
>
> —John Cleese
> *MONTY PYTHON'S FLYING CIRCUS*

Short films may have unresolved or ambiguous endings, especially if they are part of a series. Wile E. Coyote uses new gadgets in each new cartoon to try to catch the Road Runner, even though the gadgets never work. The Coyote goes on forever making the same mistakes. There is no resolution. He will return with some more gadgets in the next film that will continue to fail.

Some longer stories also lack clear resolutions. A famous example is last episode of THE SOPRANOS. All the clues were there to show what probably happened to the family after the frame blacked out, but some ambiguity remained. They may have been murdered by a mysterious man, or not. Orson Welles' CITIZEN KANE also ends ambiguously; we see nothing from the main character's viewpoint and never learn what he really wants—there are only hints. In these instances, you must provide clues in the staging and direction, so that the audience has enough information to complete the story.

Sometimes, a film's plot may be totally predictable and used solely as an excuse for a display of special effects. While there is an audience for the "wow" factor in live action, it will not work in animation. Animation already *is* a special effect. Piling more special effects on top of the animation makes the film pretty indigestible, something I call the "cheesecake effect." Most people would not eat an entire cheesecake at once. After a while, you wouldn't taste it any more. Similarly, an animated film that contains nothing but special effects will appeal to a smaller audience than one with an accessible story. An animated feature film needs a strong, well-constructed story to keep the audience interested in the characters, because it must make us believe that the special effect has come to life.

Pacing the Film

While a short film can be frenetic and fast-paced for its entire length, a feature cannot do this without losing its audience (another example of "the cheesecake effect.") You must vary the timing in a longer film, so that the audience can understand what is happening to the characters and the story. Animated films need more time to set up the suspension of disbelief than live-action films do. Audiences have to believe that art is alive and lives in a believable universe.

A short film may consist of only one sequence or be divided into one or two sequences depending on the story. Feature animation is produced like a patchwork quilt: smaller pieces (acts and sequences) make up the whole, and the design is planned in advance. It would be difficult if not impossible to complete a feature on time and on budget if it developed like a "crazy quilt" without sequences and a clearly defined story structure. An animated feature film will usually have story development and story revisions occurring simultaneously, which can feel (or be) chaotic. Breaking the picture into sequences helps keep the characters, the story, and the filmmaker's head pointed in the right direction. The main story line will always be clear if sequential structure is developed before storyboarding starts.

About 80% of the film's creation is spent in preproduction. Changes are to be expected at this stage, and it's easiest to do them in storyboard. Films are in a constant state of flux during preproduction. Storyboards will be redrawn, and sequential order may be changed. Existing scripts will be rewritten to incorporate revisions made on the boards as a verbal story is transformed into a visual one. Sequences that are approved in storyboard can go to layout and animation *"out of sequence"* (not in sequential order) while other sequences are being reboarded and revised. This practice helps minimize production delays.

Storyboarding an animated feature film is rather like having 10 or 12 cooks each mix, measure, and bake one or two precut slices of cake while changing the recipe. The master chef (director) fits the pieces together to assemble the finished cake. And sometimes the producer will then announce that he or she really wanted pie.

Acting Out: Sequential Storyboards

A feature film is divided into acts while a short film does not need them. As we have seen, both feature and short animated films can be broken into sequences. Some features are composed of sequences that are actually discrete short films unified by or based on a common theme. Examples of this type of film include

Walt Disney's FANTASIA, Bruno Bozzetto's ALLEGRO NON TROPPO, and Bill Plympton's THE TUNE. The omnibus film eliminates the need for a continuing story line. Sequences in an omnibus film may use different characters in each animated segment and take place in a variety of locations. Each will contain its own sequential structure, its own set of story beats, and may use a different style of art direction. The thread that ties varied animated sequences together in a feature film may be a narrator, as in FANTASIA, or a framing (external) story. Mr. Banks' gradual realization that his family is more important than his job provides the framing story for the seemingly unrelated animated and fantasy action in MARY POPPINS.

As we saw in the "Three Bears" example in Figure 13.3, sequences in an animated feature film are given descriptive names as well as numbers. The names are written down in sequential order before storyboarding begins. Naming a sequence gives the director and story artist a description of its action. This allows them to see the film's structure, pace the story, and rearrange sequences without having to view all of the storyboards simultaneously. (Only rough atmospheric sketches may exist at this stage.) Simple descriptive names indicate each sequence's content and story point. The sequence's name may contain puns or jokes about its content. This makes the name easy to remember even if the memory creates the occasional shudder.

It does not matter which types of names you choose for your sequences, since they will never appear in the finished production. The names simply indicate what the sequences are about. Identifying each sequence by name and number will be very helpful to you whether you are on a long production containing two dozen of them, or a short one with three or four. Sequences often go into production out of sequential order. The names and numbers keep artistic materials organized and keep the crew informed about the story's twists and turns. Even the main titles of the film will sometimes have a separate sequence name and number if animation begins before or plays under the main credits.

Breaking your story down into sequences helps you develop the film's rhythm and the characters' personalities over time. Storyboards for entire sequences of a feature film (and all of a short film) may be viewed simultaneously and changes may be made quickly. The sequential structure may need revision if several action or song sequences appear consecutively or too many sequences are set in the same location. The modular storyboard makes this relatively simple to do.

Please note: *There is no formula for constructing stories for animated films.* Use this structure as a guideline only! Animated stories, whether short or long, are planned with rough atmospheric sketches scribbled at the same time as the sequences are developed, since you have to start somewhere. Ken Anderson discusses "blue sky" story development in his interview in Appendix 3.

A–B-Sequences: Prioritizing the Action

When the sequences have been determined and the boarding is under way, each one is assigned a letter "A," "B," or "C" to indicate its importance to the story. "A" sequences *are essential to the story* and often have the most extensive and complex action. They are boarded first. "B" sequences are still important but are less difficult to animate. The "B" sequences may go into production before the "A" sequences get out of preproduction. The "C" sequences may be edited out without damaging the story. "C" sequences are put into production last, so that they may be cut from the film if time or money runs out.

- An "A" scene/sequence is an essential story point that *must be* in the film and cannot be eliminated.
- A "B" scene/sequence is also important, but it can be shortened or restaged if time and budget require it.
- A "C" scene/sequence is one that contains material that may be amusing but not essential. It can be cut without compromising the story.

Label your sequences and scenes and work on them in order of importance. Prioritization ensures that the important story points are finished. Inessential sequences may be cut, so that the film can be completed on time.

It's vital that storyboard artists be informed of story changes that develop as storyboard progresses. Continuity is also important. You must know how the sequence fits into the picture before starting to board it. If an artist does not know what happens before and after his/her sequence, the storyboards will have to be redone.

Feature animators will often thumbnail character actions and staging for all the scenes in a sequence at once, so that the acting remains consistent throughout even if the scenes are animated out of order. This is also a good course of action when planning sequences in short films. If the animator has an understanding of the story and the character, it is possible to come back to a sequence that was put on hold months earlier without making it obvious that portions of it were animated at different times. My animation of the Fates in HERCULES was put on hold after a few scenes were completed while another part of the sequence underwent storyboard revisions. I was able to keep the "actresses" in character when I returned to the Fates sequence seven months later because I had first thumb-nailed the action for every scene after viewing the story reel and the storyboards for the sequences preceding and following the Fates, in addition to my own sequence. I was able to tailor my animation so that it fits into the film's context. In animation and in animation storyboard, one works from "large to small." Get the big picture (beginning, middle, and especially the end), and then break the story and action down into smaller increments with everything fitting inside the story line like nesting Russian dolls. This will prevent your story and your animation from going off on tangents.

The script or treatment will be rewritten to incorporate modifications made on the storyboard as sequences are developed. Walt Disney Studio story man Floyd Norman describes how THE JUNGLE BOOK (1967) changed between outline and storyboard:

"The guys [in the story department] would just kick around a lot of ideas. Larry Clemmons was our official writer. What Larry would do was put together an outline of the way a sequence might "play." Then this rough script outline was handed out to the story artists who would take it and embellish it. Everything was wide open. We would try anything. It wasn't structured and no one was saying "You can't do this or that." [Story man Vance Gerry and I] were given Mowgli and the snake [sequence] and so we started working out some gag ideas. The first version of THE JUNGLE BOOK as envisioned by Bill Peet was a much darker film. This was not to Walt Disney's taste. We really just took the story and redid it. When we showed it to Walt he liked it and said, "Do more with this." He had the Sherman brothers write a song (*"Trust in Me"*). People still talk about it. We had no idea the film was that good! You never know. I guess the audience tells you."

(Interview with Nancy Beiman, August 29, 2000)

Naming Names

Characters in animated film, including incidentals, receive names for precisely the same reason that sequences do. If a scene contains multiple characters, it is far easier to direct action on "Julie and Steve" than "the pink fish with the blue eyes" and "the octopus with the bowtie and moustache" since there may be more than one mustached, bowtie-wearing octopus in a scene, as shown in Figure 13.9. The names should be easy to pronounce since you will be referring to characters by name during story pitches. "Julie and Steve" may never have their names mentioned in the film. The incidental characters in the scene are also named.

Figure 13.9

Animated characters have names. This makes it easy to pitch storyboards and direct the action, especially when there are multiple characters.

What if there is only one character in the film or sequence? It still needs a name, because constantly referring to it as "the character" is tiresome to hear and can actually change your timing during a pitch session. It is perfectly okay to give characters generic names like Dog, Cat, Tree, Man, or Woman. Don't use long names that are not easy to pronounce. This will impress no one and will slow down your pitch. The names identify the character and need never appear in the film.

Now that you have named and numbered your sequences and characters and determined your characters' arcs, you are ready to stick in your thumbs—thumbnail drawings, that is—to stage the action and acting for each sequence. But things are going to get *rough!*

13. The Big Picture: Creating Story Sequences

14

Patterns in Time: Pacing Action on Rough Boards

> "Time is an illusion. Lunchtime doubly so."
>
> **—Douglas Adams**
> *The Hitchhiker's Guide to the Galaxy*

Time seems to slow to a crawl and stop when you are listening to a dull speaker. A short lecture given in a monotone can appear to last for hours rather than a few minutes.

Conversely, a good speaker who varies his or her inflection and pacing can make a long speech fly by and leave the audience wanting more. I once auditioned an actress for a narrator's role in a film I was directing. Since I wanted the character to have a sexy voice but didn't want the actress' choice of material to influence my decision, I requested that she read distinctly "unsexy" material for the audition. The actress found an extremely dull exterminator's treatise on the life cycle of the bedbug and declaimed it in a breathy, Marilyn Monroe—style voice that reduced the crew to hysterics. She got the part.

There is an old saying that it's not what you do, but how you do it. Good timing and good delivery can make a scientific analysis of insect pests interesting, while monotonous droning speech can make a fascinating subject seem dull to the listener (Figures 14.1 and 14.2).

Figure 14.1

A monotonous voice can make a gripping topic seem dull.

Figure 14.2

Varied and well-paced verbal and visual delivery can generate audience interest in a plebian subject.

Film has a language, a vocabulary, and structure. A film's editing and pacing can correspond to natural pauses and punctuation in human speech. Evenly paced visual rhythms can be just as monotonous as speech that lacks inflection.

Some successful animated films are staged in one scene. Simon Tofield's SIMON'S CAT web series is an excellent example. Tofield makes sure that all story points read clearly and varies the timing of the action in an entertaining way. We don't even notice that he never cuts to a new scene. You may make a film "in one" like this, but you should also become familiar with the tools of filmmaking since good editing is a major component of film language.

Animation storyboards cannot simply set up the shot in the way live-action boards do. Animation boards will block in every aspect of the character's performance. Consider them rehearsals for the animated action. A new storyboard is added when any of the elements listed in Figures 14.3, 14.4, 14.5, or 14.6 change.

New scenes are needed for different camera angles in one location and to establish new locations. Figure 14.3 is an example of a *match cut*. Papa Bear stays in the same attitude in the two scenes, but the background and costume change.

Figure 14.3

Change of Scene. A *match cut* has the character action continue smoothly across two different scenes in different locations.

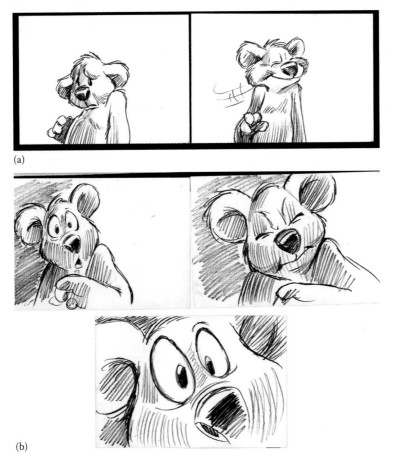

(a)

(b)

Figure 14.4

Change of Acting. In example (a), two panels are needed to show an emotional transition. In the second example (b), a camera move (*truck in*) is drawn on the storyboard to create an even stronger effect.

Figure 14.5

Change of Action. Use as many panels as you think necessary to convey the action but not too many. You aren't supposed to animate on the storyboard!

Action sequences will use many storyboard drawings to choreograph progressive movements of character and camera. Spontaneous-looking actions and "quick cuts" must be planned in advance. A flashback or montage sequence may include scenes set in a variety of locations in different time periods, featuring new characters. All of the scenes in a sequence must work together to convey *one* story point to the audience.

Figure 14.6 shows storyboards for a fast action sequence that takes place in several locations. Action sequences will use more drawings than other types of storyboards. The character in this sequence is racing through different locations, so clearly indicated backgrounds are extremely important.

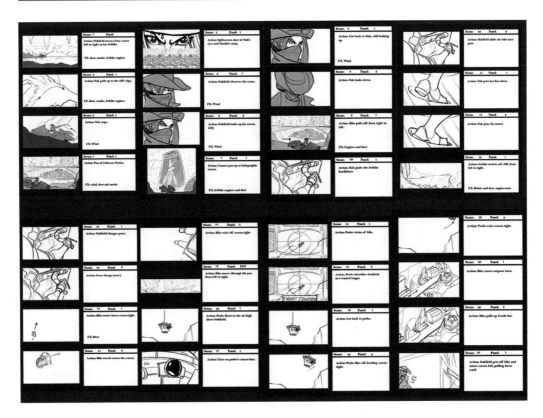

Figure 14.6

Action sequences will require the most storyboards due to rapidly changing backgrounds and rapid movement within the scenes, all of which must be blocked
on the storyboard. Camera pans will also be blocked, as shown in Scene 15.
(OAKFIELD © 2016 by Colin Searle.)

Action storyboards can include rough drafts for layouts, as shown in
Figure 14.7. In (a), the original storyboard for Scene 15 is shown. The character
was drawn on a separate level (b). The storyboard was then revised with a new
background. (c) The action was staged differently in the *workbook* (rough blocking of camera moves) for the final layout. (d) Oakfield and her "horse" will actually pan through the scene in the animatic.

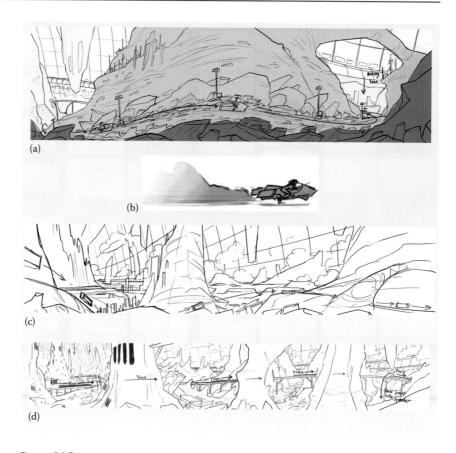

(a)

(b)

(c)

(d)

Figure 14.7

An action storyboard can resemble a small layout with separate levels that allow the character to move through the frame in the animatic. The final "workbook" storyboard for Scene 15 is broken down into background (d) and animation (b) levels. (OAKFIELD © 2016 by Colin Searle.)

Storyboard allows you to experiment with staging and timing before creating finished artwork.

The animated film's final timing and pacing are created when the boards are edited into an *animatic* (assembled into movie files with *scratch,* or temporary, music and dialogue, with camera moves and timing blocked for the animators). These pictures not only tell the story, but also make the movie. But timing and pacing will originate on the storyboards by varying camera angles and cuts. Scenes in storyboard may "play" short or long depending on staging and cutting and the number of panels that are used to convey the action.

Figure 14.8a shows three boards with identical staging. They give the impression that the pacing of the action is just as dull. Perhaps, the characters could have moved around more—but even a simple conversation can convey deeper meaning if a variety of shots are used as shown in the second example. The camera angle and perspective in Figure 14.8b are caricatured along with the characters.

(a)

(b)

Figure 14.8

Unvarying visuals can cause a viewer to lose interest in the story. (a) Different camera angles help the storyboard artist create dramatic tension within a scene. (b) Animated perspective is "forced" and deliberately exaggerated to create an emotional effect.

Vance Gerry, the great Disney story artist, was of the opinion that the story artist should only present ideas and not concern himself or herself with a cinematic approach to the story, since cinematography was the provenance of the director. In modern productions, this rule no longer applies. The industry has changed greatly since Gerry's time, and so the modern storyboard artist should be fully conversant with the language of film. The pigs' acting becomes more compelling when they are given props to work with and staging that helps establish the mood and the setting, as shown in Figure 14.9. A story is being told visually, and the dialogue is distinctly secondary to the action!

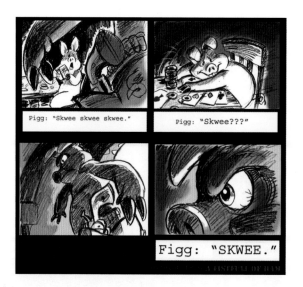

Figure 14.9

Dialogue scenes are more interesting when characters have something to do. Props and camera angles help set the scene's atmosphere. Animated camera angles are more caricatured than the angles used for live-action boards.

Stage your action in *thumbnail* sketches before proceeding to final storyboard. Thumbnails can be done on one sheet of paper or on self-stick notes. These pads enable the artist to create modular "mini-boards" without the need for pins or large display spaces or computer programs. It is possible to display the thumbnails for an entire sequence in a very small area. *Please use rectangular notes for your thumbnails rather than the square ones used in Figure 14.11*, since the rectangular note is closer to current widescreen formats used both in television and feature animation production. Different color notes can be used for scene cuts or to suggest mood changes. The sticky pages are easily replaced or removed and can be arranged in different orders with little effort. There is no need to scratch out or cut up thumbnails that were created on the same page. It's also more flexible than working digitally, since you don't need any special tools or programs to create them and can show them anywhere.

The story artist quickly roughs out several interpretations of the staging to find the one that is most effective for the action in a scene or sequence. The action sequence may contain the most drawings, but you will find that the sequences with emotional depth and acting will be most difficult to do. Sometimes, less is more in these instances. Final boards are drawn after the thumbnails establish the staging (Figure 14.10).

Figure 14.10

Camera moves can be blocked in thumbnails before final boards are drawn. (Reproduced by permission of J. Adam Fox.)

Remember that storyboard is a *script*, and animation is *acting*. Use story sketches to show emotional changes and broad actions that convey the point of each scene. The animator will create key poses for the action using the storyboard as a starting point, adding or changing material where necessary. If you drew one storyboard panel for every possible key pose in a scene, you would be *animating on the storyboard*. This slows the story artist down and does not allow the animator to contribute to the performance. Storyboard should give the animator a guide to what is expected in the performance, not every pose in the scene.

After the rough staging is finalized, full-sized storyboard drawings are worked up from the thumbnails as shown in Figure 14.11.

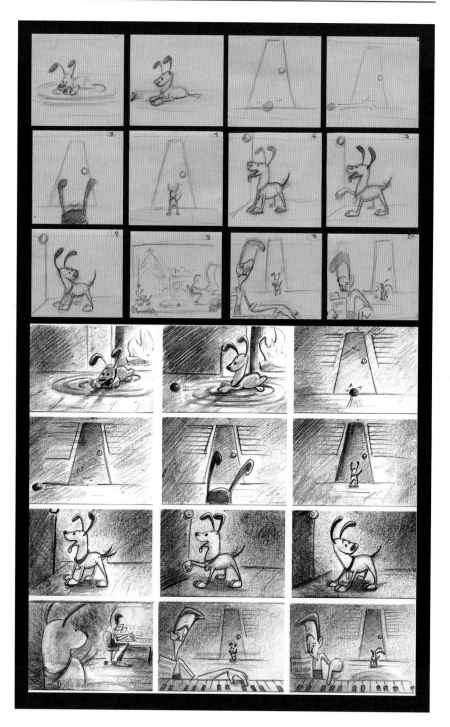

Figure 14.11

An example of rough thumbnails drawn on self-stick notes and the final storyboards for the same shots. (Reproduced by permission of Brittney Lee.)

14. Patterns in Time: Pacing Action on Rough Boards

Digital tools make it simple to include backgrounds in every panel—unless it's a very fast pan (*whip pan*) or a tight close-up, all panels should contain backgrounds (a horizon line and rough indication of necessary props are usually sufficient for all except the establishing shots). A *pan shot*, whether slow or fast, needs some indication of the background on every panel, so that the camera move reads well. Compare the slow pan in Figure 14.12 with the very rapid one in Figure 14.7.

Figure 14.12

Background indications are drawn in each panel of a pan shot to indicate that the camera is in motion.

Storyboards should contain only one idea per panel. Don't try to show all of the action in one panel. If a scene is complex and involves a good deal of acting or action, panels are added as needed, so that the action reads clearly. Here is an example of how the same action can be boarded to appear short or long. The thumbnails in Figure 14.13 are a brief indication of the action in the scene.

Figure 14.13

One or two thumbnails will convey the basic idea of a scene, but not the characters' acting. (© 2005 by Brittney Lee.)

The next figure depicts the same situation as Figure 14.13 with additional panels added, so that the characters' acting reads clearly. As a result, this scene appears longer even though the timing for the film may not have changed a bit. Note how even a simple action assumes more importance when illustrated on a series of storyboards (Figure 14.14).

Figure 14.14

The storyboards now show details of the action and acting and incidentally slow the pacing of the scene before any animation or filming has been completed. (© 2005 by Brittney Lee.)

How Many Panels Do You Use in a Storyboard?

This varies on a case-by-case basis; there is no "one way" to do storyboard any more than there is "one way" to animate. The story will determine your need. Remember that you will use a new storyboard for each change of *acting, action, or location.*

Here's a good system to determine how many panels are required for your scene. See if you can describe the action in the scene—out loud if necessary—in *one sentence*, without using the word *"and."* If you can do this, only one storyboard panel is needed for the scene (Figure 14.15).

Figure 14.15

One action, with no change in acting, can be shown on one storyboard panel.

Example: "Papa Bear checks to see if the coast is clear."

If you use more than one sentence to describe the action in the scene, or use the word "*and*," more storyboards are required in the scene.

Example: "Papa Bear checks to see if the coast is clear. He then grabs the bowl and greedily eats the porridge."

A simple action may be simply staged, as shown in Figure 14.16. There is some hint of Papa Bear's desperation, but the action comes before the acting. Four drawings convey the impression of rapid action in a short scene.

Figure 14.16

Papa Bear's basic action is blocked. The scene is short and direct.

This scene requires *multiple storyboard panels* to properly convey the action and acting that you are describing. Remember: What is on the storyboard should match what you are describing, or "pitching." There are enough panels to time the action in a Leica reel without "animating on the storyboard."

Figure 14.17 retimes the action in Figure 14.16 and expands Papa Bear's emotional performance. Papa Bear's desperation builds as he grows bolder and finally breaks down and quickly eats the porridge. The additional panels in Figure 14.17 give the impression of a lengthy scene, but the drawings may represent the same amount of time depicted in Figure 14.16's four boards. The scene's final timing will be determined by the director when the *story reel* or *animatic* is created.

Figure 14.17

Additional storyboards can change the acting even if the timing remains consistent. Papa Bear's acting is now the main focus of the scene.

Both of these interpretations are acceptable depending on whether the director wants to emphasize the acting or the action in the scene.

The number of panels used to show the progression of action in a scene depends on the story and the complexity of the scene. Timing will vary depending on what *the characters* see, and what *the audience* sees. These perceptions are not always identical, as the next example shows. Figure 14.18 is an excerpt from a student storyboard based on the beat boards shown in Figure 11.5. Sally locks Benjamin in the cellar in panels 1 through 3. It takes two panels to close the trapdoor (the action is quick, but the door is heavy; a light door might need only one panel for this action). In panel 4, Benjamin heads trustingly down the stairs toward several pictures on the wall. We, and he, will slow down here and spend time observing this new environment. There may even be a camera move trucking in on this panel so that we "follow" him down to the depths. Our perceptions (and timing) are the same as Benjamin's. As Benjamin walks past the three portraits in panels 5, 6, and 7, we see that Sally is growing older, but the man in the picture (Harold) is changing. *These*

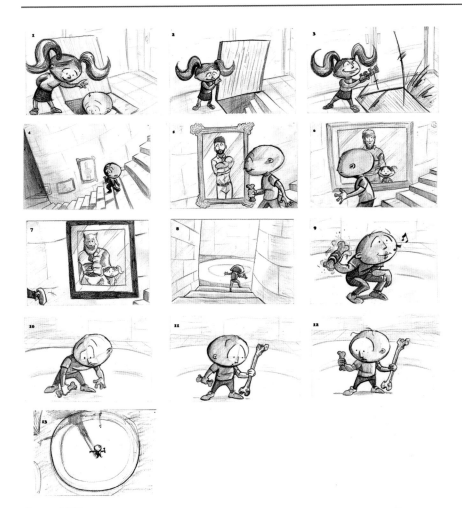

Figure 14.18

The action and acting of the characters are shown in multiple storyboard panels. The audience may understand what is going on well before the character does. (Reproduced by permission of Bram Cayne.)

panels need to be onscreen long enough for the audience to see the changes in each portrait, since we are starting to view the scene in a different time frame from Benjamin. As Benjamin moves through each frame without noticing the pictures, our perception of the situation starts to speed up. We "get" what has happened to the characters while Benjamin is still unaware. Benjamin's slow thinking is shown as he puzzles over the "props" in panels 9 through 12. The props give the audience clues showing what will happen next, so that we know the end of the scene well before he does. (The story did not have a happy ending, at least not for Benjamin.)

The use of *too few* storyboards can result in animation problems down the line. If most of the action described on a few panels and not drawn out, there is no way of blocking the action in Leica to time the sequence. This can lead to a lot of wrong turns in the acting. While the use of too many panels is "like animating on the storyboards," generally it is better to use more, rather than fewer, storyboard drawings in your projects. The ones that are not needed will be removed during the turnover session after your pitch. This is why it is so important to work rough and not get too attached to your artwork. Chances are the entire board will be redone at least once on a production. Some feature projects have had sequences reboarded 50 times!

Use camera angles that tell the story in the best and least complicated way. Don't use technique for its own sake. Extreme angles are like Tabasco sauce: a little bit goes a long way. The straight downshot in panel 13 of the previous storyboard is not as effective as a replacement panel that the student drew up after a pitch.

The downshot in Figure 14.18 is not easy to read. The location could be mistaken for an arena or a bullring. The three-quarters downshot in Figure 14.19 has the background unambiguously reading as a dinner plate. The camera angle is very important to the story in this instance.

Figure 14.19

Staging panel 13 as a three-quarters downshot rather than shooting from directly overhead clearly shows that Benjamin has "stepped up to the plate." The audience is aware of what will happen next long before the character is. (Reproduced by permission of Bram Cayne.)

Camera rotations became a cliché in recent times, but that doesn't mean you shouldn't use them. They're best used for a sudden revelation that puts the character or the audience momentarily off balance. A camera rotation in panel 13 would not be out of place as Benjamin finally understands what is going on. Comedy and horror or suspense films use the same construction; there is a gradual buildup that leads to a release, though one might use a custard pie in the face and the other, a shark attack.

A dramatic scene can become comic if the timing and pacing are pushed just a little further than normal.

DRIPALONG DAFFY, directed by Chuck Jones, contains a hilarious parody of the stark dramatic showdowns often seen in "arty" Westerns. Two gunslingers advance along a Western street. We hear only footsteps and jingling spurs. Jones cuts to one "artistic" view after another, alternating shots of the endlessly approaching duelists. Each shot is more elaborately framed than the previous one, and the camera moves farther and farther away from the actors. Midway through the sequence, the audience begins to laugh at the artificially drawn-out timing of the duel and the self-reverential staging. The too-numerous scenes become comic since the "artistic" angles upstage the action and emphasize the fact that nothing much is going on.

The lengthy build-up to the shootout (which never actually takes place) turns drama into comedy. A dramatic acting scene will become comic if the emoting goes on just a little too long. There is a fine line between pathos and bathos that should not be crossed unless the "emoting" is comic, as shown in Figure 14.20. Hold a dramatic pose too long, and it becomes funny. Underplay strong emotional scenes. Provide hints that let the audience understand what is happening. Do not drive an emotional point home with a sledgehammer. Less is more.

Figure 14.20

Underplaying drama lets the audience participate in the story. If the emoting goes on too obviously for too long, drama can turn into comedy.

Yakkity Yak: Dialogue on the Storyboard

Dialogue provides another way of timing the storyboard. It's much easier to board dialogue scenes than "free timed" comedy or action, since the dialogue sets limitations on the length of the scenes. The board artist will "play" the characters during the pitch, in effect rehearsing and timing the vocal performance with the visuals before the final track is recorded. One or two panels may suffice to show the action in a dialogue scene if the character's attitude does not change. Figure 14.21 shows storyboards for a dialogue scene that doesn't contain much action. Dialogue is neatly typed or printed on separate cards underneath the panels. The dialogue, like the storyboard panels, can be easily changed, used as a voice-over over a shot of another character, used in a different scene or eliminated if necessary. Note how it is labeled by character name even though Mama is onscreen. Two boards are enough for this scene, since the bears' attitude or body language do not change during the delivery of the line. The characters are only "talking heads." This sort of staging should be avoided since it's very difficult to sit and listen to animated characters simply talking. Directors at one studio once observed the audience's attention span during long animated dialogue scenes. After 20 seconds of animated talking heads, the audience's heads were nodding.

Figure 14.21

A long speech may be depicted on one or two storyboard panels if the character's attitude does not change from the beginning to the end of the scene. This staging is adequate but not very interesting. "Talking heads" should be avoided in long dialogue scenes.

A new board is used for each attitude change. Figure 14.22 illustrates the same line used in Figure 14.21, but in this interpretation we cut away from the close-up of Mama Bear to Baby Bear and some props. Mama Bear's lengthy dialogue is now indicated as being spoken *offscreen* in two panels.

14. Patterns in Time: Pacing Action on Rough Boards

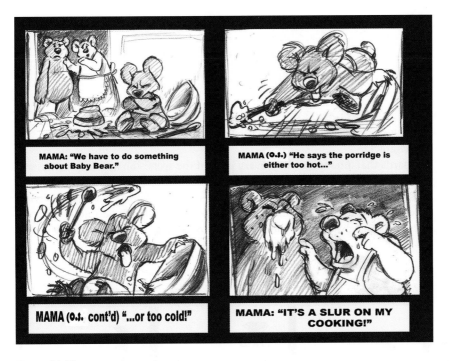

MAMA: "We have to do something about Baby Bear."

MAMA (O.S.) "He says the porridge is either too hot..."

MAMA (O.S. cont'd) "...or too cold!"

MAMA: "IT'S A SLUR ON MY COOKING!"

Figure 14.22

The scene now cuts from the complaining parents to the more interesting Baby Bear. The dialogue is spread over several scenes. Two panels are lip synched and two are marked "O.S." for offscreen dialogue.

Giving Baby Bear props to work with and cutting to the reactions of Mama and Papa Bear varies the staging. Having Mama Bear speak some dialogue offscreen (*abbreviated as O.S. on the storyboard*) eliminates "talking heads." The boards in Figure 14.22 give us more insight into the characters' performances and depict more interesting action than the boards in Figure 14.21. Animators will draw out the conflict even more when the characters begin to move.

Dialogue may either be *lip synch, offscreen,* or *voice-over.* You only need to label dialogue with the speaker's name for lip synch scenes, but a voice-over or offscreen line must also be indicated with a symbol.

A *voice-over* means that the soundtrack dialogue is used without lip synch. Voice-over is frequently used in dream, flashback, or fantasy sequences to illustrate an onscreen character's spoken inner thoughts, or when an unseen narrator is talking about the action on the screen.

A good rule to follow: if an onscreen character is "thinking aloud," without lip synch, its dialogue is labeled *V.O.* for voice-over. If a character is talking while offscreen, use *O.S.* to label the line. Unseen narrators should be labelled *V.O.* as well; if they are onscreen, their dialogue is labeled by character name or simply as spoken by "Narrator."

Sound effects (SFX) are considered "dialogue" if they are performed by an actor playing a specific character.

BABY BEAR (O.S.) "Sniff...sniff...sniff."

If nonvocal sound effects occur offscreen, they are usually labeled this way:

SFX: (Loud crash of dishes *offscreen*)
SFX: (Donkey brays and hoofbeats *offscreen*)
SFX: (Sniffling noises *offscreen*)

The last sound effect (sniffling) may be performed by any actor and not by a specific character.

Boards that attempt to show every pose in the scene can appear precious and mannered. Figure 14.23 is an example of storyboard overkill or "animating on the storyboards." These appear to be key poses used when animating the scene's action. This is fine for action analysis, but the extra panels add nothing to the story. This board artist is spending a lot of time doing something that is properly the provenance of the animator.

Figure 14.23

Six boards for one line of dialogue leave nothing to the imagination or to the animator. When in doubt, it is better to have too many boards than too few, but most will probably be tossed out or *turned over* during a storyboard review.

If the character's attitude and acting do not change much during the scene, one panel will be sufficient to illustrate the dialogue, as shown in Figure 14.24.

14. Patterns in Time: Pacing Action on Rough Boards

wicked witch: "After all, there are more of us than there are of you!"

Figure 14.24

Use the minimum number of boards that best convey the action and acting in a scene. The Witch's attitude does not change in this scene, so her dialogue can be illustrated in one storyboard panel.

But Figure 14.17 also uses a series of boards to illustrate Papa Bear's action in one scene. So what is wrong with Figure 14.23? There is an important difference between the two examples. Papa Bear's attitude changes during his scene. He is also acting and interacting with a prop. A new panel is required for each change of emotion and action. The Wicked Witch's attitude remains consistent throughout Figure 14.23. She is not given anything to do except talk. There is no need for the lengthy series of storyboards. The scene works more effectively when the action appears on one panel, as shown in Figure 14.24.

Remember that dialogue and acting will be modified during the course of the production. If you spent time drawing twenty panels for one line of dialogue when you could have conveyed the action and acting adequately with three or four, you will have much more work to toss out should the scene change. Do not waste time on self-indulgent exercises like the one shown in Figure 14.23.

Rights and Wrongs: Using Transitions

I think that most of us would find it rather difficult to read an entire book or a really long article on the Internet that contained no punctuation whatsoever so that there was no pacing, and so the book or article actually seems to consist of just one long sentence that runs on and on and on for hundreds of pages or what at least looks or sounds like hundreds of pages without any pacing or editing such as is often used to cut out irrelevant remarks or stuff that is repeated more than once, and it is also very tiring to listen to someone talking endlessly in run on sentences that contain no pauses for breath or audience comprehension, and it's especially hard to sit through a lecture by a person who drones on in a monotone all the time that is to say with the same tone of voice and equal emphasis on every word which can make the audience fall asleep quickly, and IT IS ALSO INTERESTING TO NOTE THAT TYPING IN ALL CAPITAL LETTERS IS CALLED "SCREAMING" ON THE INTERNET, and just as you wouldn't talk or write like this in real life, you don't want your film's visuals to run on and on and on without variation in a similar fashion, so just as writers will use punctuation such as commas and periods and colons and semicolons to edit and vary the timing of the read or spoken words, filmmakers will use transitions in image with fades and dissolves and in sound with audio fades and mixes to punctuate the film visually and aurally (full stop).

The boxed text is a *run-on sentence* that is badly in need of punctuation. Storyboard artists use graphic symbols to represent cinematic "punctuation"— Fade-ins, fade-outs, and cross dissolves are examples of common visual *transitions* that help pace the cutting in a film in the same way that commas, periods, colons, and semicolons do in a written sentence. Symbols for these transitions are indicated in Figure 14.25. Cross dissolves and fades are filmed in "real time" for the Leica reel. The graphic symbols are used in storyboard but never appear onscreen.

TRANSITIONS: FILM PUNCTUATION AND PACING

FADE IN

ALWAYS appears at the start of sequence of scene, NEVER at the end. Begins with black frame, then 'opens' up on scene. Comparable to opening shut eyes. Indicated as "F.I", and one triangle, on storyboard.

FADE OUT

ALWAYS appears at the END of the sequence or scene, NEVER at the beginning. Scene may fade to black (or white). Speed of fade out may vary. Compare this to a blink. A fade-in may introduce the next scene. Comparable to closing eyes; indicated as 'F.O.' and upside down triangle, on storyboard.

This is what shows onscreen.

CROSS DISSOLVE  One scene fades out as another one fades in. Indicated with overlapping triangles on storyboard; abbreviated 'x-diss'

This is how it is indicated on storyboard.

Figure 14.25

Cross dissolves, fade-ins, and fade-outs are cinematic *transitions* that show the passage of time. They are always drawn on separate storyboard panels. This makes it possible to shift or remove them if the storyboard is changed.

14. Patterns in Time: Pacing Action on Rough Boards

Use these devices as punctuation marks to pace your action and sequences. Some sequences will not use these transitions but will cut directly from scene to scene. For example, action sequences won't use cross dissolves for transitions since they take place in the "now" and increase the suspense using increasingly shorter cuts. They don't need anything to slow them down.

A *fade-in* (or fade-up) from black or white at the beginning of a scene or sequence may be compared to opening your eyes to view a new scene or bringing up the lights on a dark stage. A fade-in gradually introduces your audience to your animated universe (pictures commonly open with a fade-in). It can also indicate that time has passed since the previous sequence. Fade-ups or fade-ins only appear at the beginning of a scene or sequence, never at the end! *You cannot fade up from a scene that is already on the screen.* Fade-ins *always* start with black or white frames and gradually reveal the scene. Figure 14.26 shows the fade-out mistakenly used in an opening scene. The second example shows the correct use of a fade-in at the start of the same scene.

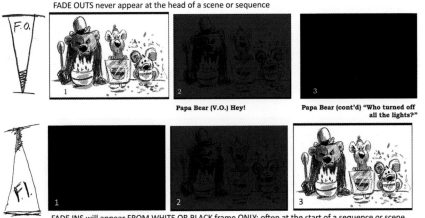

FADE OUTS never appear at the head of a scene or sequence

Papa Bear (V.O.) Hey!   Papa Bear (cont'd) "Who turned off all the lights?"

FADE INS will appear FROM WHITE OR BLACK frame ONLY; often at the start of a sequence or scene
Papa Bear: "Much better!"

Figure 14.26

A fade-out in the wrong place makes the film a lot shorter and darker. Fade-ins bring us into the story gradually depending on their length.

A fade-to-black or white (*fade-out*) signifies an ending and can also suggest a longer interval between scenes or sequences, depending on how long the black or white frame is held. As we saw with cross dissolves, the length of the transition will indicate a shorter or longer passage of time. Fade-outs are like closing your eyes or lowering the curtain on a stage. *Fade-outs are never used at the beginning of a scene or a sequence—if you put them there by mistake, you will have a very short movie.* Fade-outs can indicate the end of a scene, a sequence, or an entire film. Fade-outs lower the curtain on your onscreen "stage." Think of "The End" when using fade outs, and you won't misuse them (Figure 14.27).

Figure 14.27

And They Lived Happily Ever After comes at the end of the picture, *after* the fadeout.

Cross dissolves are the simultaneous fade-out and fade-in of two scenes. The first scene fades to black as the second one fades in. Cross dissolves may transition from one scene or sequence to another or be used within a scene (*internal dissolve*) to indicate time lapses, as shown in Figure 14.28. Cross dissolves indicate the *gradual* passage of time. The speed of the cross dissolve indicates the length of the transition; its timing is indicated during the storyboard pitch and finalized in the Leica reel. A short cross dissolve (usually four to eight frames) is called a "soft cut," since it is a less abrupt transition than a direct cut to the new scene.

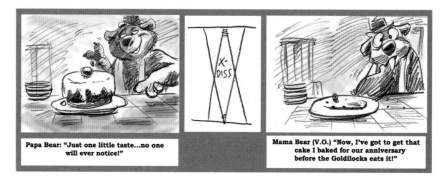

Papa Bear: "Just one little taste...no one will ever notice!"

Mama Bear (V.O.) "Now, I've got to get that cake I baked for our anniversary before the Goldilocks eats it!"

Figure 14.28

An internal cross dissolve within a scene can indicate the passage of time. The audience mentally "fills in the blanks" and visualizes action that takes place during the cross dissolve. Dialogue will be continuous in both scenes unless an "audio dissolve" is indicated.

"The curtain is lowered for seven days to denote the lapse of a week."

—**Ring Lardner**
I GASPIRI, (THE UPHOLSTERERS) nonsense play, 1922

Early live-action films were all shot in one take/scene; the use of cutting, fades, and dissolves, as developed in the films of D. W. Griffith and other filmmakers, created pacing and led to more interesting storytelling. Animation followed the lead of live action; Winsor McCay's GERTIE THE DINOSAUR (1914) was staged in one scene, while his later film THE SINKING OF THE LUSITANIA (1917) used cutting and animated transitions to stage the action more cinematically. Graphic symbols for pans, fades, and camera moves (adapted from the guides that live-action film editors customarily marked on "work prints" for their own reference) were developed at the Disney studio along with separate panels for storyboards. While digital programs may now use written descriptions of these transitions and generate the movement as the storyboard is drawn, the symbols are still in common use. It is very important that you know the correct symbols and terminology for transitions, and the most effective ways to use them. Some recent ads for storyboard artists actually make this a job requirement.

Transitions can be likened to punctuation in a written or spoken sentence that can not only vary the reader's timing and pacing of the information but actually change the meaning of the sentence if absent or improperly used. Here is a joke that uses this principle:

A woman without her man is nothing.

All words are equally emphasized. There are no indications of pacing or timing. The addition of a few commas paces it better and allows the reader to infer emphases on particular words which I have indicated in boldface.

A woman, without her *man,* is *nothing.*

Here is the same sentence with variations in punctuation.

A woman: without *her, man* is nothing.

The colon after "woman" implies a slightly longer and more "dramatic" pause than the original comma did. The additional commas completely change the meaning of the sentence!

Let's see how variations in storyboard "punctuation" can also change the meaning and timing of the animated story. Figures 14.29 and 14.30 show two versions of the same storyboard using different transitions. Fades and cross dissolves change the meaning and timing of the sequence, just as punctuation did in the written example quoted above. You may find transitions easier to understand if you compare cross dissolves to commas, colons, or semicolons, fade-ins to a slow introduction, and fade-outs to periods or full stops. The dialogue spacing underneath the boards will change the timing of the scene and the character acting.

Figure 14.29 and 14.30

Here are two versions of the same storyboard with major variations in timing and pacing through sequence" is abrupt when a direct cut; a *ripple dissolve* shows it down. Note how the spacing of the

　　　　14. Patterns in Time: Pacing Action on Rough Boards

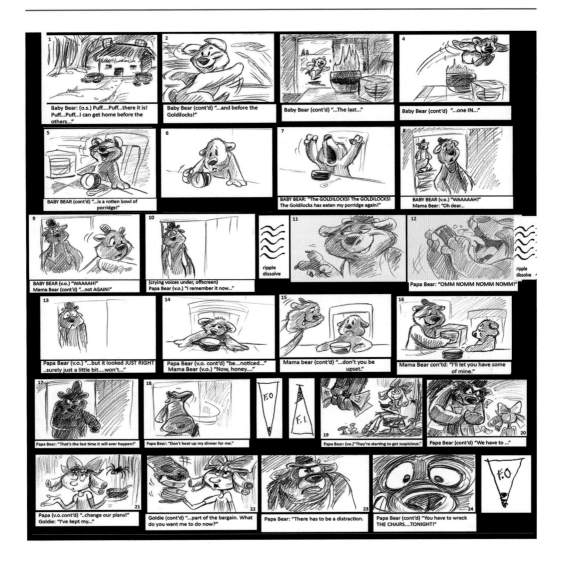

the use of transitions. Fade-outs indicate longer transitions than cross dissolves do. The "dream dialogue varies the timing and pacing on identical drawings.

Cutting without transitions may indicate a rapid transition or a "jump cut" that leaps ahead in time and space. A particularly famous jump cut takes place in Orson Welles' CITIZEN KANE (1940), where Mr. Thatcher begins the line "Merry Christmas" as a young man in one scene, and ends with "And a happy New Year" 20 years later... in the same location, but in a new scene, cutting in the middle of the action and matching it perfectly. We see the passage of time in Thatcher's greatly aged features.

Cutting directly to black frames without a fade out indicates a very abrupt transition and is called a "*blackout*" in both live action and animation. A white frame can also be used for a "*whiteout*." They are used to end a sequence or indicate a rapid change in a character's mental state (Blackouts often appear as a character loses consciousness). Camera rotations, camera moves, jump cuts, and quick cuts also serve as punctuation marks. They may be compared to exclamation marks and all-capital letters. Use them only for occasional emphasis. Do not use them simply for their own sake.

Now, there is one type of graphic transition that DOES show onscreen in the final film. Graphic symbols for "*Whip*" or "*flash*" pans that move rapidly from one location to another without cutting will appear onscreen in animatic as a *placeholder*, since the finished background hasn't been created yet (Figure 14.31).

Figure 14.31

A *whip* or *flash* pan indicates a rapid camera move. This is the only graphic transition that actually appears in the animatic and the finished film. An indistinct or out-of-focus background will be prepared for the length of the whip pan, while the start and end fields will have finished artwork. These pans may be vertical, diagonal, or horizontal, as the scene requires. (© 2012 by Maya Shavzin.)

Ripple dissolves are often used to indicate *flashbacks* or transitions to *dream or fantasy* sequences. The symbol of three vertical or horizontal wavy lines will only appear in storyboard and not in the animatic, since computer programs make it easy for the storyboard artist to create the ripple dissolve in real time (Figure 14.32).

14. Patterns in Time: Pacing Action on Rough Boards

| Papa Bear: "That voice! I heard it for the first time..." (start ripple dissolve) | (end ripple dissolve) Papa (cont'd)..."On Noodle Beach." |

Figure 14.32

A ripple dissolve can be used to indicate a transition to dream or fantasy states, or a flashback to a character's memory of an earlier event. This graphic symbol will not appear in the animatic.

Always remember that the people watching your film must understand a complex visual language in real time, at the same time. Your technique must help the audience understand your story and not distract from it. Here's an example of how fast cutting and rapid transitions may cancel each other out.

I worked on a film that contained an upbeat song and dance sequence. The story reel was assembled in the style of a live-action music video, with extremely short cuts averaging 12 frames or one-half second in length. The scenes were each illustrated with one storyboard panel. The sequence worked well when the boards were assembled into the Leica (*up on reels*) but proved extremely confusing to watch when it was fully animated. The artists were mystified at first but finally understood that we were victims of visual overload. We viewed one storyboard drawing *per scene* in the story reel, so we were able to absorb the information it contained in very little time. The action became difficult to follow when a dozen animated drawings played in the 12 frames formerly occupied by a single panel. Each shot featured a new background and characters. The song provided story continuity, but the quick cuts competed with the rapid-fire lyrics. It officially takes *four frames for the audience to visually register a cut.* This sequence's rapid pacing, constantly changing settings, and complex visuals meant that each shot needed more than four frames to register with the viewer. All of the short scenes were lengthened by an average of 12 frames each, so that the sequence would read, and since the song's length remained constant, some scenes had to be cut to accommodate the new edit.

A live-action music video *can* use very short shots. A live-action film's audience does not need time to suspend disbelief and accept the characters as "real" beings. Music videos are usually not part of a longer film and usually do not need to worry about story continuity. There are of course exceptions to this rule: John

Rights and Wrongs: Using Transitions

Landis' video for Michael Jackson's THRILLER (1984) has a strong story structure and is edited like a live-action movie without the rapid "MTV" cutting that became associated with this medium.

Pace your scenes using a variety of short and long scenes where required. Use filmic punctuation, such as fades and cross dissolves, to avoid visual overload. The story must be told in a clear and understandable fashion. There is no set blueprint for a film's construction, and interpretations of story materials will vary by filmmaker and culture. Variable pacing will maintain an audience's interest in the story.

Climactic Events

A feature will build from small climaxes in Act One to stronger ones that illustrate the complications developing in Act Two. The strongest climax will usually occur in Act Three. Think of the story line as a roller-coaster where the twists and turns gradually build toward the biggest thrill just before the recovery at the end of the ride. Figure 14.33 shows a sample chart from the story of *The Three Bears*. A series of small climaxes leads up to the major conflict. The Bears' emotional roller-coaster is on a higher level at the end of the sequence than it was at the beginning.

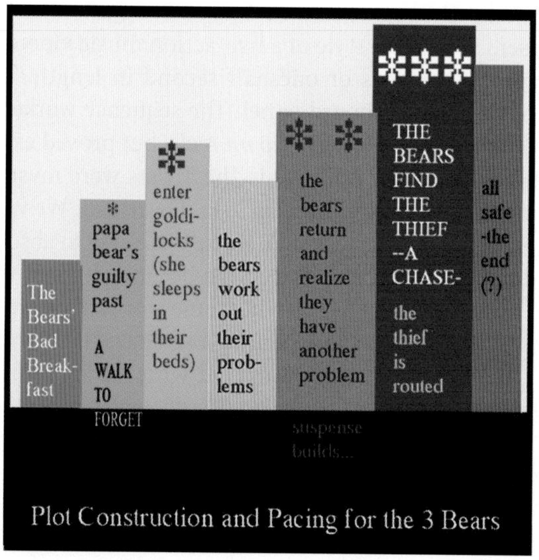

Plot Construction and Pacing for the 3 Bears

Figure 14.33

The story climaxes of THE THREE BEARS build and gradually become stronger with the strongest one occurring near the end of the story. The denouement, or summing up of the story, comes afterward and lets us down from the emotional high.

Climactic charts are not commonly used in storyboard, but you may find it helpful to sketch one out when plotting an original story for a longer production. The strongest climax should come just before the story's denouement. If the major conflict occurs in Act Two, the film's third act can literally be anticlimactic. (Some films are constructed in this fashion. Circumstances alter cases.)

A script, if it exists, is a framework on which the story is built. A good story man or woman will "*plus*" written material with visuals that translate verbal descriptions into images. Good boards develop the characters' personalities and the plot in equal measure. Avoid literally illustrating a script. Your visuals may lead you in another direction as they develop. A script suggests dialogue, story outline, and some character traits, but the boards bring these materials to visual fruition.

Storyboard takes a tremendous amount of work but your technique should never show onscreen. Everything in a film should develop from the characters' conflicts and seem to *happen by chance*. If you hit your audience over the head with a story point, it, and they, will ache.

We now come to the climax of the storyboarding process: blocking the action for the animated performance.

15

Present Tense: Creating a Performance on Storyboards

You are now ready to begin creating in-depth storyboards that flesh out the acting and actions of the characters. If you are working on your own film, you will have your outline, beat boards, rough character models, and atmosphere sketches completed by this stage, and your sequences should be clearly defined.

If you are on a professional production, you will most likely be working in a totally different system. A television storyboard artist will be handed a model pack, or "Bible," with all characters, props, and backgrounds already designed. Each artist will be assigned a script for a sequence or for the entire show and given a deadline to finish boarding it. All characters must be drawn accurately or *on model* and camera moves and background detail must be clearly indicated on the boards.

Feature storyboard artists work as a team or crew under a story head with each artist handling one sequence of a film or working with a few pages of a script or outline that was written in advance. The story head works out the sequences and beats with the film's directors, creates the beat boards, and decides which artists will board which sequences. Atmospheric sketches and rough character designs may not yet exist. Each artist will work separately from the others but will have some idea of what the rest of the picture is about, so that their sequence fits into the story. The story head reviews and approves the thumbnails for each sequence, and the artists then draw rough boards that are presented to the directors in a *first pass*. If this goes well, the rough boards may be reworked and detail added, turning them into *presentation boards*. It is far more likely that they will go through many rough revisions before they are finalized. Feature films spend an average of two years in development. Some have taken longer (Figure 15.1).

Figure 15.1

Feature films can take a long time to complete if their story problems are not worked out at the beginning of production. (Reproduced from *Son of Faster Cheaper* by permission of Floyd Norman.)

Commercial animated films were not always produced this way. In the early days, the story men and women were the writers of the picture. They drew thumbnails of the characters and the staging, wrote story outlines, and then worked their thumbnails up into finished boards. The writers and directors at the Warner Brothers cartoon studio often worked in groups and bounced ideas off one another. Writers such as Mike Maltese and Tedd Pierce would eventually put the witty dialogue for Bugs Bunny and Daffy Duck directly on the storyboards. The final script was written out for the voice artists to read during recording sessions. Walt Disney Studio story man and art director Ken Anderson stated that he would write his own outlines for feature films, sketching the character designs at the same time, and that the storyboard always took precedence over the script. In the instances where a feature began with a writer's treatment, it was not uncommon to have the story change 180° by the time the storyboards were completed. (A transcript of my interview with Ken Anderson is included in Appendix 3.)

The *story head* (or *head of story*) on a modern feature film will act as a "third director," in the words of story head and director Brenda Chapman. The story head has specific responsibilities: he or she will focus entirely on the story, while the directors are responsible for every aspect of the film. The story ideally is a collaborative process, with the writers working directly with the artists and the directors having final approval.

A story head will pick their *crew* of artists, give them their assignments or *handouts*, and ensure that the artists function as a unit. He or she keeps track of each sequence and notifies the crew of developments and changes, sometimes on a daily basis. At times, the story head will provide rough thumbnails for the storyboard artist to use, along with a description of the characters' attitudes and acting. Most of the time the artists are given free rein to interpret the material in their own way. Individual artists will be assigned to sequences that play to their particular strength. Some will excel at action scenes while others might be better "cast" on comedy scenes. Story artists will write or replace dialogue and add "business" that helps flesh out the written material. They may revise the script and create or delete characters if the story seems to require it. Freedom to do this will depend on the production, but the better films I've worked on welcomed constructive change, or *plus-ing*, at this stage of development. Scripts that are set in stone tend to produce weaker films.

When a story man or woman receives an assignment from the story head, he or she will first rough out thumbnails to experiment with staging. In Figure 15.2, two different sets of thumbnails have been drawn up for a short sequence. One version is staged in medium shot and the other is staged entirely in close-up. The dialogue is written under each frame. The two interpretations might be combined in the final film.

Figure 15.2

The sequence is thumbnailed in two alternate views. The final may use elements from both versions.

The story head will review the thumbnails with the storyboard artist. If the story head approves the roughs, a rough storyboard will be created for the director(s). This board will be "*pitched*" in a *first pass* and changes will be suggested in a *turnover session*. The process will be repeated until the story is acceptable to the directors, at which time the boards may be left rough or highly rendered *presentation boards* may be drawn to replace them, depending on the production and the people involved. Some directors will use extremely rough storyboards and others might require more polished examples for the *animatic* or *story reel*. Storyboard pitches are discussed in detail in Chapter 17 and the story reel is described in Chapter 18.

If the characters have not yet been designed, rough *placeholder* characters as shown in Figure 10.1, are used on the boards. The storyboard artist will have a major influence on the final appearance of the characters since they are drawing the acting that will be required in the film. Storyboard drawings that best convey the characters' personality and typical actions are frequently copied and pasted up into "*model suggestion*" or "*action model only*" sheets. Character designers and animators receive copies of these suggestions as a reference guide. The drawings and designs will be refined and standardized as the rough model sheets are created but the action sheets can be used for acting reference by the animators all through the picture (Figure 15.3).

Figure 15.3

Storyboard sketches are selected for expressiveness and pasted up into an "action model only" sheet. This may be used as reference by the animator all through the picture since it conveys Papa Bear's acting range very well. The model sheet will try to retain the spirit of the storyboard drawings even if the character's final design bears little resemblance to the storyboard sketches.

Portions of the script will be rewritten if the material is not working successfully on the storyboards. If there is a major story change, the art direction and character design may also have to be reworked.

A good story artist is open to change, since this is the one thing that is guaranteed to happen on all productions. The story man or woman has to know what to change so that the story baby is not thrown out with the bathwater. Sequences will be deleted if they no longer work, and will be replaced by new ones that may be replaced in turn. It is essential that the storyboard artist not take the reworking or deletion of his or her art personally. Storyboard is about change. There is nothing wrong with changing your drawings. It's highly unlikely that any storyboard will get it right the first time and it's not uncommon to have to redo entire boards if the story artist's vision does not coincide with that of the directors.

Adaptations of existing work have a basic story that is already worked out; original stories must find their own way. When the story is not yet set, many sequences will be experimental. Storyboard artists will thumbnail many rough sequences and much of this material will go unused in the final film. But, as with all animated work, it is best to change the story while the film is still in development rather than try to make repairs later on. Changes to animated films become more expensive the later they occur in production. Some films have had their entire stories changed when they were well into animation. Years of work and a good portion of the budget were wasted. If the story is well conceived and develops in a believable fashion, much heartache and waste may be avoided. But it is essential for the directors, producers, and story head to agree on what they are trying to say.

It is a common practice to hire "name" actors to do the character voices, caricature them in the character designs, and assume that the audience's recognition of the voices will carry the film. This can be a "crutch" in the opinion of story man Ken Anderson. Or, it can add genuine depth to the character. Jiminy Cricket, Cruella de Vil, and Shere Khan's final designs were based on caricatures of the actors who did their voices.

"It's a dangerous situation to get into, basing a whole conception of character around a voice talent," says director John Musker. "We did write [the Genie in ALADDIN] for Robin Williams, not knowing whether he would do the voice or not" (interview by Nancy Beiman in *CARTOONIST PROfiles*, no. 97, March 1993). Had Robin Williams not been available, the part would have been rewritten, although the basic story of ALADDIN would not have been affected. Voice acting is 50% of the animated performance, but the visuals and the story construction should be supplemented by the soundtrack, not the other way around. A strong animated story and good characters will carry the picture so that its success does not depend on audience recognition of celebrity voice talents.

Working with Music

Animation and music go together like peanut butter and jelly. The popular cliché of the animator is that of the frustrated actor. I maintain that we are frustrated *dancers*—we work out story in motion, like ballerinas, though in most cases without the tutus. A good *scratch track* will help you time your action when you are assembling your *story reels* or *animatics*. This is discussed in Chapter 18.

Animated musicals have been with us since the beginning of sound film. What makes the good ones work? The secret is this: the songs don't just "happen." You will find that the songs in successful animated musical films describe the characters' dreams and motivations or comment on the action. Poorly timed songs can stop a story dead in its tracks. Remember to never lose sight of your story. Never have someone burst into song just "because they can" unless you are doing a parody of a movie musical.

Story beats for musical films illustrate a few lines in each verse of the song. Each verse might have one or two beats. Songs, like poems, have recognizable beats that can be translated into visuals. If you are working with instrumental music, block the action to the musical themes (Figure 15.4).

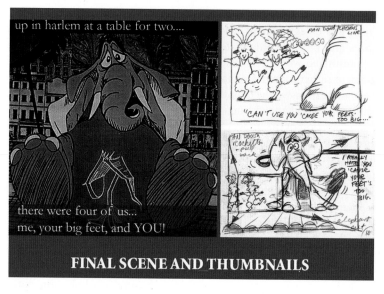

Figure 15.4

My film YOUR FEET'S TOO BIG was edited to the witty song lyrics by "Fats" Waller and to the rhythm of the music.

Visualizing the Script

So what does a story artist do when handed a couple of pages of a script? A feature film will have a script at an early stage, though it will be subject to change depending on what develops on the boards. Let us use a familiar story to illustrate one way of adapting a written script to a storyboard. Here is a short excerpt from a hypothetical script based on the Sherlock Holmes story *The Adventure of the Abbey Grange* by A. Conan Doyle.

SEQ. 1.1 (HOLMES, WATSON)

DARKNESS.

FADE UP and PAN to a gaslight that illuminates the frame as a hansom cab pulls up in front of a dark building. It is 2 a.m. on a rainy London night in 1897.

SHERLOCK HOLMES:

Stop here, driver.

The cab comes to a stop and SHERLOCK HOLMES rushes rapidly out the open door.

EXT. 221B BAKER STREET—NIGHT

Lightning illuminates the house number as we hear a door slam.

INT: WATSON'S BEDROOM—A FEW MOMENTS LATER

The room is in near-total darkness. There is an indistinct figure in a bed. Rapid steps advance upon the stairs and a door bursts open. A figure with a candle stands in the doorway for a moment, contemplating the scene.

SHERLOCK HOLMES:

Watson!

Holmes' face is illuminated by the candle. He is a thin-faced, wide-awake man dressed in the traditional deerstalker and cape.

SHERLOCK HOLMES:

Sir Eustace is dead, his head knocked in with his own poker!

Holmes advances toward Watson's bed with the candle.

SHERLOCK HOLMES:

Come, Watson, come! Into your clothes and come.

Holmes pulls the blankets from the bed, revealing Watson in pajamas. Watson does not get up. Holmes rushes to the dresser to get Watson's clothing and tosses it onto the bed.

An animated script will not contain extensive descriptions of the background since that is the story artist and art director's job. Only a bare-bones description appears for now.

Adaptations of literary stories are notoriously hard to do. Some are far more visual than others. Some provide clues to the character's personality. Sherlock Holmes is a familiar character with established mannerisms. Here are the points you should consider when translating any written story to storyboard:

- What is the tone of this story? Is it dramatic, comical, satirical, or tragic?
- What do the characters feel? Are they happy, apprehensive, or indifferent?
- Whose viewpoint will we see the action from? Do we identify with a particular character? Are they large or small? This will determine the camera angles.
- How does the action progress, and why does it happen?

This example is only an exercise. In an actual production your story head or your directors would tell you how they wish the story to be interpreted. You would also be able to read the entire script to see how matters progress in earlier and later scenes.

The first step is to break down the script "by idea," drawing extremely rough thumbnails for each setting and determining which area of the frame will be the center of interest. Create a "concrete poetry" sentence that describes the action in the setting, writing directly on each object in the panel as shown in Figure 15.5. Illustrate sentences, not words, and don't include dialogue. There are two main settings in the sequence: (a) the exterior of Holmes' and Watson's house and (b) Watson's bedroom.

An animated sequence is also constructed like a sentence. Use the concrete-poetry method to clarify your thoughts and emphasize what is primary and what is of secondary importance in the sequence. Holmes is the active figure so the sentence and staging in the *Abbey Grange* excerpt focuses on him.

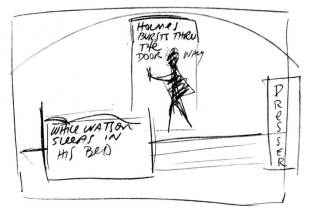

Figure 15.5

A sentence describing the setting, characters, and action is written inside the thumbnail panel. "Holmes bursts through the doorway while Watson sleeps in the bed." Once the stage is set, the action can begin.

I decide that this story will be staged as a comedy. I will contrast Sherlock Holmes' frantic action with Watson's immobility. I decide that Watson doesn't want to get out of bed because he has had too much to drink the night before. Does the script say this? No, but since this is my own production, I have perfect freedom to add additional material to flesh the action out. The same material could just as easily be staged dramatically. The director or story head will guide you on a professional production.

I next draw thumbnails in silhouette to examine possible staging and then rough out the action with the pictures and dialogue on separate panels as shown in Figure 15.6. I decide to keep the final action in silhouette for artistic reasons. Instead of following the script directions literally, I add some material with Watson going back to sleep and get Holmes over to the dresser before his last line so that he doesn't see Watson's reaction to his wake-up call. The last shot offers an explanation for Watson's behavior.

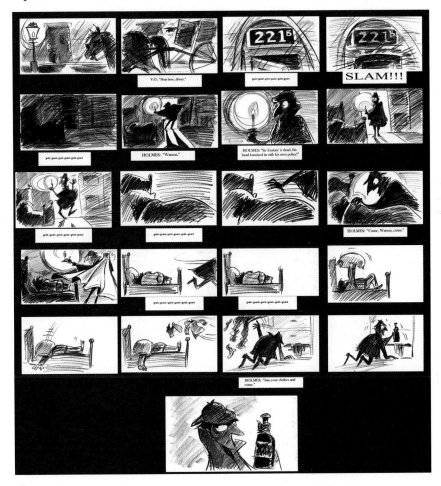

Figure 15.6

The rough boards show how the script has been modified. Holmes' reaction to Watson's disinterest adds a pause that was not indicated in the script. Written sound effects give a rough idea of the timing even though this won't be finalized until the boards are cut into the *Leica* or *story reel*.

You should always work for clarity in your drawings. The staging and acting should never be open to misinterpretation. Add another storyboard drawing to clarify the action or acting if the meaning of a scene is in doubt. It is preferable to have too many boards than too few to convey the story. The boards must direct the viewer's eye where you want it to go and not have distracting elements in the frame.

Since the characters in this story appear in silhouette on many of the boards, I use a spotlight effect from the doorway to frame Holmes, who remains in shadow throughout. He is the center of interest, since he is the greatest contrast in the frame and appears in the optical center. Light from the candle directs your attention toward Watson's bed, where I'd like you to look next. When the action becomes more frenetic, I draw the characters on the white panels without rendering the backgrounds at all. We accept that the action continues in the same dimly lit room. I was able to build on this ludicrous start by having things go from bad to worse. Holmes eventually wakes Watson with a hotfoot causing his friend to leap onto the chandelier, which falls, hitting Holmes on the head. The ending showed Watson solving the crime and getting "the girl" while Holmes is recovering (and still wearing the chandelier).

Note that characters' expressions and details show even when they are "in silhouette." I am not using absolute blacks since I want you to see the facial expressions as well as the action. This doesn't mean that you can't use absolutely black silhouette on storyboard; each story situation is unique. In this story, it was important to see Holmes' expressions even when he was in the dark room, so the silhouettes are in medium values to make them readable. Your situation may differ. Remember, there is no one way to do a storyboard any more than there is one way to perform a scene. Use the methods and techniques that best suit your story (Figure 15.7).

Figure 15.7

Silhouette values were kept in the medium range to better convey the farcical action in this absurd interpretation of the classic Sherlock Holmes story.

Before the *pitch*, I'll draw rough character designs for Holmes and Watson or paste up action model sheets to show at the same time as the storyboards. I will frequently pitch all the artwork to another artist beforehand to see if everything is *reading* well. When I am confident that the sequence is ready to show, I pitch the boards and character artwork to the (hopefully) appreciative audience. Chapter 18 lists things to do and not to do during a storyboard pitch. Wish me luck.

Exercise: Try thumbnailing the script from *The Adventure of the Abbey Grange* in a different manner and mood than I have done. After you have finished, design rough model sheets for Holmes and Watson based on your storyboard sketches. Can you make these familiar characters seem new and different?

16

Color My World: Art Direction and Storytelling

> "Griselda woke up *feeling blue*. The *violet vault* sparkled with a billion *points of white* as the blotched banana of the moon rose behind the *gray ramparts* of the Castle Preposterous. Suddenly she espied Cyril and Cynthia gamboling through the forsythia. Griselda turned *green with envy* and then *rose* in a *red rage* since she'd never approved of gamboling...."
>
> **—"*Purple Prose*," excerpted from the unpublished romance novel *Love's Annoying Ache***

Color can convey symbolic meanings that add depth and resonance to characters and stories. An animated character can literally start out "blue," then turn green, and red in rapid succession. Color changes describe a character's emotional state even when they appear outside of a story context (Figure 16.1).

Figure 16.1

Color symbolizes the women's emotional and financial state. Illustration by Nancy Beiman for the film IN DEBT WE TRUST. (Courtesy of Globalvision Inc.)

Some color symbols apply to settings rather than characters. It is possible to *see things in black and white, look at the world through rose-colored glasses, have a red-letter day, live in a golden age,* see something happen *once in a blue moon,* or find yourself in a *gray area.* Many animated films use color very creatively. Consider how color, or the absence of color, can help tell your story (Figure 16.2).

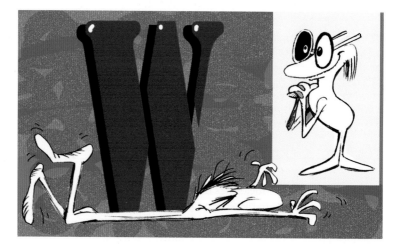

Figure 16.2

One character has a *Red-Letter Day* while another is in a *gray area* trying to *see things in black and white.* Stereotypical colors convey meaning whether used on characters, props, or backgrounds.

Fishing for Complements

I recommend purchasing a rotating color wheel that allows you to compare and analyze *warm and cool, primary, complementary,* and *split complementary* colors. This will become an indispensable tool. Some wheels are specially designed for interior decorators, and others are intended for use by Web artists. You may need to get more than one wheel, depending on your choice of medium.

A color reference library, or morgue, is a useful tool for the art director. I've used snippets of magazine photos that showed the color effect I wanted when pitching to clients. Keep your eyes open and your bookshelf and files updated with interesting books, pictures from magazines, stamps, postcards, and anything else that might provide good color reference for your project. I also like to get paint chips from a hardware store. These are helpfully filed by hue, often with four or five different values on each chip. Note the many shades of "white" offered. Certain companies have published detailed guides offering advice on which color combinations work best with particular types of décor. Others suggest palettes for specific historical periods. Many interesting effects can be obtained with little effort by juxtaposing two or three paint chip samples and comparing the different values and hues (Figure 16.3).

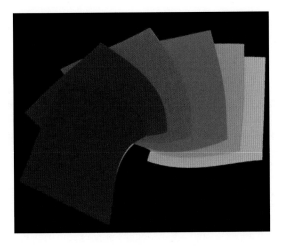

Figure 16.3

This color palette was based on paint chips obtained from a hardware store.

I recommend doing outside reference since not everything appears on the Internet! You will find inspiration in fabric patterns, items that you may use every day (remember Sherlock Holmes's admonition that you "see but do not observe"—take a good look at what is around you), and natural objects.

Color should not be an afterthought to your production design. The right colors can create an emotional mood that helps you tell your story more effectively.

Colors can stereotype as easily as character designs. A yellow sun shines in a bright blue sky, a gray thundercloud hovers over a wine-dark sea, and white snowflakes tumble across a velvety blue background punctuated by yellow light shining from chill-gray cabin windows. It can be as much fun to work against stereotypes when planning your art direction as it was when planning the character designs.

Sometimes, you need to use color in traditional ways. Goldilocks has walked into the wrong room. Her embarrassment is shown by adding a bit of red to the storyboard (Figure 16.4).

Goldilocks: "OOOPS! I am so embarrassed!"

Figure 16.4

Red is added to the black-and-white storyboard to convey Goldilocks' emotions and embarrassment.

Warner Brothers Studio art director Maurice Noble said:

> We had less to work with, [the cartoons] were spontaneous, and we had fun designing them. Chuck [Jones] gave me leeway and all of a sudden I was my own boss. I tried to be fresh in designing with color for each cartoon. I believe… that the graphic style was more fun to look at…. The graphics of animation stretch in *surprises* and that's what animation is all about…. The graphic style started because [the artists] began to realize that they could have more fun with it. It's like any other art medium…. What's the difference between a Picasso and a Van Gogh? I'm not comparing our talents to [theirs], but on the other hand maybe we *are* the modern artists. I do believe that animation is a fine art…. I think it still has a long way to go if we go back to graphics and forget the computer. When I give talks I always emphasize there is a difference between pushing a button and drawing. You can put down plenty of ideas quickly with a pencil.
>
> —**Interview with Nancy Beiman**
> *August 2000*

You can read more about Maurice Noble's theory of color in *THE NOBLE APPROACH: Maurice Noble and the Zen of Animation Design,* by Tod Joseph Polson (Chronicle Books, 2015.)

Saturation Point: Colors and Tonal Values

Color saturation, or intensity, is the equivalent of the gray and black values used on tonal storyboards.

Storyboards usually use shades of gray tone. Color is used as an accent. At times, it will be necessary to do an entire storyboard in color. Everything depends on the story context.

A quick way of testing the readability of your color palette or background is to view it through narrowed or half-closed eyes as you did when testing the grayscale values on your storyboards. Lowering the light that reaches your eye also lowers the intensity of the color values. If the colors and objects now appear to merge, there is not enough contrast in your composition, and you will have to change values or hues to make it read better. If certain areas are so contrast, they appear to "pop off" the backgrounds, be sure that that is where you want the audience to look at first. A strong color accent in the wrong place can distract the viewer from the center of interest (Figure 16.5).

Figure 16.5

The bright color accent on the wall distracts us from the characters in the foreground. Toning down the value of the background color corrects the problem.

Ken O'Connor, the great Disney layout and story man, maintained that *tonal values were the most important elements of the scene even when the composition was in color rather than in black and white.* If the tonal values read well in grayscale, according to Ken, just about any color combination would work in the shot. Legibility is the most important thing, no matter what the medium is. Viewing your color choices in grayscale will help you see whether the colors you have chosen for your backgrounds provide the same amount of contrast that their black-and-white equivalents would do.

Ken O'Connor would view his color compositions through a red gel filter to gray them down. Nowadays, this comparison may be arranged with the click of a button. Let us see what happens when a color illustration is converted into gray tonal values using the "grayscale" command in Adobe Photoshop. It is very important to use the *grayscale* and not the *desaturate* command when transforming your artwork. The gray tones that result from desaturation will not be accurate. Figure 16.6 shows color values that have been grayed out using the two different methods.

original color   grayscale   de-saturated

Figure 16.6

This color image was put into grayscale and then changed with the *desaturate* command in Adobe Photoshop. Always use the *grayscale* command for accurate tonal values.

If you get into the habit of viewing your color artwork in this fashion, your characters and background elements will read well in every scene. You can also test your compositions by viewing them in reverse (*flopped*) in a mirror, or turning them upside down (Figure 16.7).

Figure 16.7

Looking at your artwork from a different perspective will help you make your values and composition read better. Turn it upside down or mirror it, so that you can view it as an abstract design.

Color sources can be anywhere. The palette in Figure 16.8 was taken from an antique ceramic tile. The swatches are proportionately scaled to each color in the composition. These colors may be used in a completely different context. This figure shows them applied to a character rather than a background.

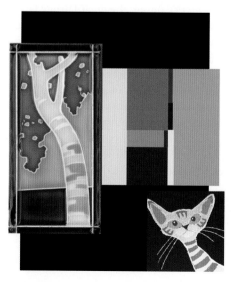

Figure 16.8

An antique German ceramic tile and a small cat colored with a palette based on the tile. (Nancy Beiman collection)

One of the signature-style goofs from the "Decade That Taste Forgot"—the 1970s—was the use of blazing-hot, fully saturated, split-complementary colors in large areas. A violent repeated pattern was often applied in a contrasting and equally saturated color. Nothing appeared in moderation. There is a reason why some colors are called *loud* (Figure 16.9).

Figure 16.9

This split-complementary color scheme uses four equally hot colors "screaming" at top volume.

Hot, fully saturated colors can cancel each other out when liberally applied to characters or backgrounds. They work much better when used in small areas as accents. Oddly enough, the same hot, blazing 1970s palette we saw in Figure 16.9 *does* appear in the natural world, as shown in Figures 16.10 and 16.11.

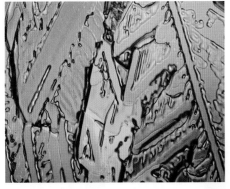

Figure 16.10

Garish hues become attractive when values and saturation are modified. (*Urea* photograph reproduced by permission of Alycia Yee.)

Figure 16.11

Flowers use brilliant hues to attract insects. The flower's contrast with the duller stem attracts humans. (California Poppies and Lupine photographed by Nancy Beiman.)

Line is "lighter" than color. Figure 16.12 shows the same character in final line and in its original computer-generated imagery (CGI) rendering. The rendered version reads as a solid shape; line reads as the outline of a negative space. The rendered animation will appear slower than the line version even if the animation timing does not change. *A line will always "move" faster than a solid.*

(a)   (b)

Figure 16.12

(a) Color reads as a solid shape, (b) while line will read "faster." (Reproduced by permission of Joseph Daniels and Jedidiah Mitchell.)

Colors can animate. They may advance or recede, as in Figure 16.13. We are shown two squares, one of which appears to have a larger center than the other.

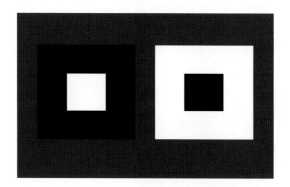

Figure 16.13

The two squares and their centers are exactly the same size, but our eye makes the central white square appear larger than the black one.

16. Color My World: Art Direction and Storytelling

Advancing and receding colors used in combination may produce startling results when used on an animated character. In Figure 16.14, cool body hues contrast with the much lighter, warmer eye color so that the character's eyes appear to glow.

Figure 16.14

Color can be used to create glowing metallic effects or glowing eyes, with no need for special effects.

Colors may also appear to advance or recede in relation to another color. This contrast can actually create a feeling of motion in a still composition as we saw in Figure 16.13. Cooler hues can indicate early morning or late afternoon, while warmer ones suggest midday. Very close monochromatic values depict eventide, fog, or distance if they are cool and dark; bright sunlight if they are light and bright (Figure 16.15).

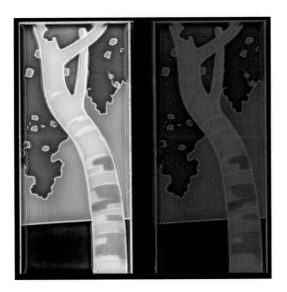

Figure 16.15

The changing time of day may be implied by color changes on the same background.

Color changes are often combined with the weather. How many climactic emotional or physical confrontations in animated films take place during a sudden thunderstorm?

Figure 16.16 is an example of a cliché. The emotional use of color need not be obvious to be effective.

> Mama Bear: "Yes, it is a bit melodramatic, and no, he isn't really dead."

Figure 16.16

No matter what the time of day, no matter what the season, violent emotional conflict in an animated film often coincides with the sudden arrival of a lightning-and-thunder-storm.

Color adds another dimension to film and raises some interesting questions. How do you determine which color schemes work "when" and 'where'? Take color cues from your story. A tale set in the Caribbean will use brighter and more intense colors than one set in Iceland—or will it? You'll start with nature, but then art takes over. The inspirational color for the Three Bears' house might be found in a piece of pottery or a fine-silk scarf. Inspiration can come from anywhere. An icescape may use colors that are as fanciful as those in Maurice Noble's haunted house if they work within the context of the story. Can color indicate a change in emotional moods a bit more subtly than a lightning-and-thunderstorm? Yes, but it requires a script—one that is not written, but *painted*.

Writing the Color: Color Scripts

> "As the light changed from red to green to yellow and back to red again, I sat there thinking about life. Was it nothing more than a bunch of honking and yelling? Sometimes it seemed that way."
>
> **—Jack Handey**
> *Deep Thoughts*

After the boards are completed, *color scripts* are created. The simplest method of doing this is to take all of the color keys out of each sequence and place them together (following the story continuity) on their own storyboard. They can then be viewed all at once much like a story beat board and modified if necessary. In the example shown in Figure 16.17, you can see that there is a great difference between the color keys since the main characters end up in very different locations.

Figure 16.17

The color keys from every sequence in a film can be copied and mounted in sequential order on their own storyboard. This is the simplest way of creating a *color script.* (Reproduced by permission of Maya Shavzin.)

The color script can also be determined before storyboard begins. In my film THE OTHER EDEN, color was essential even at the storyboard stage. No black-and-white artwork was ever produced for this movie, which was also boarded digitally to save time. All storyboards were, effectively, color keys, but I had a specific range of colors in mind. At first, I made a swatch showing how the palettes would change as the film progressed (Figure 16.18).

Figure 16.18

A simple gradient indicates how the colors will change as THE OTHER EDEN progresses. The warming color was intended to symbolize global warming.

Each storyboard panel in THE OTHER EDEN was colored as it was drawn, creating a *color script* that is excerpted in Figure 16.19. The shift from "blue" to "orange" became more and more pronounced in each scene. It wasn't just a simple shift; an intermediate pink color (representing a warming Arctic) appeared, as well as black and pure white. The general color progression was based on the gradient, but the variations helped to keep it from looking mechanical. Textures also became more foggy and blotchy as the film progressed to better symbolize the deteriorating environment. Also note how the warm orange color shifts from the living creatures in the first panel to the dead, polluting chimneys in the last one. The last blue/green in the film appears in the tigers' eyes.

a simple color script: color changes set in advance

Figure 16.19

The *color script* from THE OTHER EDEN is very simple. It is a progression from cool to warm colors and from natural blues and greens to "artificial" neon oranges and pinks.

Color and lighting design begins at the very start of preproduction. Atmospheric sketches are created in black and white and in color to determine the story's location and time period and provide story crew, character, and prop designers with visual reference to flesh out the script or outline.

The art director designs the color script to indicate how the film's color palettes vary when influenced by mood, time of day, and location. It is planned in advance like the gradient for THE OTHER EDEN but is far more complex. Storyboard panels are selected for color keys, and the art director paints color versions. They are sometimes painted directly over copies of storyboard drawings for precision of color, since the color temperature of digital monitors may vary. The finished color script will resemble a filmstrip with little detail; it will chiefly consist of blocks of color. The next illustration shows a painted color script that was created after the storyboard was finished but before lighting and rendering began on the CGI film. (Figure 16.20)

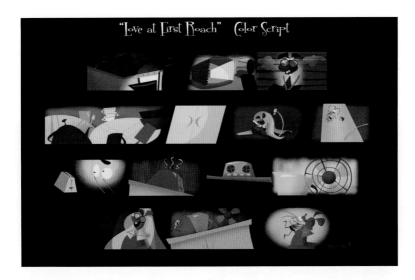

Figure 16.20

A *color script* shows how the color evolves from the first sequence of the film to the last. The art director determines the palettes and indicates transitional colors where necessary. (Reproduced by permission of William Robinson.)

The color script is a valuable guide for the coloring, lighting, and rendering of the film. Much of the final production in this example shown in Figure 16.21 bears a close resemblance to the color script, although some modifications have been made.

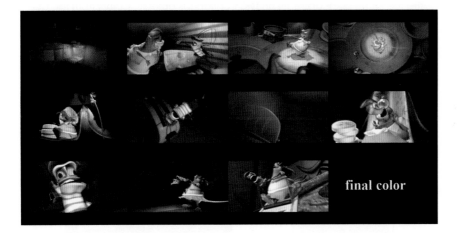

Figure 16.21

Frames from the finished CGI film show how the color keys were modified in production. (Reproduced by permission of William Robinson.)

The art director determines which color dominates each sequence and indicates transitional colors that help maintain continuity when the scene shifts to a new location. Each sequence may have a different dominant color. A dominant color from an earlier sequence may appear with different values or in different proportions in a later one to maintain the visual flow. This is known as a *color bridge*. Color bridges link to other related colors. For example, a yellow-orange shape that is near a yellow-green one has the "yellow" in common. The yellow hue creates motion within the composition since our eye will travel from one object to another via the "bridge". Our eye is attracted by contrasts in hue in the same way that tonal contrasts attract it in black-and-white storyboard drawings. This concept applies equally to still drawings and motion picture art direction (Figure 16.22).

Figure 16.22

The eye can be directed around the frame by *bridges,* areas in the composition where the same color appears on two contiguous objects. Colors from the background are repeated with variations on the characters in this still from SITA SINGS THE BLUES. (Reproduced by permission of Nina Paley.)

The art director will also create proportional color charts for each scene. Colors appear as simple blocks. The different sizes of the blocks indicate the proportion of the color that is used in the scene. Lighting color (especially important for CGI films) will also be indicated with a proportional grid as shown in Figure 16.23.

Figure 16.23

A color grid will be created for each sequence that is more complex than the gradient in Figure 16.18. The size of each square indicates the proportion of that color in the overall composition. Lighting effects are indicated separately if a CGI production is being art directed.

16. Color My World: Art Direction and Storytelling

Color can be composed, like music. It can be harmonious or discordant, soft, or loud. Color may be classical, romantic, jazzy, or modern. Use it creatively so that your visual compositions don't fall flat.

You can suggest temperature, atmosphere, and even humidity through the use of color.

In Figure 16.24, the color script uses hot, saturated tones to convey the dryness of a desert planet. The color palette changes when Oakfield enters a bar. A suggestion of temperature change (and the presence of drinks) is indicated by the use of slightly cooler greens and grays.

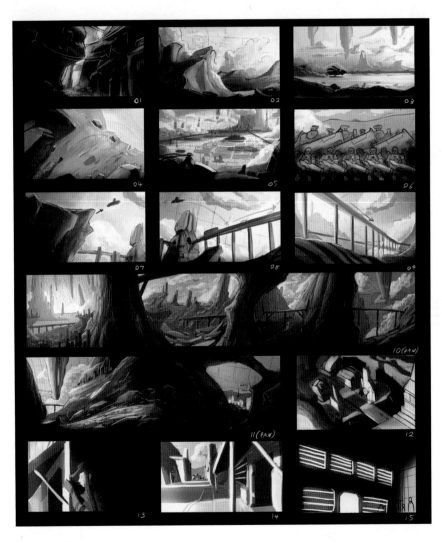

Figure 16.24

Panel 15 of this color script changes the location from a desert landscape to a bar that suggests a slightly cooler industrial atmosphere. (OAKFIELD © 2016 by Colin Searle.)

The color script for KONGO shown in Figure 16.25 uses a similar change in palette to show the contrast between heat and coolness. The blazing sun in panel 1 illuminates the next five panels and motivates the characters to fight over the water, a splash of blue that contrasts dramatically with the monochromatic orange backgrounds. When the characters land in a hidden lake in the last panel, the heat is still implied by the background light, but the water and the growing plants suggest relief and new life.

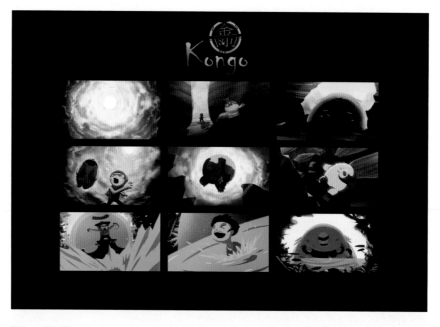

Figure 16.25

The last four panels of KONGO'S color script also indicate the contrast between heat and coolness. (© 2013 by Yacheng Guo.)

O Tempora, O More or Less

Color can create a sense of place and time. An art director must research period styles and colors. Some color combinations are suggested by art that is contemporary with the film's setting. Historic painters are a terrific guide for period color. You'll find that artist contemporaries from one country paint very different types of light. Palettes also vary from country to country, and artists will reproduce the color of the local foliage and even the sky with great accuracy. Monet's hues are excellent representations of the colors of the nineteenth-century French countryside while Turner utilizes a grayer, equally accurate palette for his English landscapes.

You may also use the work of modern illustrators and painters as a guide for period films. Paintings and illustrations can give you the colors of a country or a culture from the distant past. Museums usually have brochures about their collection that contain color reproductions, or postcards of specific paintings. Old auction catalogues are a terrific and cheap reference source. They are sometimes available in secondhand bookstores. Anything and everything are grist for your color and design mill. You should never feel restricted by this material, but it provides great reference for possible color combinations and artistic styles.

Here's a little design secret: *A film that is set in a particular era need not use only contemporary material.* Any object, particularly architecture, dating from a period *earlier* than the movie's time frame may be utilized in your background design and art direction. For example: a story set in the 1950s may show cars from the 1930s and 1920s. A story set in Victorian England may take place in medieval buildings. Oddly enough, some animated films that used contemporary design styles and fashionable color now appear more dated than films that use a mixture of design elements from various time periods. Nothing dates faster than modernity (Figure 16.26).

Figure 16.26

A period piece may use design elements from earlier time periods. This implies that settings grew over time and avoids the "newly minted look" that can occur when characters, backgrounds, and props all date to a brief historical period.

TOY STORY contains many elements of a 1960s universe, such as period toys and Swedish Modern furniture, but its laser-shooting spaceman and themed restaurant (and video game in TOY STORY 2) date from the 1990s. The mixture of styles gives the TOY STORY films a period quality without making them appear dated. This is the same technique that Ken Anderson used for ONE HUNDRED AND ONE DALMATIANS. Complete color scripts for the Pixar films appear in Amid Amidi's book *The Art of Pixar: 25th Anniversary: The Complete Color Scripts and Select Art from 25 Years of Animation* (Chronicle Books, 2011). (Figure 16.27)

Figure 16.27

A mixture of styles and period elements may be used for comic effect as shown in James Montgomery Flagg's comic strip NERVY NAT. Nat, a New York street tough from the 1850s, discusses 1912 political issues with some fifth-century mythological mermaids. (Nancy Beiman collection)

I do not recommend referencing artwork from other animated films, since these may be familiar to your audience. Another art director has already researched the period and assembled color palettes and design elements from various sources. Find your own reference from your sketches, illustrations, photographs, and observation of life. Adapt the reference and redesign it, so that your work does not slavishly copy the work of someone else. Specific cartoon or illustration styles should be viewed through the subjective lens of your own judgment and experience. Look through your own eyes, not someone else's. Artistic interpretation will make a style *yours*.

You now have rough character designs and color and atmospheric sketches that can be presented to an audience along with your storyboards. It is time to step up to the Pitch in Chapter 17.

SECTION III
Presentation

17

Show and Tell: Presenting Your Storyboards

"You have to get the story point across in the first 10 seconds of a pitch."

—Ollie Johnston
(to author)

The day for the story pitch has arrived. Sometimes, it's the day after you get the handout! Your first consideration will always be "readability" whether you have had one day or a month to finish your assignment. The boards are the most important part of the pitch but the quality of your presentation is nearly as important. A bad presentation will hurt a good storyboard. You're providing the acting and the timing for the action, so your commentary is 50% of the pitch and has to communicate as clearly as the boards do.

Your objective is to convey the story point clearly to the audience, in real time.

Be prepared. *Number your panels* so that they do not get out of order. Be sure to pin the panels correctly beforehand. You won't have an opportunity to change the order during the pitch (Figure 17.1).

Figure 17.1

Number the storyboard drawings, so that you are able to reassemble them in the correct order should a few fall off the boards. (Drawing from *Son of Faster Cheaper* by Floyd Norman reproduced by permission of Floyd Norman.)

Pitch Etiquette and Procedure

Memorize the Dialogue and the Action in Each Panel   It is not good to stand and read dialogue off the small cards that are pinned under the panels. It's even worse if you forget it completely and freeze up or "die" in the middle of your pitch. Say the same dialogue that you have on the boards. *Use one sentence to describe the action in each panel.* If your panel shows Sherlock Holmes bursting through Watson's bedroom doorway, it's enough to state, "Holmes bursts the door open— Wham! Pit-pat-pit-pat," and let the drawing do the rest.

Do not use extraneous material. Stick to the story and keep it simple. The pitch should run approximately the same time as it takes to perform the action in the sequence. Anecdotes, useless *factoids*, back story, and other stuff that doesn't matter will only slow down the pitch and bore or confuse your audience. Use simple descriptions of camera moves; don't give them a technical lecture (Figure 17.2).

Figure 17.2

Know the action in each board, and memorize the dialogue before the pitch. Be completely familiar with the material. (Drawing from *Son of Faster Cheaper* by Floyd Norman reproduced by permission of Floyd Norman.)

17. Show and Tell: Presenting Your Storyboards

Make a Joyful Noise   You should provide appropriate noises and sound effects where necessary. If you cannot reproduce the exact sound of a planet imploding, simply say "Bang!" Sound effects can add a lot to the presentation, so it helps to be a bit of a hambone. Don't be nervous and don't worry about looking a little ridiculous—the audience should be concentrating on the boards. You are literally just a background noise (Figure 17.3).

Figure 17.3

Provide any necessary sound effects with your own voice. Don't go overboard, but use whatever works in the context of the storyboard.

If your boards illustrate a musical composition, you can have it playing in the background while you offer a description of the action or simply play the music without commentary while you point to each panel of the boards. Don't be completely dependent on having the musical accompaniment during the pitch.

What If You Make a Mistake? Keep Going   You may repeat the sentence, with the correction, but never, ever, stop a pitch and say "I'm sorry, I'll read that again," or "I meant to say…." You will distract the audience and lose your momentum.

Props can be useful. I've seen a story man recite his entire pitch with the aid of a puppet. Another one unrolled a ball of string around the story room and rewound it to a different knot as he made each point of his pitch. If you feel comfortable using additional materials and feel that it will help your pitch, use them—as long as they do not completely upstage your boards and your story.

Rehearse the Pitch   Be familiar with the story and the dialogue so that you can do the pitch without peering continually at the boards—you should know what happens next, since you drew them! Make sure you can pronounce the dialogue and the characters' names; rewrite the dialogue, and rename the characters if you can't.

Don't use a lot of "ums" and "aaahs"—they are a sure indication that you did not rehearse the pitch.

Time Your Pitch   Vary the pacing and your tone of voice to indicate changes of action and build the suspense. There is nothing worse than a pitch that is delivered in a droning, monotonous voice. *Show enthusiasm for the material.* If you don't think it is good, why should anyone else?

Refer to Characters by Name   If there are two or more characters of the same sex in a scene, it is most important that we know which is being referred to during a conversation, or a pitch (Figure 17.4).

Oliver Hardy: "Do you mean to say that the money that he gave to you that you gave to him that he gave to me was the same money that I gave to him to pay HIM?" *Stan Laurel:* "Well, if that was the money that you gave to him, to give to me, to pay to HIM, it must have been the money that I gave HIM to give to you to pay my rent! Didn't I?"

Jimmy Finlayson: "You're all NUTS!"

—Laurel and Hardy
THICKER THAN WATER (Hal Roach Studios, 1935)

Figure 17.4

Daphne Pollard, Oliver Hardy, Stan Laurel, and Jimmy Finlayson lose track of who they are talking to in THICKER THAN WATER (1935).

Using character names during the pitch will avoid absurd exchanges like the quote from THICKER THAN WATER, where it becomes impossible to tell one character from another. (Remember to give your characters names that can be easily pronounced!) "He" or "She" may be used when a character is alone in a scene, or when the action continues after we have been informed which character is in the scene. (For example: "***Goldilocks*** *enters the dining room and looks around.* ***She*** *picks up a newspaper and sits down in Baby Bear's chair, waving hello to Baby Bear, who is sitting in Papa Bear's chair.* ***Baby Bear*** *grabs his bowl of porridge and leaps out of the chair.* ***He*** *drops the spoon as he runs out of the room.*")

Test the Boards before You Pitch   Pitch the boards to other storyboard artists, to animators, to your mother, to total strangers, to be sure that everything reads well before you meet your final audience. You're too close to the thing to be able to judge it objectively, so a second or third opinion becomes necessary. I've received some excellent story suggestions from nonanimators. After all, the ultimate audience for the project is ordinary people who are interested in hearing a story, not animation professionals. Rework and revise any inconsistencies or omissions before you go up before a highly critical professional audience. Be sure that all story points are reading clearly. You will probably change your boards more than once while rehearsing them. It's impossible to predict how directors and producers will react before you actually present the materials. If you are working with a *Head of story*, they will have signed off on the boards before you pitch. If you are working alone, trying the boards out on an auditor who is not familiar with the material will help ensure that they read well to someone other than you. You will, with practice, be able to make your pitch easily and coherently (Figure 17.5).

Figure 17.5

Rehearse your pitch with the help of someone else. Be sure they are able to give you feedback, so that you know when something isn't working as well as it should.

Good story people are excellent actors. They keep the audience's attention focused on the story from the first frame to the last. Make the pitch entertaining enough to hold the audience's interest. Avoid ironic commentary on the artwork. Never make disparaging comments such as, "This isn't any good," or "I meant to do this instead of that." *Never apologize* and never tear down your own work—that's the director's job (Figure 17.6).

Figure 17.6

Believe in your story. Don't point out weak spots in your own boards.

Your panels should be printed out and pinned to large storyboards that are mounted on the wall, or they may be pinned directly on the wall if the surface is suitable. They should not be displayed on a tabletop or handed around like playing cards. (I've seen both.) The storyboards should be a neutral color. Black, gray, cork, or off-white are common. Pin the drawings separately from the dialogue panels, since they may be rearranged. Get a simple pointer. A yardstick will do. Don't use your hands. Stand with your back to the board, a little to one side. It is okay to look at the storyboard and occasionally make eye contact with the audience while pitching. Never obscure the board by standing in front of the section you are pitching, and never turn your back on the viewers. Your pointer will enable you to reach across the boards to pitch more distant panels without doing this. At times, you may have to walk forward or backward while pitching. If you keep the audience interested in the story, this will not be a distraction (Figures 17.7 and 17.8).

Figure 17.7

A pointer will enable you to pitch the boards without turning your back on the audience. Be sure that the boards are never obscured.

17. Show and Tell: Presenting Your Storyboards

Figure 17.8

You may want to do character voices for the different parts. Sometimes, the character projection doesn't end there!

If you do have to walk to the other side of the board, do so quickly and quietly and continue with your pitch in the same one of voice as before.

If you feel comfortable doing character voices, by all means do them. Story men will play women and story women will play men if they feel it will help the pitch. If you do not wish to do this, simply pitch the boards using your normal voice. Your inflection should help convey the action in the drawings. Don't mumble and don't read in a monotone. Speak clearly and loudly enough for the audience to hear you but not so loudly that you're audible next door. Keep a positive attitude. Smile. Act like you're enjoying yourself.

I have seen instances where story men and women got "into character" with costume as well as voice talent. I was once only allowed to pitch my designs while wearing a huge felt high-cocked hat that I'd purchased as reference for the creature's costume! Use your judgment. Neat clothing is perfectly suitable for a story pitch.

Introduce Yourself and Your Sequence at the Beginning of the Pitch A brief introduction will allow you to connect with the audience. (*"Hello, I'm Joe Zilch and I am pitching Sequence 22, if Only Mama Bear Could Cook."*) If your sequence is part of a larger film, it is good to let them know what comes just before your bit. (*"This sequence takes place right after Papa Bear's flashback to his first job in the pickle factory."*) Give them enough material so that they see how the sequence works in context, but don't make things too elaborate. This is a pitch for a film, not a novel, and backstory is usually limited to one or two sentences. Ollie Johnston told me that the main story point had to be apparent to the audience in 10 seconds or less. If you are pitching *beat boards,* state your *log line* first (the single sentence that sums up the meaning of the story as described in Chapter 4). The drawings and your brief commentary should be able to get the point across.

If you have character design sketches, pin these up on a separate board. It can help if you introduce the characters before beginning your pitch, especially if this is your *first pass* on the boards. Be sure to write the characters' names on all of the sketches.

It Is *Polite to Point*   The pointer (which is usually about a meter or three-feet long) allows you to point to a wide area of the storyboards without obstructing the artwork. If it is used correctly, it shows the audience where you want them to look. If you point it at the storyboards, you are calling attention to each panel, and they will look there. If you wave it around in the air, you are calling attention to yourself, and the audience will look at you instead of the boards. This is not what you want. If you dislike public speaking, don't worry. It really is "not about you." Rest assured that if you use the pointer to indicate the panels during your pitch, the audience will be totally focused on the story and will *not* look directly at you. But if you are using the pointer to practice for a twirling exhibition, you will upstage your own artwork (Figure 17.9).

Figure 17.9

Do not use the pointer in a way that calls attention to yourself. The audience will not look at the storyboards if you put on a competing show.

Don't smack the pointer up against the story panels. You are not mad at them—at least not yet—so don't work out your frustrations or nerves in this fashion. The noise will distract your audience from what is on the boards. Point to each panel in turn and *hold the pointer steady on the panel, touching the artwork,* while you say the dialogue and describe the action. Then *slide* the pointer to the next storyboard. Bouncing the pointer up and down on the panels is distracting and very counterproductive (Figure 17.10).

17. Show and Tell: Presenting Your Storyboards

Figure 17.10

Don't beat up, around, or on the storyboard.

Work in Real Time   The pitch is pretty much a rehearsal for the picture, and each scene ideally should be pitched in the same amount of time the action will take when it is fully animated. You will have to explain the action occasionally, but be sure to keep all explanations *brief*. If you have to describe the action at length, chances are you did not draw enough storyboards to get the story point over in the first place.

Don't drag things out or your audience might fall asleep. (I've seen this happen during a dull presentation.) Don't be pretentious. Keep your story points simple. Do not give convoluted explanations of the action and lengthy biographies of your characters. All that matters during the pitch is what is on the storyboard. If your story does not work, all the explanations in the world won't help you (Figure 17.11).

Figure 17.11

If you're talking too much, you probably did not draw enough panels to convey the story. Your audience can, and will, lose interest. Avoid saying "Um" and "Aaah"— you should know your story by heart.

Don't Rush   Take the necessary time to get the story point across. Don't run words together trying to cram a lot of information into a short-time frame. Be sure to pace the story pitch. If you are nervous standing in front of the audience, remember that they are looking at the storyboard, not at you. Imagine that you are telling an interesting story to a familiar friend who has heard you speak before. Speak clearly. Project your voice so they can hear you. There is no need to shout (unless you absolutely have to). Let the drawings carry half of the presentation. Give the audience time to see what is going on (Figure 17.12).

Figure 17.12

Don't rush through at high speed.

Director Jack Kinney wrote of a story man who got so "into" his performance that he actually ran out the door while describing the character performing this action on his storyboard. (The other artists locked the door behind him and went to lunch. They sensed that he was a show-off and reacted accordingly.) Act, but don't overact. You will distract attention from the storyboard and you won't impress your audience (Figure 17.13).

Figure 17.13

Don't overdo things.

Digital Pitches

All of the above elements also apply to digital pitches where the panels are individually projected as you narrate the pitch. In this instance, you will have to hold the image on the screen for the same amount of time that it takes for you to describe the action and acting; and it won't be possible to see all of the panels at once, as is the case when they're pinned on a board. This is why many professional productions will print out digital panels and mount them on a storyboard for presentation. It is very useful to see all of the panels at once, but some studios will not use this method. You must follow the requirements of the production. Pitching will require you to develop a sense of timing, regardless of how the boards are presented.

After your pitch, you'll get down to the *real* work—*turning over* the boards and revising them!

The More Things Change: The Turnover Session

Story people learn to welcome change. A *turnover session* is where you find out just how much change you and your boards can take. All storyboards are changed at least once. Never take these changes personally. Everyone has to change their storyboards. Your only consideration should be that the story is read in the clearest possible way.

Turnover sessions happen immediately after the pitch. The audience, which may consist of other story men and women, animators, the directors, and the art director, will make suggestions for additional action, revised staging, or new lines of dialogue. They may be drawn on self-stick notes and stuck on top of the original boards. The sketches will be very rough. If the changes are approved, you will incorporate them into your reworked boards prior to the second pass, or pitch.

If the directors do not like one of the existing panels, one or more panels of your board will be *turned over*. The deleted board(s) will be pinned so that their blank backs face the viewers, and the new drawing(s) will be stuck on top of them. In the event of a pure digital pitch with panels displayed onscreen, I normally display all of the panels in the folder at once as large, consecutively numbered icons, then add a subfolder called "OLD" and drag the "turned over" panels into this folder. I do not recommend deleting them (nor do I recommend throwing out turned over panels in a storyboard pitch) since you may need them again at a later date when the boards are changed. In this type of digital pitch, it is not possible to add new drawings during the session, but notes are taken and the revisions are created by the storyboard artist after the turnover is completed.

You may be asked to insert close-ups for a reaction shot or place your camera farther back to get more of the action into the frame. Someone may suggest an entirely new piece of acting or business that will lengthen the sequence. On occasion, you will be told to *flop* a scene. This is not an indication of failure. Flopping a board means that the action will be staged as a mirror image. Sometimes, entire sequences have their boards flopped. The advent of computers has made this a lot easier for the story people to do. In the old days, they just had to draw everything going the other way. Now, boards can be scanned and reversed automatically.

Plan to make at least two pitches for your boards. That is, if you are lucky. Some directors might make a few small changes or *tweaks* and get the boards *up on reels,* or shot and timed to a soundtrack in an *animatic* or *Leica,* before making a final decision on the staging. The boards might be sent back to you at a later date for reworking if the story changes. At the Walt Disney Studio, the boards were pitched "until they got it right or until they ran out of money," according to story man Floyd Norman. Constructive suggestions from your colleagues and friends will help foster a team feeling and make your boards stronger (Figure 17.14).

Figure 17.14

After the turnover session. Most sessions won't be as dismissive as this, but some panels always wind up on the "story room floor." Don't take it personally.

Once the turnover session is over, your storyboard panels may have been repositioned so that they appear in different orders from when you started. Other panels will have been "turned over" and eliminated from the sequence. You will need to renumber your panels to indicate the new arrangement. The numbering is often done on removable stickers, but you can change the numbers that are already there (use pencil for all panel numbers, if working on paper). Digitally drawn boards must be numbered consecutively, so that they load in the correct order before you do the pitch. Check the order of the panels before you pitch … you won't get a chance to rearrange them after you have started! Some digital storyboard programs automatically number your panels for you as they are created. If new panels are inserted later on, percentages will be used, as shown in Figure 17.15. (Red numbers are used solely for this example. Your numbers should not be in color and should not be so large as to distract from the drawing.)

Figure 17.15

Storyboard numbers will change after the turnover session. New panels inserted between two older ones will be numbered with a decimal point.

The BBC reported that 3000 adults who took a survey of "most-feared" incidents rated public speaking higher than financial ruin and death itself. If you prepare your pitch properly, you should acquit yourself well speaking in public and avoid the other two problems (Figure 17.16).

Figure 17.16

Pitching a storyboard is rather like public speaking, but it need not be a dreaded occasion.

18

Talking Pictures: Assembling a Leica, Story Reel, or Animatic with a Scratch Track

Congratulations! You have just pitched your boards and character concepts and had them approved—possibly with a few small *"tweaks."*

After a feature film sequence has been reviewed in a *turnover* session, a small removable sticker is placed in one corner of each storyboard drawing indicating the sequence, scene, and drawing number (Figure 18.1). Shorter films can have the scene and drawing numbers written directly on the boards, as shown in the second panel of Figure 18.1. Boards that are drawn on paper only receive final numbers after the turnover since they may have been rearranged during the pitch, and some panels may have been removed. Before this time, numbers are on the reverse in case the panels are accidentally mixed up on the storyboard or in storage. Storyboards, if created or scanned into a digital graphics program, must be labeled according to file protocols so that all of the panels can be imported into a computer editing or storyboard program in the correct order (001, 002, 002.5, 003, etc.).

Figure 18.1

When a sequence is approved, each storyboard panel is identified by a removable sticker listing the sequence, scene, and drawing number. Shorter films may eliminate the sequence numbers, and write scene and frame numbers directly on the boards. Digital files must be numbered with correct file protocols. Some computer programs will do this automatically. Don't assume that you won't need to know how.

Dialogue changes made during the turnover session are noted and incorporated into the recording script, which is finalized only after the storyboard is approved. When the script is ready, the voice actors record the dialogue in individual or group sessions depending on the project. The recording script is broken up into short numbered sections, so that the actors do not read the entire script in one take. The editor and director then assemble the best takes from each section into the final track. Retakes of lines or portions of lines may be recorded during the session, or new dialogue may be added in later recording sessions. These are called *pickups*. If a character actor is not available for a session, a dialogue *scratch track* may be recorded by another actor or the director and used as a placeholder until the pickup session is recorded. Scenes with scratch dialogue tracks will not be put into production, since the synchronization will not be accurate for the animator.

At this stage, the storyboards are transformed from still pictures into motion pictures in a process known as *getting it* (a sequence or project) *up on reels*. This term is used even though the story reel is now created with computers instead of animation cameras and reels of film.

The numbered storyboards are imported into a digital editing program (assuming they were not created digitally in the first place). Dialogue panels and screen directions are not scanned since the dialogue, and the camera moves will be included as part of the *Leica* or *animatic*. The director(s) and editor assemble the boards into a *Leica reel* (*story reel*) or *animatic* and time or *slug* each panel to the dialogue and a musical *scratch track*. All film is edited to scratch tracks, since the final scores are generally one of the last things that are completed on the production. (Song sequences are an exception to this rule.)

A *story or Leica reel* is constructed of storyboards that are timed, or *slugged,* to the *scratch music and dialogue* tracks. Camera moves may be shot, but the drawings are not modified. Cross dissolves, fades, and simple camera moves such as pans, trucks, and rotations created in the editing program replace the graphic symbols used during the storyboard pitch. (Note: There is no such thing as a "zoom" in animation. A zoom is a lens used in live-action photography.)

An *animatic*, rather than merely timing the storyboards, uses simple movements and special effects to give a more precise idea of the timing and acting in the final animation. Like the Leica, it will use a scratch music and dialogue track. Techniques can vary from simply panning a character across a panel with the aid of a computer graphics program to animating character drawings, background layouts, and overlays to create a feeling of three-dimensional motions in the frame and convey the action in the scene. Animatics, formerly much more expensive and time-consuming to construct than storyboard Leicas, are very common now since digital programs make it easy to create them.

Filmmaker Elliot Cowan's short film series THE STRESSFUL ADVENTURES OF BOXHEAD AND ROUNDHEAD has won many animation awards, and a feature film was produced in 2012. Here, he discusses the creation of digital animatics. (All artwork for Boxhead and Roundhead is hand drawn in Photoshop and animated in After Effects.)

You are producing a feature film with characters who formerly only appeared in short films. Did you rework their characters or add anything to the original personalities?

ELLIOT COWAN: Making the shorts by myself gave me the chance to develop B&R in a very organic way.

I was trying very hard to avoid the usual cartoon pairing—an angry one and a dopey one.

I feel that I was able to give their relationship shades of gray rather than painting them entirely in black and white.

The important thing I wanted audiences to feel was that even though they may have different personalities, they are very close.

They love each other and rely on each other for different things.

I made the decision to have them speak in the feature script. (Note: All the short films with these characters were made without dialogue.) I think I was able to explore this further.

Everything in the feature is an extension of things previously touched on in the shorts at some point.

What sort of design or production research do you do for a short film? Does it differ for a longer picture?

ELLIOT COWAN: I don't have a lot of time to make my shorts.

When you are working and have a child and a mortgage, it is not easy to find the time to animate your own material.

When I am planning an animated project, I try and keep it within parameters that ensure I can complete something satisfactory in a goodly amount of time.

It's one of the lesser reasons I've made so many B&R shorts—they are relatively simple for me to put together, so I can get on with the business of timing, editorial, and acting.

I also believe strongly that the best way to get a project done is to do it yourself.

Over 10 or so shorts, the only other folks working on them were the musicians and on one film, a sound engineer.

The shorts are all in black and white, and I felt that introducing some color to the feature would be beneficial.

I turned to my very good friend, superstar production designer Neil Ross who produced some beautiful concept art.

Did you write an outline, treatment, and script for this project before beginning the digital storyboard?

ELLIOT COWAN: I wrote both a treatment and a script.

At the time of writing this, I've just completed draft number six of the script, and the story has changed somewhat.

When I make my shorts, I do not board or write them.

Which sequence is shown in this animatic? Will you produce an animatic for every sequence?

ELLIOT COWAN: This is part of the opening.

Although plenty of folks know B&R from the shorts, I felt that I needed to write something that dropped those who didn't know the characters straight into their world.

It's likely that I'll create animatics for the action sequences.

What influenced your choice of music for the scratch track?

ELLIOT COWAN: The track that plays at the end is called "Zydeco Boogaloo" by Buckwheat Zydeco, and it inspired the whole script, believe it or not.

Music and animation are essentially the same thing, I think.

They pair beautifully, because it's particularly easy for us to time our action to the music.

When I first heard the track, I imagined B&R in some kind of chase sequence.

The same thing happened with the shorts.

The Infernal Machine was inspired by a Tom Waits song that I cut the film to originally.

Safari was inspired by a track by Eels.

It's hard to say exactly how I got from the zydeco tune to the story.

These things are hard to trace.

What advice would you have for an independent filmmaker seeking to produce his or her own film?

ELLIOT COWAN: If you want to make your own shorts, the best advice I'd give is to get down to the business of making one.

If you've never made an animated film before, then start simple, basic, [and keep it] short.

Over-ambition is the enemy of new filmmakers.

[Story idea] "A man walks into a room and something happens to him."

Make [your film] 10 seconds long. Ten seconds is very manageable.

Then make another film about the same guy, but something different happens to him.

After a while you'll have a series of them, and people like that kind of thing.

You'll learn a million times more about timing and animation and cutting over a series of teeny shorts than you will slaving away at some epic you'll never finish, or never finish well.

The animatic for the first sequence from the BOXHEAD AND ROUNDHEAD feature can be viewed online at http://www.youtube.com/watch?v=Tw5aE4A 6fps%26feature=youtu.be.

THE CRUMB FACTORY, an episode of THE STRESSFUL ADVENTURES OF BOXHEAD AND ROUNDHEAD that features music by They Might Be Giants, can be viewed online at http://www.youtube.com/watch?v= 89ot4uLkYvI (Figure 18.2).

Figure 18.2

Stills from an animatic for the feature film THE STRESSFUL ADVENTURES OF BOXHEAD AND ROUNDHEAD. All artwork is digital, and scene elements will be used in the finished animation. (Reproduced by permission of Elliot Cowan.)

Animatics and Leicas require that the storyboard artist has good layout and scene-planning skills. Digital programs and compositing make camera moves much easier to shoot than was formerly the case when animators had to shoot all levels simultaneously, one frame at a time, and use cumbersome camera stands to create the illusion of depth and movement. While camera mechanics were formerly created in layout, digital tools make it easy to preview them in the storyboard and animatic stage. Twisted or distorted perspective, combinations of 2D and 3D graphics, and bold camera moves can create effects that were formerly only achievable in high-budget feature films. Figure 18.3 shows the camera starting on the young cat in the doorway (field A). It then trucks up to the ceiling (field B) and rotates around the chandelier (field C) before descending toward a heroic feline statue on field D. The storyboard panel is larger than usual to allow for the camera moves, and the background detail is downplayed in the "pass-through" areas. The illusion of depth was very convincing when this camera move was shot for the animatic. The flat layout appears to work in three dimensions when the camera moves are added in real time.

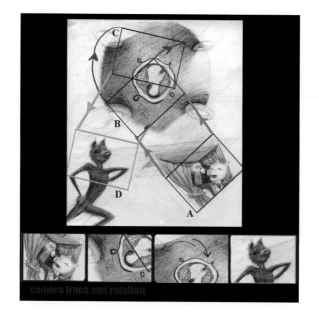

Figure 18.3

A complex camera move can be planned on one storyboard. This atmospheric establishing shot's background is detailed in areas where the camera lingers; less important sections are modeled with tonal values. (Reproduced by permission of Sarah Kropiewnicki.)

A *scratch music track* is often assembled from a variety of sources including classical and jazz music and soundtracks from other films. The scratch track sets a tempo for the editing, and the action that will be retained in the final music track. The musical excerpts (*Cues*) should define the mood and pacing of the sequence, or part of a sequence. (Cues rarely change "by scene.") The scratch track is a script for the composer. New music cues are used when there is a change of pace in the action. The scratch track is only a timing device, so the musical excerpts do not need to blend perfectly with one another. Cuts can be abrupt. Sometimes, as with the Boxhead and Roundhead animatic and my short film YOUR FEET'S TOO BIG, one musical track will actually provide inspiration for the story line.

Choose instrumental music with a tempo that matches the visual rhythm you wish to use for the film. Animators often use classical "*program music*" (music that "tells a story," such as THE NUTCRACKER SUITE by Tchaikovsky) since there are many tempo and key changes, and a variety of musical instruments are used. Music with evenly timed, repetitive themes and tempos is usually not used in scratch tracks, though there are always exceptions to the rule. *It does not matter if scratch track music is copyrighted*, since it is used only in preproduction and will not appear in the final film.

Popular songs can call attention to themselves and be distracting, though they are sometimes used as ironic commentary on the action. Soundtracks should convey the emotional moods of the film and support the visuals, not distract from them.

Stanley Kubrick used 1940s' love songs on the soundtrack of DR. STRANGELOVE [1964], with the most sentimental tune, WE'LL MEET AGAIN, playing over scenes of warplanes and nuclear explosions. These were in fact the scratch tracks for the film and were retained in the final. Sheridan student Kyu-bum Lee found the scratch music for his senior project so entertaining that it was retained as the final track for the finished film. DEATH BUY LEMONADE, like DR. STRANGE-LOVE, uses cheerful, happy sounding music as an ironic commentary on the dark story. The music cue was copyright-free and downloaded from the Sheridan animation department's server, so it was possible for Kyu-bum to use it without permission or fee. DEATH BUY LEMONADE can be viewed online at http://vimeo.com/15071571 (Figure 18.4).

Figure 18.4

The Grim Reaper appears in a sunny setting, with equally sunny music, in DEATH BUY LEMONADE. (Reproduced by permission of Kyu-bum Lee.)

Never use copyrighted music for a final track unless you have received written permission to do so from the copyright holders, They Might Be Giants kindly allowed Elliot Cowan to use their song CRUMB FACTORY as a cartoon soundtrack, but buying song rights can be an expensive business. It is strongly recommended that you use either recordings that are in the public domain (only those recorded before 1923 will qualify), purchase a license to use "canned music" from a vendor or (the best choice) have original music composed for your films.

The tone of the picture can be changed by varying the scratch track. LOVE AT FIRST ROACH by William Robinson was originally timed to a 1930s jazz scratch soundtrack. Its final track used French accordion tunes that helped turn a dirty kitchen into a romantic bistro. The two tracks shared a common tempo but created different emotional moods for the same visuals. The film's running time did not change when the music was replaced (Figure 18.5). LOVE AT FIRST ROACH can be viewed online at http://www.aniboom.com/animation-video/20066/Love-at-First-Roach/.

Figure 18.5

Parisian accordion music sets the atmosphere better for this romantic date than the original jazz scratch track. (Reproduced by permission of William Robinson.)

A song sequence will usually have its final soundtrack recorded before storyboards begin. Dialogue is changeable. Songs are *locked down* when they are recorded. Even a scratch version of a song will have the same tempo as the final version and lines will rarely be inserted, edited out, or rerecorded. This is the reason why musical numbers are frequently the first feature film sequences to go into production.

Sound effects are usually recorded *wild* after the music and dialogue tracks are completed. The ones that are a bit difficult to record in the studio (explosions, bullets, etc.) can be purchased and downloaded from online vendors. Sound effects are *laid down,* or *slugged,* in a simple mix with the main soundtrack. Visual effects such as explosions and puffs of smoke are added to the reel with computer graphics programs if they are necessary for the story. If not, they are left for later and the storyboards carry the visuals alone.

Previsualization, also known as *previz,* adds a new string to the story artist's bow. Originally developed for live action, it has become an important part of computer-generated imagery (CGI) preproduction. Previz can be described as a CGI animatic created in the third and fourth dimensions with roughly modeled characters and backgrounds and in-depth camera moves. It closely resembles the *pop-throughs* shot by stop-motion animators using the finished puppets and sets. Previsualization artist Jean Pilotte describes the technique:

> 3D implies volume and perspective in shades. The fourth dimension that *previz* brings is movement in time. A *leica* doesn't move like a real camera in space. So, the true *pre-viz* is the one that moves the characters and the camera…. Once [it is] edited together [it] brings continuity of motion and camera planning to the [computer-animated film]

Previz is an elaboration on the storyboard and not a substitute for it, since it occurs at the end of preproduction after all story elements have been finalized. A previz artist must know how to translate a two-dimensional storyboard into three-dimensional camera moves and also have excellent editorial skills. The timed animatic or Leica is the last stage of animation preproduction. When the visual and audio materials are edited to the director's satisfaction, the project is finally *up on reels* and the Leica is *locked!* And that, according to director David Hand, is when the film is finished. Everything that follows is built on what was developed in story and design.

This Is Only a Test: Refining Story Reels

"If people don't want to go to the picture, nobody can stop them!"

—**Samuel Goldwyn**

Screen your story reel or animatic for family and friends. Screen it for total strangers. You'll need a second and third and fourth opinion just as you did when you practiced pitching the storyboards, but now the film does the talking instead of you, and it must stand or fall on its own merits. Stuff either works or it doesn't. (Don't tell the audience what they should be seeing. If they can't follow the story, it's your problem, not theirs.) Ask your viewers for their impressions after the screening. See if their interpretations coincide with yours. If not, ask for suggestions on how the material could be improved. Take notes. Revise the boards and story reel accordingly, and screen it again for the same audience if possible. See if the problems are solved. Once everyone reads everything consistently, you're done—for now.

A feature film will "screen and screen again" as the story is developed. Sequences may be added or dropped after different test audiences view the same material. Sometimes, a secondary character may reveal its "star potential" and have its part expanded as a direct result of an audience's response during a test screening.

There is no blueprint, no one way to create an appealing story. I like to use the words of story man and layout artist Ken O'Connor as a guideline for story creation:

We never achieved a formula. It was an interesting thing; I did [boards and layouts for] between 75 and 100 [theatrical] shorts, and you'd think that after a while you'd get the thing down to a routine, you know?... But we never succeeded at all. Every picture brings a whole new set of problems, and you simply can't make it like the last one, in my experience.... It's aggravating, but it's also very stimulating to me.

—**Interview with Nancy Beiman, 1979**

19

Team Storyboard: Working on Group Projects

Teamwork is the ability to work as a group toward a common vision, even if that vision becomes extremely blurry.

—Author Unknown

Two People, Three Arguments

Storyboarding is a team enterprise. Unless you are making a personal film, you will usually be working with a director who has a particular vision for the film. On longer projects, or on continuing ones like television series, you may be working with a story "crew" of up to a dozen people. You may not only have to share artwork with someone else, they may actually be working on the same assignment. At Disney Features, storyboard revisions were routinely assigned to a different artist from the one who originally drew them, since a new pair of eyes could look at it objectively. This practice also familiarized the story team with every aspect of the story rather than just their own sequences.

Some television projects have "story teams" of two people. Each artist will receive a few sequences from the same episode, and the team must make the story work seamlessly. Communication will be necessary. This is a very important part of the development process. I was once on a film whose two directors did not meet with one another while storyboarding their sequences. One of them boarded sequences where a town was populated with animal characters.

The other one's sequences showed the same town inhabited by human characters. There was no explanation that the town actually worked on two different scales, and that humans and animals shared the same spaces. This caused confusion in the finished film (Figure 19.1).

Figure 19.1

Story artists sometimes work in isolation. It's very important to know what happens before and after your sequence, so that it fits into the context of the picture. The head of story or director informs the crew when changes are made. If there is no communication continuity problems may develop.

As we saw in Chapter 17, the storyboard and character designs are pitched to an audience repeatedly during the development of the project. This allows the story man or woman to see how the action "plays"—whether the designs are working, whether the boards are communicating the story point—and make changes where necessary.

If the film is your personal project, you are the one who decides whether to accept the suggestions for change that your coworkers/teammates/instructors might make after a pitch. You're the director and you call the shots. But commercial films are big, long, expensive things that require more than one person to complete them. It is just as important to communicate with your crew as it is to communicate with an audience.

You don't have to agree with everyone all the time, but you need to listen to other people's opinions and modify your ideas when requested to do so. Everyone on a crew works to make the film appear to be a coherent whole rather than a series of separate pieces. The more people there are working on a project, the more opinions there are. A good filmmaker or director listens to them all, and sometimes a great idea may come from an unexpected source.

Remember that it is all about what is ON the screen. Revisions must be made before the film is finished. You are not going to be standing in a theater or in someone's house with a pointer explaining to an audience what they should have seen, or taking the film back in order to revise a few scenes (Figure 19.2).

Story team assignments vary by production. You may be one of many people pitching variations on the same idea. Or you may be on a team where everyone is suggesting different ideas for a group project. If the teamwork is good, everyone "brainstorms" or "bounces ideas around" in a story meeting, with rapid suggestions and scribbled sketches coming fast and furious. This is one of the most creative

19. Team Storyboard: Working on Group Projects

Figure 19.2

The story has to communicate with the audience, and animated filmmakers must also communicate with their colleagues while the film is being made. Once the film has wrapped, you don't get to revise it.

parts of filmmaking but it means that you should not be averse to changes to your work. You must be willing to consider alternatives, or at least listen to them, and support other artists when their ideas are chosen instead of yours. You may be asked to redesign your characters in the style of another artist. Your boards may need to be redrawn because the director has changed the story. Perhaps your sequence does not work out of the previous sequence of the film (if this happens, you have not been talking to your teammates to learn what happens before and after your sequence!). Always accept suggestions for change gracefully. Similarly, your teammates should behave in a professional and courteous manner when you make suggestions of your own. No one should behave as if the other person was trying to destroy the film. Everyone should want to make the film as good as it can possibly be.

On a professional production, the directors have final approval of all ideas. Some directors welcome suggestion for change. Others do not. You have to do what the director wants, even if you think you have a better idea. If they don't think so, just smile and do it their way. Your pride and ego must be sublimated to the directors' vision. Remember, it is the director's movie, not yours.

Changing the storyboard *is not about you*. Changes are made to improve the film. Storyboard exists BECAUSE it makes it easy to change the artwork. You are not *entitled* to anything in a studio. If you don't accept suggestions for improvement in your work, you would probably be better off working for yourself. Chances are you will be.

Story Team Etiquette

Kevin Richardson is an experienced animation director and producer who has also worked as an overseas animation supervisor. Michael Cachuela is a character designer and storyboard artist who has worked on many feature films. They have some excellent advice for aspiring, or perspiring, filmmakers who are working on a group project. Believe it or not, "playing well with others" is one of the most important skills that you can have when working at this job or *any* job.

- Avoid an "us" board artists versus "them" (the management) discussions or thinking. It takes a village to make a movie.
- Draw a hard line between brainstorming ideas from evaluating them—every idea is a good idea, until it isn't when you evaluate it.
- Avoid repeating yourself—rather ask the team if they understood your idea. And don't take it personally if nobody jumps on it.
- Don't take anything personally. It's not about you, it's about the film. It's what's best for the film.
- Focus on the story, not on making pretty drawings. Your sequence might get cut anyway, so don't overwork it, or get attached to strongly to it.
- Share your work. Get feedback. That doesn't mean you always have to take it or use it—but your peer's ideas gives you more fodder.
- If you feel blocked, just board anyway. Being idle and stewing is worse, so just draw! It's okay to throw away your drawings.
- Rather than criticize, offer a helpful suggestion. You won't be perceived as a negative person but rather a person with ideas.
- Don't judge an idea until you've seen it play in the reel. It might be great once it's played in the context of the entire movie.
- Melodrama works in the story but not in the story meeting situation. Avoid nonverbal disapproval like eye rolling, sighs, or any indications of negative judgment on the work of your peers. That's your team!
- If you think the story sucks, find a constructive way and venue to help make it better. Remember: it's not your story. Find the balance between owning it and realizing its not your story.
- Remember the rules that apply to any relationship, small or large scale—be respectful.
- If other departments or your team mates don't use a specific idea of yours, let it go. There are thousands of decisions made on a film, if you are on the story team, many of your ideas will get used—so don't worry.
- Celebrate milestones and small successes of your team mates and yours, too. Make work FUN for yourself and those around you.
- Remember the director is giving birth to her or his baby—find a way to support the story and the director with great work and helpful advice—which they may take or not. Never deviate from this mode or line of thinking.

—Kevin Richardson and Michael Cachuela

Making, but Not Taking, Things Personally

"A symphony orchestra is composed of 100 egomaniacs, each of whom believes that they play better than everyone else. The only thing that unites them is their common hatred of the conductor."

—Melvyn Beiman
Principal oboe/English horn,
New Jersey Symphony Orchestra 1962–1981

As stated earlier in this chapter, you must be willing to accept change and explore different avenues when working in story and development. You may not like the crew you are assigned to. You may not think the project is ideal.

Since it's highly unlikely that everyone you work with will be a friend of yours, you will have to keep the "personal" element out of your interactions and deal only with matters pertaining to the film. Remember, if you are working on a project that is not your own, you and everyone else on the show are illustrating someone else's vision. You aren't required to like everyone who is in the crew, but you are required to do your job as well as you can and behave in a professional manner toward your coworkers.

And if another artist is not treating you with professional courtesy...they might not be working in the studio much longer. Some studios list "plays well with others" as a major qualification when hiring their artists.

Animation is a very time-consuming art form and people spend months working on things that might appear on screen for only a second or two. Stress levels can be high especially with tight deadlines. It's essential to have a respite from work so that you don't take out your artistic frustrations on your coworkers. Likewise, minor events in your personal life should not be allowed to affect your work. (Studios and schools will work with you in the event of major disruptions.) It is essential to deal with emotional matters outside of work lest they make it difficult for you to complete your assignments. Whether you unwind through meditation, exercise, talking it out with a friend (who should under no circumstances be working in animation, *especially* not in the same studio!) is up to you. I like to ride a bicycle, walk, call friends to talk things over, and play with my two cats. Mindfulness training is also a great thing for animators. A problematic mountain may turn into a molehill if you are able to distance yourself from it and view it objectively with someone else's help if necessary (Figure 19.3).

Figure 19.3

Outside interests can help you deal with tensions that can occur at work.

Switching Story Gears

The creative ferment on a project can be exhilarating if the directors *know what they want*. There is nothing worse than a project where the director does NOT know what they want and the story and artwork are reworked again and again. There isn't much the crew can do in these instances but carry on as best they can and make changes when requested to do so. Projects that do not resolve are said to be in "*development hell.*"

Sometimes no matter what you do, the characters don't seem to come to life and the story stalls since there is no center or anchor for the film. In some cases, the story may be reworked with a different hero, or a different approach may be used—*is the hero comic rather than serious? A mixture of the two? Would the story work better if a different character's viewpoint was used?* There are many examples of these changes in feature animation, as you will find when viewing the special feature "deleted scenes" and "alternate openings/endings" on digital video releases of animated films. I always recommend watching these special features…you will see that most changes were done in storyboard. That's when the changes *should* be made.

In a short film, it's a bit easier to start over with a different idea if the first one isn't working. If you are pitching ideas at a studio or a school, you are often asked to bring two or three presentations consisting of beat boards, character lineups, and treatments, so that you have more than one chance to sell an idea to whoever gives you the green light to make the film. But, as with a feature film, you have to consider your budget. A student film's budget is *time*. If you continue to change your story when you are in production, the film may suffer in quality or be unfinished when the final deadline falls due (Figure 19.4).

Figure 19.4

Ready or not, here it (the film) comes.

A group project doesn't have to resemble "factory work" any more than a computer-animated film has to look like something that has been made by a machine. When all of the artists on a picture work together, with a director who can clearly indicate what is expected from each, the relationship is indeed like that of a good orchestra, with each artist's work contributing to a creative vision—*playing well with others.*

19. Team Storyboard: Working on Group Projects

20

Maquette Simple: Modeling Characters in Three Dimensions

"Sculpture is really a drawing that you fall over in the dark."

—Al Hirschfeld, THE LINE KING

Charles Philipon, editor of the French satirical magazines *La Caricature* and *Le Charivari*, commissioned the first *maquettes,* or three-dimensional models of a fanciful or imaginary figure. *La Caricature's* April 26, 1832 issue announced a "Celebrities" series of caricature portraits. Philipon stated that the political figures would first be portrayed *en maquette* and the drawings would be based on the clay sculptures. Staff illustrator Honoré Daumier was assigned to produce the artwork. He created more than 35 unbaked clay caricature *maquettes* of contemporary politicians that have survived until the present day. Legend has it that Daumier created the *maquettes* from life by sneaking lumps of clay into legislative sessions. More probably, he drew thumbnail sketches from life and then exaggerated the subject's features in clay. By using *maquettes* as models, Daumier was able to instill a lifelike three-dimensional quality into his highly unflattering drawings. A lithograph that Daumier drew from one of his caricature busts appears in Figure 20.1.

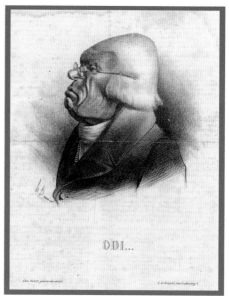

Figure 20.1

"Odi..." (Odier) was caricatured first in clay and then drawn by Honoré Daumier in May 1833 for *Le Charivari's* series of political portraits. (From Nancy Beiman collection.)

Maquettes were first produced at the Walt Disney Studio in the 1930s to enable the animators to draw animated characters from any angle. A special model department was established at the request of Walt Disney by Joe Grant, a top caricaturist, character designer, and story man. Some maquettes for the Seven Dwarfs had movable wooden joints, but plaster or clay soon became the standard construction material. PINOCCHIO's maquettes included full-sized functioning clocks for Geppetto's workshop and a life-sized wooden marionette of Pinocchio. A fully articulated wooden maquette of Bambi as a fawn had its construction based on traditional wooden artist's models.

The practice of creating character maquettes was revived for THE RESCUERS in 1972, and they have been sculpted for major characters in most subsequent films. Many studios have continued the tradition by creating maquettes in clay or polymer plastic prior to modeling them on a computer. Maquette builders are increasingly using specially designed "digital sculpting" programs like MudBox and ZBrush, but they all trained first by creating three-dimensional sculptures. A thorough understanding of art-in-the-round is needed in order to be successful at the digital equivalent.

Maquette production starts as character turnarounds, and construction models are being finalized. Turnarounds provide a three-dimensional view of the character for the sculptor to work with (Figure 20.2).

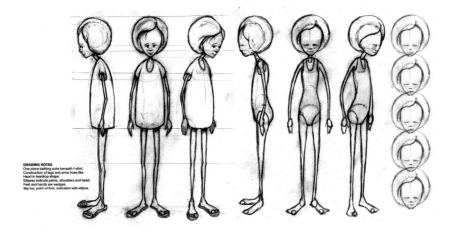

Figure 20.2

Turnaround and construction models are essential tools for the maquette maker. Action poses show the personality and mobility of the character. (Reproduced by permission of Jim Downer.)

The model sheets may change as the maquette *evolves* weak design features out. The maquette is baked and cast only when the final model sheets are approved.

Scale drawings for computer-generated imagery (CGI) characters have the arms spread out at a 45° or 90° angle as shown in Figure 20.3. These drawings are then imported into the CGI program and used as modeling guides. A maquette for a CGI character will often be sculpted in a *modeling pose* or a neutral stance. Maquettes may be scanned, digitized, and cleaned up in CGI so that the computer model is identical to the original design.

Figure 20.3

CGI figures use modeling poses that typically have the arms extended to the side of the figure. In this example, the modeling pose is intentionally hunched, which will restrict and distort the character's body movements. (Reproduced by permission of Nathaniel Hubbell.)

The character designer next draws the character in the pose that is desired for the maquette. The drawing is the size of the actual maquette. Turnaround drawings and details of costumes or features may also be provided to the sculptor (Figure 20.4).

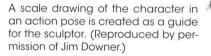

Figure 20.4

A scale drawing of the character in an action pose is created as a guide for the sculptor. (Reproduced by permission of Jim Downer.)

The maquette drawing must be large enough to allow a wire armature to fit inside it and also leave room for the aluminum foil padding and clay or polymer "skin" that will be placed over the sculpture's wire "bones." A polymer figure must also be able to fit into an oven.

Next, twist medium gauge wire into a simple armature. Aluminum wire is used in Figure 20.5 and steel wire is used in Figure 20.6. Steel wire is stronger and more appropriate for standing characters.

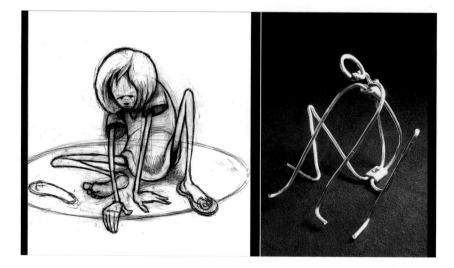

Figure 20.5

Aluminum wire is used for this seated figure's armature. The armature is smaller than the maquette drawing. (Reproduced by permission of Jim Downer.)

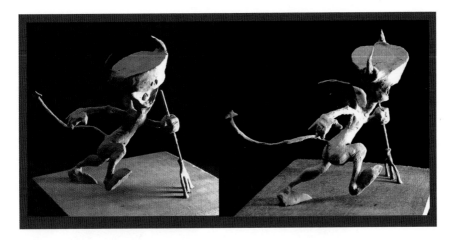

Figure 20.6

The little devil is supported by steel wires inside his pitchfork. Armature wires extend through the feet and pitchfork into the wooden base. The resulting triangular support has considerable strength. (Reproduced by permission of Jeremy A. Galante.)

If you are sculpting a standing character, *it is very important to attach the wire armature to a solid wooden base before proceeding further. Do not use plywood.* Secure the wire feet firmly to the base with staples, nails, or other metal attachments. You may drill holes in the wood and feed the wire feet through it, attaching it to the bottom of the base to secure the figure more firmly. Another method involves making a small loop at the end of the legs where the feet should be and allowing a small section of wire to project downward from the loop into the holes drilled in the wood. Wires or wooden dowels may be camouflaged inside clothing or an object that the figure leans on for additional support as shown in Figure 20.6.

> *WARNING:* Polymer plastics such as Sculpey must be baked in a cool oven in order to "set." If your maquette sculpture is to be made of polymer plastic you *must* use only *SOLID* wood for the base. Do not use plywood, particle board, or any type of plastic as a base for polymer figurines. Use *only* aluminum foil to bulk up the armature but *not* paper, Styrofoam, or rag, since these materials will release poisonous gases, burn, or melt during the baking process.

A satisfactory base can be made from a piece of scrap wood obtained at a lumber yard or hardware store. If you are working with Plasticine or air-hardening clay that does not need to be baked, you may use plastic, plywood, or particle board bases without danger. The wire frame is then bulked out with aluminum foil. (*Do not use flammable materials. A list of what to avoid is provided in the previous box.*) Foil padding reduces the weight of the figure, conserves modeling material, and makes the resultant sculpture more resistant to breakage. The heat-conductive foil center bakes the maquette from the inside out and enables the polymer to set faster. The padding should be ½ inch to ¾ inch smaller than the drawing so that the clay "skin" may fit within its outline. A figure made of air-drying clay typically has its armature bulked out with strips of rag (Figure 20.7).

Figure 20.7

The wire armature is bulked up with aluminum foil padding. *No plastic or paper padding should be used in a polymer sculpture.* (Reproduced by permission of Jim Downer.)

The weight of the polymer plastic can cause it to sag slightly on the wire frame during baking. The material also will contract slightly as it cools. A foil center will maintain its shape and keep cracking and crazing to a minimum. Use enough foil to create a rough body shape for the character, but not so much that it completely fills the outline of the scale drawing. You must leave room for the "skin." Maquettes may be precisely proportioned by creating a wooden or cardboard negative outline of the scale drawing and ensuring that the finished maquette fits inside it. This technique is associated with "creature labs" and monster-movie model makers. A cartoon character maquette will usually be sculpted "by eye" with frequent comparisons to the scale drawing(s) as modeling progresses.

Modeling material is applied after the armature is completed and attached to its wooden base. It is very important to follow the directions on the box regarding time and temperature when baking polymer plastic. Low temperatures work best since they minimize cracking. The polymer will be very hot and malleable after the figure is taken from the oven, typically after a 20-minute baking period.

Polymer plastic must be baked at a *low temperature* in a standard convection or radiant-heated oven. *Never put polymer-plastic figures, with or without wire and aluminum armatures, in the microwave.* Air bubbles in the polymer compound may explode, damaging the sculpture. Toxic chemicals may be released, damaging the sculptor. Read the directions on the polymer material's package and follow them to prevent serious consequences. Certain types of polymer clay are now designed for microwave use. Be SURE that you have the right clay before using the microwave!

Once the maquette has been baked, it should be allowed to cool overnight. When it is completely cool, the sculpture and base are painted in one medium shade of gray water-based acrylic paint. *Do not use spray or oil paint on polymer compounds.* This neutral color allows values created by light and shadow to define the character's form in the same way that tonal values create contrast and depth in storyboard drawings. Sculpey modeling clay is now available in gray and brown shades that eliminate the need to paint the finished maquette (Figure 20.8).

Figure 20.8

The armature is attached to a wooden base. Polymer material is sculpted over the armature in conformation with the scale drawing and the figure is baked. When it is cool and dry, the maquette and its base are painted with a medium-gray acrylic paint, which allows light and shadow to define three-dimensional forms. Decorative elements, such as patterns on clothing, are added at a later stage of production. Plasticine figures are not painted. (Reproduced by permission of Jim Downer.)

Maquettes are used at several stages in hand-drawn animated film production. Animators use them to scale and distort characters. Art directors and background artists use them to determine how the quality of the light in the painted settings affects the characters. CGI lighting directors will literally use maquettes as models when creating the lighting for a sequence.

Figure 20.9 is an example of a polymer figure that I created in a sculpture class at the Walt Disney Studio. The maquette is designed to portray different emotions. It wears a cheerful expression on one side of its face and an alien, homicidal one on the other. The character's expression appeared to change when the light source was raised or lowered in relation to the sculpture. The planes of its head

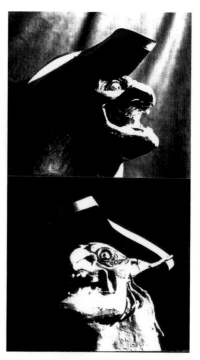

Figure 20.9

This maquette had two different expressions sculpted on either side of its face. The expressions were designed to intensify as the light source changed. (Maquette sculpture by Nancy Beiman.)

were carefully constructed to create shadows that created a more or less threatening appearance as the light source changed. I accomplished this by shining a strong light on the maquette, while the sculpture was actually in progress and emphasizing or diminishing individual planes as required.

Not every character will work as a sculpture. A maquette has never been made for Mickey Mouse since his nose, ears, and other elements of his design do not turn in three-dimensional space. A "pure" graphic character does not need a three-dimensional representation. Simple, rounded characters such as the one in Figure 20.10 are usually animated without the use of maquettes.

Color

Figure 20.10

A maquette was not considered necessary as an animation aid for "Mozart," since his design is very simple. (Reproduced by permission of Brittney Lee.)

A maquette helps you determine how your character's volumes turn in space and also enables you to "evolve" any lingering weaknesses or inconsistencies out of the character design before it is too late to change it further. A maquette is the last checkpoint on the long road an animated character must travel before it goes into production.

21

Build a Better Mouse: Creating Final Model Sheets

Keep It Clean

Animated characters have it rough. They're pushed, prodded, pulled into and out of shape on storyboards, forced to line up on size-comparison sheets, and put through their paces on action model sheets. Their outlines are erased, redrawn, re-erased, reworked, reviewed, and redone. Their innards are exposed, their skeletons analyzed, and their clothes removed or left as transparent shapes over their naked bodies. But even the roughest animated character can clean up their act.

In hand-drawn animation, *Cleanup model sheets* standardize surface details, line quality, and the appearance of all characters. It is the Wardrobe, Makeup, and Hairstyling Department of animation. Inconsistencies in design such as *cheats* must also be labeled on the cleanups (Figure 21.1).

Figure 21.1

Animated characters can sometimes lose their appeal when the *cleanup* line is not handled with sensitivity. Cleanup drawings must retain the lively, animated quality of the rough. (Reproduced by permission of Nina L. Haley.)

Sometimes an animated character retains its rough, unpolished mannerisms and lines into the final color production. Color may be applied as a texture that moves continually as the figure animates. This shifting technique is called *boiling*. A rough line and boiling color on character and background can give a lively and vibrant quality to the images, creating a pleasing stylistic effect. Bill Plympton's films (YOUR FACE, THE GUARD DOG, IDIOTS AND ANGELS, CHEATIN') are excellent examples of this technique. Figure 21.2 shows two consecutive frames of a character that was designed to *boil* when animating.

(a)   (b)

Figure 21.2

He's *boiling*, but he's not mad. The shifting color is an artistic effect that can create a pleasing complement to the *rough* outline of the character.

Like all effects, boiling is best used in moderation.

Hand-drawn animated characters are typically cleaned up with the classic *wire line* that is thinly and evenly applied on all sections of the drawing. A *weighted* or "thick-and-thin" line is occasionally used on an entire character but more typically is restricted to outlines or limited areas of a design such as a female character's hair (Figure 21.3).

Figure 21.3

The rough composition is very different from its final *cleanup* shown to the right. A *weighted* line gives a solid feeling to the cats' body outline. Interior lines are drawn with a *wire* line. (Reproduced by permission of Nina L. Haley.)

Cleanups must retain the animation and life of the original drawing. If hand-drawn animation is *on model,* the assistant needs only add details such as stripes, buttons, and flyaway hair that the animator or designer may not have included on the rough drawing. Rough animation that is fairly tight often has a lively, interesting quality that is maintained when the drawings are painted without cleanup, as in Figure 21.4.

Figure 21.4

This rough drawing was "tight" enough to be painted without additional cleanup. Note the nonphoto blue construction lines that drop out when the figure is scanned and painted by computer. (Reprinted by permission of Brittney Lee.)

If a rough is extremely sketchy, the cleanup artist may completely redraw the image, reducing or inflating incorrect volumes and adding details while standardizing the line weight and removing construction lines. The cleanup must retain the poses and composition of the rough sketch.

Hand-drawn television shows require the storyboard artist to draw *on model,* maintaining proper size relationships and volumes. No evolution is allowed. Cleanup standardizes the character volumes and appearance according to the model sheets and maintains the consistency of the design throughout the picture.

If your cleanup model differs from the original rough or volumes are inconsistent, you should redraw the character's construction in a new color on a separate level. Red is commonly used, though nonphoto blue is also permissible. Black line cleanup is drawn directly on top of the red sketch as shown in Figure 21.5.

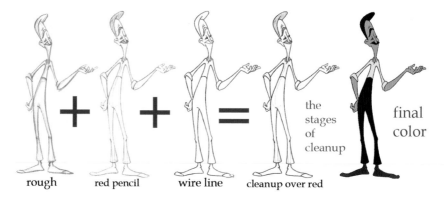

rough   red pencil   wire line   cleanup over red   the stages of cleanup   final color

Figure 21.5

"Rough" roughs are first redrawn in red or blue to make sure that volume and details are consistent, then cleaned up with the final line. (Design reproduced by permission of Brittney Lee. Cleanup reproduced by permission of Nina L. Haley.)

You may clean up on the same level as the red sketch using a new color and dropping out the rough line. Leaving the artwork rough eliminates the need for cleanup. This look can be very appealing if the animator has drawn important details on the roughs. My film YOUR FEET'S TOO BIG was animated rough and stayed that way in the final (Figure 21.6).

Figure 21.6

My rough animation for YOUR FEET'S TOO BIG was xeroxed on cel and painted without benefit of cleanup. Today, I'd paint it on a computer in half the time at one-tenth of the cost.

A computer-generated imagery (CGI) character is constructed by importing concept drawings into the computer program and projecting the design into three dimensions via the modeling process in a digital sculpting program. The character's modeling poses show the same pose in different angles. Suzette, the rat was designed on paper and drawn in action poses showing the range of motion that her CGI incarnation would need to perform. Computer graphics programs won't correct shifting volumes or add missing costume details. But they will keep your characters on model throughout. This means that it is very important to get the models and rigs right before you start animating, so test animation of the designs on paper is recommended, including changes of facial expression (Figure 21.7).

Figure 21.7

Action models of Suzette show the range of motion her CGI incarnation must perform. (Reproduced by permission of William Robinson.)

Figure 21.8 shows Suzette in modeling poses drawn after her model sheets were finalized. Her design was set before it went into the computer. Or was it?

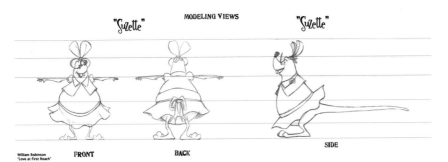

Figure 21.8

Front, back, and side drawings of Suzette's modeling pose were imported into the computer and used for the final model. (Reproduced by permission of William Robinson.)

Suzette's design was considerably modified after the model poses were imported into the computer. Her arms were lengthened, so that they would be better able to hug her cockroach boyfriend Pierre. She got a nose job. Other details of her anatomy changed as she was modeled and rigged and transformed into a three-dimensional character.

The model drawings were the starting point for a character design that was finished in the computer. Only Suzette's clothing remained consistent with the original drawing, as shown in Figure 21.9. Suzette appeared in a student film, so *evolution* of the character design at this stage was allowed and encouraged. This is now becoming more common in feature films. Disney's WRECK IT RALPH was one of the first CGI films to evolve the characters as they were being modelled.

Figure 21.9

Suzette's arms were lengthened, and her body proportions were changed from the model drawings as she was modeled in CGI. (Reproduced by permission of William Robinson.)

A CGI character that is to be combined with live-action film is tested by digitally combining a rendering of the character created in a 2D graphics program with one still frame from a live-action shoot. If there are design changes, another rendering is completed and recomposited until the look is finalized. Modeling, rigging, and texturing are the costliest parts of CGI animation, so testing the design in a less expensive format allows CGI designs to *evolve* before they are *locked down* for good.

CGI characters may be rendered with an outline that mimics the "wire line" and eliminates interior shading so that the figures resemble painted or drawn animation. Special shaders can reproduce the look of brush or pen lines. An example of a CGI render in the style of Chinese brush painting is shown in Figures 21.10 and 21.11.

Figure 21.10 and 21.11

This character was sculpted as a maquette (Figure 21.10), then animated in CGI (Figure 21.11). The final render combined the CGI with hand-painted backgrounds and line to create the look of Chinese brush paintings. (Reproduced by permission of Joseph Daniels and Jedidiah Mitchell.)

The artists emphasized the film's graphic look using transparent color, flat lighting, and a digitized rice-paper background. Elaborate graphic effects can be animated more quickly on computer than by hand. *The machine need not create art that looks machine made!* (Figure 21.12).

Figure 21.12

Backgrounds were painted conventionally, then scanned, and modified in the computer. A rice-paper texture was applied digitally, and the CGI-animated characters were rendered so that they resembled watercolor paintings. (Reproduced by permission of Joseph Daniels and Jedidiah Mitchell.)

22

Screen and Screen Again: Preparing for Production

As I mentioned earlier, workbook and previz are a transition between storyboard and layout. *Never* make the mistake of going directly "from script to previz" *without storyboard*, as one ill-fated CGI production once tried to do. (It did not work, and the film ran way over budget when the inevitable changes came.) Storyboard is the visual script for an animated film. How can you build the digital placeholder sets, scale the characters, set up a camera move, or design the shot if you only have a brief written description of the action in a scene and some concept art as a guide? How, without a storyboard, can you remain focused on your story and (as Hans Bacher memorably states in Chapter 9) not be distracted by the endless variations offered by the very technology that was designed to help you make the film more efficiently? Writing cannot truly describe what we see on the screen. Writing *tells*; Film (of any kind) *shows*. Storyboard shows AND tells.

You have now officially ended preproduction. The *production* is about to begin. Layout, background painting, modeling, rigging, texturing, character blocking, rough pass animation, final tie down, backgrounds, color, texture, lighting, special effects, compositing, final render, musical track, sound design and edit, final mix, digital formatting, export… *Production and postproduction* work actually show on the screen. But it won't make a coherent film without good storyboard, design, and direction. When you work in preproduction, you are scripting, designing, casting, and directing the animated movie. Your work gives production artists something to get their teeth into. You may even shift over to production once preproduction is finished (as I have done on many films). Story problems are dealt within storyboard stage, so that the picture won't need to rework the characters, settings, and animation after the animation is 40% completed (and there are films that have achieved this dubious distinction). Changes can and will continue to be made to story if you are working on a commercial production. Sequences may be added or more likely dropped if directors and producers and budgets demand it. A well-run feature project will have some sequences in production while others are being revised, so that the film can be completed out of sequential order.

If you're working on a personal film, you have completed the boards and timed the story reel or animatic to a scratch track. You have prioritized the sequences so that the expendable "C's" go into production last, and your major efforts go into the "A's and B's". The character models are finalized, modeled, and rigged, and the production design is set. Layout, the first stage of production, is the cinematography of animation. Good layout *pluses* the storyboard staging, choreographs the camera moves, adds depth and design to backgrounds, and sets the stage for the animated actors. Layout and previz are blending more and more with live action in modern animated films. You may work with live-action cinematographers when you are designing your camera moves or lighting virtual "sets" in two or three dimensions.

And after that, it is *finally* time for the animators to create memorable performances that are based on the storyboard "script and rehearsals." Animated scenes (line tests or low-resolution renders, whichever is applicable to the project) are cut into the Leica/animatic as they are completed, replacing the scene's storyboards, which are now placeholders for the animation. This keeps the scenes at their correct lengths and the animator informed about what comes before and after each scene. The acting, editing, and story continuity will be consistent. Now the Leica/animatic becomes a *work picture*. As production progresses, more and more animation appears until all of the Leica/animatic boards have been replaced, and the sequence is fully animated. The work picture is then revised yet again as color scenes are cut in, replacing the rough animation and low-resolution renders, until the work picture turns into the finished film. The same technique is used to produce short and student films. Cut your scenes into the Leica/animatic as you finish animating them and replace the scene's storyboards as you go. A work picture will keep your scenes from running too long, and you can review them in continuity rather than one at a time outside of story context. If you made your film's big changes at the storyboard phase and built a solid story with good direction, you will make smaller and fewer revisions to the final animation.

And don't forget to save often and back up your files every day.

This book ends where most others begin.

I stated in the Introduction that animators were magicians. Like magicians, we work hard to make the impossible look easy. Our reward is a symphony of color, sound, and motion, and the pleasure of working in the most fascinating art form of the last hundred years. Best of all, in animation, the magic is real. It will come to you with practice. Good bye, good luck, and have fun!

And so Goodbye!

Appendix 1: Discussion with A. Kendall O'Connor[*]

Ken O'Connor worked as a story man, art director, and layout artist at the Walt Disney Studio. He began on short cartoons in 1935 and worked on most Disney films up until THE LITTLE MERMAID in 1989. This interview was conducted by Nancy Beiman at the California Institute of the Arts, while she was a student in Ken O'Connor's layout and storyboard class.

Ken O'Connor, photographed in 1987 by Nancy Beiman.

[*] Excerpts, February 15, 1979, © 1979, 2005 by Nancy Beiman.

NANCY BEIMAN: When you were doing tonal studies, did you always have the color of the final background in mind?

KEN O'CONNOR: No, I'd say not. Not always.

NANCY BEIMAN: These layouts are highly rendered. You brought in one which was sketchier.

KEN O'CONNOR: Well, circumstances alter cases here all the time…. I think of the pure line effect, then the tone, then the color. It evolves that way sometimes; of course, there are no real hard-and-fast rules. Inspirational material, in this case Maxfield Parrish-like inspirational paintings—had been done before this was done. So you've got that in mind, you see. You know what shade of lavender you would reasonably use for the shadows, and you've seen the inspirational painting.

NANCY BEIMAN: I was wondering whether tonal rendering layouts was a general practice, or was it just done for the sheer pleasure of doing it?

KEN O'CONNOR: No, there was very little done for the sheer pleasure of doing it. There are a number of reasons for rendering, there's no simplistic answer…. This thing in line wouldn't impress a director anywhere near as impressively as a tonal version of the same landscape. And then, of course, the end product of layout is something for background. So the background man has to think in values, tonality; and you give him the best send-off you can. If you hand the background man just a line drawing, he's got to do all the thinking of the values, the light scheme; where's the light coming from, where do you want the dramatic emphasis? We put in flashes of light and dark where we wanted it.

KEN O'CONNOR: You can see how your eye tends to go to [a certain area]. That's where the layout man wants you to go. Everything else is subservient. The tonality tells the background man to keep that in mind when painting. You bring one thing out, powerfully, and play that other down tonally.

NANCY BEIMAN: In animation, when you use reference material, the general guideline is to look at it once and never look at it again. Would you do the same thing when you were researching backgrounds?

KEN O'CONNOR: I would get every piece of reference I could lay my hands on before I started. Which frequently wasn't much time, I might say. I'd go to the library; go to other artists who kept scrapbooks; I'd go to my own collection at home. I keep a clip-file with maybe 200,000 clippings classified by subject, I imagine. I'd gather everything in like a big vacuum cleaner, almost regardless of exactly how valuable it would be—then I'd try to go through a period of absorbing it…. Then I'd regurgitate it as layouts.

NANCY BEIMAN: How long would this take you, on the average?

KEN O'CONNOR: Very variable—a matter of hours on a short film sometimes; a matter of months on a picture like PINOCCHIO or THE RESTLESS SEA. Before we did THE RESTLESS SEA, we sat down and read books for maybe two months. We were not up on such things as, for example, the differences between zooplankton and phytoplankton, or internal waves. These things are not in the average man's vocabulary, you see. We had to study a great deal because this was to be authentic. Having got all the reference together, I would hang onto it right through the picture ... I'd often pass it on to the background men.... As far as I was concerned reference was a thing to be used the whole time.

NANCY BEIMAN: Would you caricature it?

KEN O'CONNOR: Yes, I'd try to make it appropriate to the picture. In this picture (FANTASIA) you can see that it is a very decorative style.... We warped everything towards the idyllic, romantic, classical, decorative mood in this particular sequence. We went in other directions depending on the mood of the picture ... There were certain key backgrounds painted from layouts which the other background men were expected to follow stylistically ... we did a lot of conferring with the director, the head animator, and the background man as much as we could.

NANCY BEIMAN: Is it better to have more camera moves, or cut to a new shot?

KEN O'CONNOR: I think everything should be judged by what the scene calls for. I think there's probably a certain amount of ignorance today that's behind a lot of lack of use of the camera. We studied live action very closely, and stole everything we could from it ... I'll give you an example. Alfred Hitchcock, in some of his suspense pictures, used what he called a "fluid camera." He kept it moving the whole time. It resulted in a flow to the picture that you don't get by "cut, cut, cut," you know. If you are building up toward a collision, or going to a battle, you build the tempo with shorter pans and faster cuts to get a staccato effect. It's like music; staccato versus legato. That's the way we thought of the thing.

NANCY BEIMAN: How did they manage to get sequence directors to work together?

KEN O'CONNOR: Well ... certain things tend to pull [a picture] together. One is model sheets, so the characters, at least are consistent. Another is a good lead background painter who can see to it that the appearance of the thing doesn't suddenly jolt when you cut from one sequence to another. People respond to repetition, gradation of size and shapes, and airbrush gradations. These are things we know that people just love to see.

NANCY BEIMAN: Aren't curves also supposed to be something audiences respond to?

KEN O'CONNOR: Well, men respond to curves all the time. (Laughter.) Yes, if you play them off right—a curved line against a straight line, that's the strong thing.... Curves versus straights is a basic, and good, principle.... Different styles are good for study.

NANCY BEIMAN: You were talking about contrasts. A cartoon character, no matter how realistically animated, isn't real.

KEN O'CONNOR: Well, we've tried to get consistency. We've tried to make the backgrounds look like the characters, and the characters look like the backgrounds. I like experimentation and contrast too... there was a fashion for a while to take colored tissue paper and tear it up and use it for backgrounds. Frank Armitage used that in THE RESTLESS SEA.... It all depends on how much you want to convey the idea of the third dimension. Characters are, at Disney, normally animated in the round. They seem to be round, so the idea has been to try to make the background seem to have depth too. If you get it sketchy and flat, it won't achieve that. It might achieve something else, and I'm all for checking that out. Originally they used watercolor washes in pastel colors so that the character would kick out. Then they got more depth into the thing. Poster colors can really make the background go back… I started the switch on THE MOOSE HUNT. We painted the characters in flat colors and then painted the rocks, and trees, and bushes in… poster technique. With the right values it did go back….

It's always been a two-way stretch to try to make the characters and the background so rendered that they seem like one picture on the screen, and not like two disparate objects; the second direction of the two-way stretch is [that the] character must read and be seen as separate from the background. The primary thing is to have the character legible. This can be done by line design and color and sometimes by texture contrasts.

In other words, if you have a large, smooth character, you can put a lot of little texture things in the background for contrast…. Separating characters from backgrounds [while relating to them at the same time] has always been the big struggle….

NANCY BEIMAN: Do color key artists have a background in front of them so that they can relate characters to the background?

KEN O'CONNOR: No, color key starts at the story sketch stage. The color [modelist] has frequently seen the storyboards and so has a general idea of the color and tonality of the *probable* backgrounds. Background painting is frequently one of the last functions to happen [on a film]. The character is one of the first, so they have to get some sort of a model early on.

NANCY BEIMAN: When you have nighttime and daytime sequences in the same picture, do you design characters with colors that would fit in with practically any type of lighting?

KEN O'CONNOR: Some of the characters are naturally difficult. Pluto is difficult because he's sort of an intermediate, middle-value tan. This is the sort of color you're liable to use in a background quite a bit; so you want contrast. You've got to push the background down or up relative to his value. Some characters have built-in contrasts. A penguin, for example; put it on a dark background, only the light will show up, and vice versa. You can get contrasts within the character. You know that part of it is going to read, whatever you put it over. That could be important.

[Character colorists in the model department] would design what they thought would make a good character. A king, lion, whatever, would be designed for itself. Later they frequently had to be adjusted for color to go with the backgrounds that showed up. But they had good basic design and good tonality.

NANCY BEIMAN: There's a design principle which states that dark colors are "slower" than light ones.

KEN O'CONNOR: Yes, the "heavy" is heavy in the value sense as well as in the mind.

NANCY BEIMAN: How useful are inspirational paintings?

KEN O'CONNOR: There's an evolution that has to go on. When you do thumbnails [for storyboard] you find out that these [artists] are not concerned with, for instance, screen directions. We would change things around. These [sketches] are not too specific. They just have the atmosphere and feeling which they thought would be good [for the picture]. Almost none of [the sketches] have survived.

NANCY BEIMAN: Are there problems that are common to both short and feature films? Was there any difference other than that of scale?

KEN O'CONNOR: Nancy, you're full of questions like a dog is full of fleas…. Well, a lot of difference was time… And there were essential differences in tempo. Short films had to be finished in six or seven minutes, so the story man had to gear his mind up to a rapid tempo and so did everybody else. Features have more opportunity for pacing—slow, fast, and climactic drops, rises, and dramatics and so on.

[Short-film] tempo is fast underneath, and scenes had to be shorter. Action was faster and we tried to get as much quality as we could into them, but due to time and budget they were necessarily simplified.

NANCY BEIMAN: I was wondering if you could comment on some of the early "Silly Symphonies," some of which had rather slow pacing.

KEN O'CONNOR: This was probably because they were geared to the music. But "Silly Symphonies" were different from the Mickey or Donald cartoons. They were into prettiness, beauty, and that stuff. They were more into the look of things rather than the story, such as the Plutos and Ducks and so on were.

NANCY BEIMAN: Would you do as much research for a short film as for a feature?

KEN O'CONNOR: Oh yes, I would do as much research on everything as I had time for, and that means getting data from every available source.

NANCY BEIMAN: On the shorts, what kind of story construction worked best for you?

KEN O'CONNOR: Normally the simplest story was the best…. This sometimes affected the features such as DUMBO, where the story is very simple… Simplicity in story didn't mean that our settings or our drawings were simple necessarily. THE UGLY DUCKLING was a simple story… but we had a really complex forest and pond and all the hunter eyes there… I didn't lay that out but wish I had.

We had shots down to eight frames in length in SNOW WHITE AND THE SEVEN DWARFS, where she's running through the forest and the trees came at her. Simple things were done here because there's no point in putting massive [detail] behind an 8-frame scene. It would never be seen. Contrariwise, if you had a 15-foot scene you would try to elaborate the background so that the eye didn't have to look at a blank wall for that length of time. Circumstances alter cases.

NANCY BEIMAN: Could you talk about some of the short films you worked on?

KEN O'CONNOR: Oh boy, that's like picking out of the Sears Catalog! Well, I liked CLOCK CLEANERS, because we got violent angle shots. There were some who felt that perhaps the layout man put in angle shots just for the sake of putting in angle shots! However, the picture called for it.

NANCY BEIMAN: What characters did you work with?

KEN O'CONNOR: I worked with all the characters. I was with Freddy Spencer right from the very beginning when he was first developing the Duck, before the Duck became cute.

NANCY BEIMAN: Would you try for a different feel for each series, to get them to differentiate from each other? Would you do a different background for the Goof and the Duck?

KEN O'CONNOR: You fit the setting into the story each time. In MOVING DAY (1936) the story largely dictated the set [as well as] the action.

The story man didn't necessarily have to work the [backgrounds] out thoroughly, but the layout person did.

Silhouette value was something that [director] David Hand was very strong on, and it was particularly important to make the characters legible so that Walt could read them.

NANCY BEIMAN: If you were doing an atmospheric thing wouldn't you have to sacrifice some silhouette value to get the proper effect?

KEN O'CONNOR: Sometimes in a sinister or mysterious film you'd play silhouette down and it would be hard to see because that was part of the story... you'd see mysterious, dark figures moving through patches of light. Dramatics controls everything. But in a normal cartoon, we made things very clear and very plain.... [The characters] had to show up as strongly as we could make them, and silhouette value was [stressed] by the layout person and animator particularly.

I know of no law that is invariable. I think every rule is made to be broken. But you have to work on general average, and in general average you'll come out ahead by stressing silhouette value. When we have quick action, the audience has to figure things out very fast. [In life-drawing class Don Graham would say,] "Now black it in." Doing this to your drawings was oddly revealing because you'd [sometimes] find that you just had a blob that didn't express anything. It's very good training... and not only for animated cartoons.

"Circumstances alter cases."
  "Now, that's better than a poke in the eye with a sharp stick!"
  "That's clear as mud!"

—**Ken O'Connor**

Ken O'Connor with self-caricature bust, 1987.
(Courtesy of Nancy Beiman.)

HAIL GLUTEUS MAXIMUS

Appendix 2: Caricature Discussion with T. Hee*

T. Hee was a noted caricaturist at the MGM, Warner Brothers, and Walt Disney Studios. He worked in story and character design on films such as MOTHER GOOSE GOES HOLLYWOOD, THE RELUCTANT DRAGON, and NOAH'S ARK, and was sequence director on "The Dance of the Hours" sequence of FANTASIA and PINOCCHIO's sequences with the Fox and Cat. He created storyboards for UPA cartoons including MR. FUDGET'S BUDGET, THE OOMPAHS, and GERALD McBOING BOING on PLANET MOO. The interview was recorded at the California Institute of the Arts, when I was a student in T. Hee's caricature class. We never learned his real name.

T. Hee at the T. Hee ranch, 1982. (Courtesy of John Van Vliet, reproduced by permission of John Van Vliet.)

---

* February 23, 1979 (edited), © 1979, 2006 by Nancy Beiman.

NANCY BEIMAN: It's very interesting. This is the only art form that you need a machine to view it with.

T. HEE: One frame at a time. Consequently, you see the motion. [But] you can create motion through *design*.

T. HEE: [You can] express a situation through a variety of little actions... or one tremendous action carrying right through. [Edgar Allan] Poe used to say as he began to write a story, that "it wrote itself." I talk to animators who are like this. They start a scene, and as they start working with it, this character takes over and becomes the one who leads him or her to the final action. Each one of us sees things completely differently.

NANCY BEIMAN: Would it be good for [an animator] to have a set of guidelines, the way Japanese art has?

T. HEE: I think that each one of these [woodblock] artists had their own interpretations of what they were seeing. And this is the same thing that should be evident with people in an art school. Why *be* exactly like someone else? Create your own art that has a strong sense of identity. This is the only way that you can progress. If you try to copy and imitate you will find that somebody else who is *creative* will keep pulling ahead [of you]. If you're copying and trying to do what somebody else did you will find that you are always two or three steps behind this other person.

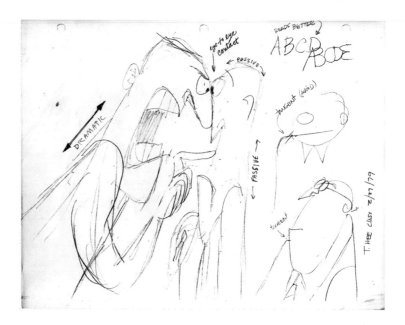

A drawing by T. Hee depicting motion in design. Certain parts of the figure read *faster* or *slower* than others. The eye is led around the composition in the direction indicated by the arrows and captions. The composition and pose of the figures convey a sense of motion in a single drawing. (Nancy Beiman collection)

NANCY BEIMAN: You once said that you can always tell when a drawing had been taken from life and when it had been thought up out of your head. How would you be able to do that?

T. HEE: You had an assignment where you made caricatures of each other using clay. They have a life because they were *of* somebody who existed. Just to make a caricature without any kind of relationship to something that exists, that has life and action and vitality, will ensure that it will not have that liveliness.

NANCY BEIMAN: How do you design something that doesn't exist? Say, something that has no relation to anything on this planet. It's totally alien. Do you have to try to relate it to something that you are familiar with?

T. HEE: I think most everything is related to something else. There isn't anything that is original all by itself. No one describes those Martians, and so forth, exactly the same.

If you think long enough about a certain thing, it will make a picture in your mind…. The fact that you try to capture something that is real is better than having something that you made up. It will help you to give it life. Life aspects are the factors that make things on the screen appear convincing.

To make a caricature of *anybody* is one hell of a challenge. I think you have to forget yourself, forget everything, and think in terms of what this person has that makes them different from everyone else that you've seen. You have to look at that person and look at another person and see how they contrast.

Sammy Davis Junior caricatured by T. Hee. (Nancy Beiman collection)

It's difficult to make a caricature of somebody, unless you *know* them. So to get back from reality and work from that base is, I think, the only way to do caricatures. Look at dogs or animals and people in the zoo and really study them. I think studying the differences and uniqueness of each individual creature that exists is the way to do it.

NANCY BEIMAN: Would you find that it is harder to caricature someone when they are aware of you? Would you rather hide in the corner, so they wouldn't see you and be off guard?

T. HEE: No, I think that it's better if they are busy doing what they're doing. They're not pretending to be something that they're not. Try to get them as they are. *You're being caricatured right now.* (General giggles from class.)

T. HEE: You got a whole million questions?

NANCY BEIMAN: No, only about four.

T. HEE: Okay, I came out with four answers this morning.

NANCY BEIMAN: You have been talking all morning about a different way of seeing that a creative person must develop. Is this something that you are born with or can you train yourself to look at something objectively?

T. HEE: I think it's something you are either born with *or* you can train yourself to do. If you could train your brain to record little details, well, it would be just a delightful thing. You can do it by going into a store and looking at the… textures of materials and how things are put together. Put colors together and see how they work, or go look at bark on trees to see how one is different from another. Start training yourself to observe things. That's why I think that little kids have it made—little tiny ones, about two feet tall—they fall down in the grass and experiment. They're tasting and really getting close to the earth. When we grow up, we lose all sense of that; we look in windows as we go down the street [and we are] straightening ties or pulling a skirt down. We don't look up and see what's up there with those buildings….

… I think that everything you've ever seen or ever done or heard as a child is still there with you. It's not something that you're going to destroy. Your contemporary approach can open up your mind to recall these things and become involved in more things.

IMPROBABLE INTERVIEW #1980
Caricatures of Nancy Beiman interviewing Buster Keaton, by T. Hee. Photo at left was taken by Enrique May the same day this interview and caricature were created

Caricature of Nancy Beiman interviewing Buster Keaton, by T. Hee. T. told me later that "I drew both of you from life, only about 50 years apart!" The photograph was taken by Enrique May, at T. Hee's request, on the same day that T. drew the roughs for my caricature. (Nancy Beiman collection)

I believe very strongly that if someone is going to draw a horse they must go look at a horse; touch the horse… and get in back of a horse [but far enough back, so that you don't get kicked] and get *on* a horse. Then you know what a horse is! But you cannot draw a horse by simply taking a look at one that goes down a street. You have to really study it and apply every bit of creativity you have within you to capture that horse….

I am for learning everything you can about the human form. But you will never do all your animation [or design] based exactly on the training you received [in life-drawing class]. You have to observe from life.

You have guidelines, but if you were to take an animal and give it human characteristics—put clothes on it, turn it into a fat man or a skinny guy—it becomes a caricature. You don't have to make it too realistic…. Your best action will come from a caricature body. If the legs are short, you are confined to a certain kind of action. But if it's a high-waisted thing with long legs, then you've got something else. Go to some extremes to change what would be considered "normal" placement of proportions on the body. Unless you are going to be doing "lifelike" animation, you should be getting into this offbeat type of thing. I think you can get away with all kinds of exaggerations. People will accept your "giraffe walk" because they don't know the basis for the movements. Most animated animals are human beings in animal skins.

NANCY BEIMAN: I'd like to talk to you about inanimate objects. If you are caricaturing your backgrounds and they are *not* moving, but one "inanimate object" is moving in the foreground, would it have a different design quality from the rest?

T. HEE: I think I would give them the same degree of caricature, so that they would be related to one another. The one doing all the activity looks like everyone else but acts differently. If it looks different from the articles on the wall, there will be no correlation between the objects in the scene. There should be a marriage between the objects in the background and foreground.

NANCY BEIMAN: Cartoon characters tend to be stereotypes. Pretty girl. Handsome hero. Characters that are going to be nice, "look" nice.

T. HEE: Well, designs come from an expression of the character. It can't be pinned down. "All villains have to be big and strong." I don't think so. I think they are stereotypes. The easiest way out is to make them big and mean.

There are degrees of nicety and villainy that you can play with. Once I was working with Frank Capra. He and his associate, Joe Sisten, were talking about a villainous character. They said you could not really laugh at a villain unless you liked him. So what they tried to do was have a bit of action happen to the villain that… made him seem a human being, not all bad. Then, whatever he did after that, you could laugh at… If you make him all bad and show no aspect of weakness or likeability, then you've got a dead character….

Caricature of Walt Disney (circa 1940) by T. Hee. (Nancy Beiman collection)

Of course, if you have all funny villains, you wind up with Dom DeLuise characters, a Mel Brooks picture. There have to be gradations of villainy and heroics.

I think that we are intrigued by villainy. The villains are usually the important people in the picture. They make drama happen. If you don't have drama, you don't have much of a story.

You get to know the characters and realize who they are by spelling out their characters, a little bit at a time, by their actions. Charlie Chaplin was the guy who was trapped with a villain in a snowbound cabin in THE GOLD RUSH. The villain fantasizes about Charlie turning into a chicken. He was at risk of being decimated and done away with. He was the hero dealing with this crazy madman.

NANCY BEIMAN: The villain in that picture wasn't really that mean.

T. HEE: *But he could be at any minute!*

NANCY BEIMAN: Chaplin was also the guy who had a millionaire friend who liked him when he was drunk but couldn't stand him when he was sober.

T. HEE: You cannot say, "This is what makes a villain; this is what makes a hero!" There are all kinds of gradations!

T. Hee at Cal Arts, early 1980s. Caricature by Ralph Eggleston; photograph by David Fulp. (Reproduced by permission of David Fulp.)

Appendix 3: Interview with Ken Anderson[*]

Ken Anderson worked in story and development on many Disney features. His art direction credits include FANTASIA, ONE HUNDRED AND ONE DALMATIANS, THE SWORD IN THE STONE, THE JUNGLE BOOK, and THE RESCUERS.

NANCY BEIMAN: Ken O'Connor's been bringing in a lot of stuff that you did. You seem to have done practically everything! My main questions will be about story, since we don't have a lot of information on how to recognize when a story has good potential for animation.

KEN ANDERSON: You don't mind if I ramble a little bit?

NANCY BEIMAN: No.

KEN ANDERSON: In the last 15 or 20 years, the emphasis has been [in the right place] on animation. There is a tendency to specialize. [But] there is no reason why a good animator can't also be a good story man. I have to go back to the beginning to make my point a little more clear. We were all animators. We were interested in animation as an art form and also as a way of expressing ourselves. And we were, or are, more or less, all frustrated actors. We *feel* acting, and we also *feel* art and design, and try to put that over [in the films]. Everyone of the animators in the early days was also an "idea man." Some of the animators were more interested in telling stories than others were. I believe that everyone who is involved in animation should also be involved in story. Which is what intrigues me with your question; it's a bit unusual, because it seems to me that that [ability] has been lost sight of in the industry.

There is no way that I've ever heard of that is a "sure thing" in constructing a story. But there are a few guidelines that I learned, not things that I knew instinctively. I had to learn them through experience.

---

[*] by Nancy Beiman (edited), © 1979, 2006 by Nancy Beiman.

If you are considering making an animated feature, you must remember that the animation medium is predominately a pantomime medium. The most important thing in it is body language and expressiveness, put over by the way the characters move. This should not be overwhelmed by an excess of dialogue. The moment that this happens, you have an audio, or radio, medium, and you really don't need the pantomimic gestures to put it over. The virtue of the medium as we know it today is that it is worldwide. Pantomime is understood everywhere, even though certain little gestures, in certain countries, mean the opposite. The basic movements of the human body—recoiling in fear, laughter, and so on—are all recognized universally, so pantomime has a very broad base of communication.

Ken Anderson and friend. (Reproduced by permission of Cyndy Bohanovsky.)

Walt said something that stuck in our minds. He said, "You don't write a Disney feature. Building a Disney feature is a lot like building a building, with building blocks. Our building blocks would be 'personalities'." It would be better for our purposes if those personalities were abrasive, or if there was some sort of conflict between the protagonist and the antagonist, because this gives you more room for entertainment and communication. In the early days, we discovered that a true story line or "clothesline" for an animated feature would work best if the story line was extremely simple. If you could go from A to Z in as simple a direction as possible, you could hang more entertainment on that simple story line. It is very easy to explain why "this" problem created "that" problem and then "that" problem all built and led, in consecutive order, to a finish. The extraneous things that were least entertaining and least helpful to the development of the story line would be gotten rid of. The better ones, we'd keep.

NANCY BEIMAN: Did you write the treatment first?

KEN ANDERSON: Oh yes. Your treatment—it's not a script, because we don't get too involved with dialogue, we just get involved in the "clothesline."

We weren't trying to pass ourselves off as writers. We were writing a theme. If we can hang sequences on the clothesline, it's going to work. Simple stories are *defined.* This is the [type of story] that you should try to have. But it's not easy to come by.

NANCY BEIMAN: Nearly all animated films—I can think of very few exceptions—have been made from children's books. There is a lot of very good fantasy being written for adults. Has there ever been any attempt to develop something like that and would there be a potential for this type of story?

KEN ANDERSON: Yes, I think so. I'm sure there are many doors to be opened that can be opened. But we didn't consider SNOW WHITE AND THE SEVEN DWARFS to be a child's fantasy. Adults then weren't so afraid to be associated with things that children liked. During the past 20 years, it seems that adults before the age of 50 don't want to be associated in any way with something that is perceived as "childish," and after 50, there's no hope!

NANCY BEIMAN: Movies have become more diversified instead of appealing to a family audience.

I really would love to know how you go about taking a story sketch and breaking it down into camera angles. How do you know when one shot is going to work better than another?

KEN ANDERSON: I think that in order to plan the story sketch, you have to be primarily an animator, whether you are actually going to animate the scene or not; unless it is a purely scenic shot where the animation is incidental, where there's some lovely establishing mood that has to be established. Otherwise you can't create something in story sketch if you are not thinking of animation. There is an ideal way, I think, of working. It involves thumbnailing *entire pictures.* I would go through breaking down sequences and scenes, and how they would be animated. I'd do my own version of how the dialogue and staging would work best for particular actions. Thumbnails have to coordinate sound, picture, dialogue, and you have to be able to decide whether the script is useful. Nine times out of ten an animated feature cannot be written. It has to be visualized. The thumbnails could even be shot and timed. We would add scratch dialogue. And this became a "Bible." We'd do the whole picture, not just sequence by sequence. Each animator would be given a copy of this book [of thumbnails] for the whole picture before he came onto it. The animator would say, "I have a better way of doing this," and could substitute his own way of what the thumbnail action should be. Everyone should build the building if they can, and if theirs was better, it would become the version that was used.

NANCY BEIMAN: I sometimes have trouble distinguishing the thumbnails from story sketches. You use several different drawings for a scene where the storyboard might use only one.

KEN ANDERSON: It depends on who is doing the story sketch. In this case, it was Bill Peet.... He had a feeling for putting over scenes, too. Everything here is a re-evaluation. In most cases, there was no prior storyboard sketch for them. There was just writing. Bill's story sketches were undoubtedly a help.

NANCY BEIMAN: Would you work with inspirational drawings?

KEN ANDERSON: That's right. I also did some of them, and some of the story-boards, though more of those were done by Bill Peet. I took the story-boards and developed them a step further.

NANCY BEIMAN: So your cutting is determined by motion?

KEN ANDERSON: Yes, by putting over the idea of motion. I would make many, many sketches [for each scene in the sequence]. It wasn't just blind searching, because the minute you know what your story situation is, what you are trying to put over, you begin to have preferences: should it be real close, long shots, should you be looking down or up? Every part of your experience is used to interpret that particular instant of movement.

There are all sorts of reasons for angles—it might be a low angle, if the viewpoint is Jiminy Cricket's. There are reasons for moving the camera. You maintain a mood with the camera angle and the station point.

NANCY BEIMAN: Were you influenced by live-action directors?

KEN ANDERSON: Absolutely. I used to go to the movies *all* the time and make sketches and drawings of how they put over certain things, [thumb-nails of] staging in live-action pictures. Walt got hold of that and one day, we began to have classes on this very thing, cutting, staging, and storytelling with light. All the good pictures communicated with the audience. Today, I find many pictures that have confused cutting—too fast, or with people going in different directions. They do that on pur-pose. They don't want you to know what's going on. They really don't want you to catch up with them until they can surprise you with the ending. It's a different way to put things over than my training.

NANCY BEIMAN: Have you ever tried to do this sort of cutting in animation?

KEN ANDERSON: Sure. I think there's no holds barred for anything that you can do to intrigue and entertain an audience. Obviously the new film held my attention, or I wouldn't be talking about it. It was just hard to fol-low. We were afraid that if we did not let the audience know very clearly what story point we were trying to make, we could lose them for maybe a whole sequence.

NANCY BEIMAN: Is there a tendency to be a little over-obvious in the staging of animated cartoons?

KEN ANDERSON: I think so. Almost so that it becomes boring. But I think that no one is really equipped to do the cutting that is being done today, unless they understand the staging that we were talking about earlier which is very basic. If you understand how to communicate, then you can deviate from it in the same way that knowing the scales on the piano enables you to play a complex piece of music. You can bang on a piano and make a lot of sounds that may not have any relevance to the people who are listening to you.

NANCY BEIMAN: You were sole character designer on the later Disney pictures. I notice in the thirties and forties, character designs seemed to be more of a group effort. Do you get better results when you have a group of people to bounce ideas off of?

KEN ANDERSON: Oh yeah. From the very beginning, every one of us over-lapped into everything on the picture. It was a real delight. Everyone was involved in learning all the other facets of the production. Then you gravitated toward whatever your strengths were. Frank Thomas never gave up! He was a story man, an animator; he was interested in background painting and everything else, which is the way it was supposed to be. Ollie [Johnston] was the same. And I never got over animating, either! We interacted in every way. And some of us, because of the immensity of the project, found we had to level on something, because if you kept bouncing around you'd never get anything done. I found that I liked to level on the overall picture, the characters, and the story situations. I gravitated on my own accord to the story department. I liked mood and locale also. But I kept animating scenes on my own, just so I wouldn't forget how!

The day is coming when any person can make a film all by himself. And that is the optimum. But then if you have many artists, as in the great ateliers, each making their own painting or sculpture, the atmosphere is very invigorating. Many animators could work in one studio on their own projects. Think of the variety of films that will occur!

When writing for animation, if any one of us wrote the lines, and we knew which actor was going to play the part, we'd say, "This is what we want but we want it to come out of *you*. If you see a better way to say it, you should build on it." That is part of the building block process I referred to earlier. There's another thing to take from Walt: making a feature, to him, was like planting a seed. You want to have a plant with one beautiful bloom. You plant the seed and fertilize it, and prune it to make sure that the strength is not going to the wrong buds. You allow one beautiful bud to bloom, and you've got your feature picture. But you don't stand around and admire it; you plant another seed.

NANCY BEIMAN: What sort of problems would be posed by work in short films as opposed to features?

KEN ANDERSON: The short film doesn't need to hold a person's attention for a long time, so you can get away with a lot more; be a little offhand, less concerned with what is going to happen in subsequent sequences. It's a comparatively short piece of film, and so its problems are extremely simplified. You can hang a short film on one character. You don't necessarily need two or three, although it's better to have at least one foil.

NANCY BEIMAN: Well, the advantage is that you don't have to make your point quickly in a feature. The disadvantage of a short is that you have to make your point in six minutes or less.

KEN ANDERSON: That's true. It works both ways. You can concern yourself, if it is a musical short, primarily with entertainment. Some of the earliest Disney shorts were nothing more than movement to music.

NANCY BEIMAN: If you have a good story, how do you make a presentation out of it? Do you work your story sketch up immediately from thumbnails?

KEN ANDERSON: First of all, I will probably start visualizing the characters, making drawings, so that I will have something to make little thumbnails from. It's almost the same as writing a book. But you can't write a story without characters, and you can't get characters without the story! You have to have something to illustrate, and so I start fooling around with the characters. They keep changing—they keep getting better, as the story develops.

NANCY BEIMAN: Would you do a script treatment of the story after you had actually started drawing characters, or would you do them at the same time?

KEN ANDERSON: My script treatment would probably be done more or less coincidentally with the characters. Each one leads the other. As you find a simplified version that you are likely to work with, you are likely to see a flowering of certain portions of it. This gives you an impetus to move on to something else. One thing takes precedence for a while, then the other catches up, and so you finally arrive [at a finished story with characters set]. The written form is just a nice simplified version of a treatment. You should make it clear and very simple, so that your story evolves through the relationship of the characters. Each entertainment situation will help the story progress.

NANCY BEIMAN: Do you occasionally find the story going in a different direction when you start doing your thumbnails?

KEN ANDERSON: It certainly has happened.

NANCY BEIMAN: Your script is not the final word?

KEN ANDERSON: Oh, no. The chances are that the script will be superseded by storyboard, to the extent that when you get through, your original writer may not recognize the story that has turned into something quite different from what you started with. This is not so much an intention as a development. It grows so far away from the original that it demands new writing. The story JEREMIAH became LADY AND THE TRAMP.

NANCY BEIMAN: Do you like to write original material as opposed to adapting something that has already been written?

KEN ANDERSON: I think that nowadays, you don't have to rely on a presold story to a presold audience. If you have a great story, if you can get it produced and distributed, you would easily succeed. Animated films can be made using a wholly different way to reach the audiences than they used in the past. I sure hope that this happens. I don't think we are at the "end."

NANCY BEIMAN: The color in modern films tends to be more garish than formerly. Older films used more muted tones. Violent colors are appropriate for a garish character like Medusa, but every character seems to be that way nowadays. Sometimes, the characters do not seem to fit with the backgrounds.

KEN ANDERSON: In ONE HUNDRED AND ONE DALMATIANS, everyone suggested using muted grays on the backgrounds since this film took place in England. England is not a country that is associated with garish colors, considering the weather that they have. I found that [the limited palette] was a strength; it brought us full circle to SNOW WHITE AND THE SEVEN DWARFS, which had been designed in earth colors. BAMBI looked as good as it did because of the art of Tyrus Wong. Ty had a beautiful way of emphasizing a highlight in a forest and let it melt off into color tones, so that you felt you were seeing a whole scene where only a part of it was actually painted.

Somebody has to have control over the color and style of each picture. Eyvind Earle's personal style of painting had a tremendous influence on SLEEPING BEAUTY; the characters were influenced by the backgrounds which were done first, with the strange angular design, and the characters came along later. And there was Mary Blair, who was just a natural colorist. Earle came to his color combinations mathematically.

NANCY BEIMAN: In character design, is it good to have a "studio style" or to keep experimenting?

KEN ANDERSON: Inherently, for your own growth, and for the growth of the medium, it's wise to keep experimenting. We never tried to come up with a "style." It's simply that certain shapes and forms are easier to move. Certain shapes make it easier to get expressions.

NANCY BEIMAN: What sort of reference do you use for character design? What if you were designing a mythological creature that you could not see in a zoo?

KEN ANDERSON: I research everything I can. For an actual creature, I get every photograph or book that I can find. I immerse myself in as much knowledge of the creature as I can, make it a part of me. Then I decide that some things have to adapt, but I can make the adaptations based on what I know. The material leaves me better prepared to come up with something new. For mythological creatures: in the back of my mind, I would think of an actor (say, Wallace Beery) when designing a particular dragon. So I was drawing dragons with that feeling of Wallace Beery. Shere Khan, the tiger in the original THE JUNGLE BOOK was a terrifying menace. He doesn't appear until the last two sequences of the picture. We had to see why everyone else was afraid of him. I was stymied but had to come back with something. I thought of Basil Rathbone, but he was no longer around even at this time, so I used him as an inspiration. Shere Khan didn't even have to show up, he just *was*. I didn't try to draw him to look like a caricature of Basil Rathbone but to have that quality of high-and-mightiness, so that his appearance told you that he was this kind of creature. Walt looked at the drawings and said, "Oh, I know who that is, that's George Sanders." Milt Kahl, who loved it, developed the design much further but they were based on the sketches I did. So this is an example of a design that was based on a well-known person.

The vultures in [THE JUNGLE BOOK] were based on some of the animators! They wound up as the Beatles, but at the start, they were caricatures of the animation crew. Many times you are in danger of falling into the trap of caricaturing an actor or actress. What you really should do is create a new character that has the actors' attributes that help put over your story point. You never know where anything that influenced you is going to show up. And it will be subconscious, unless you are trying to do a conscious imitation of the style.

NANCY BEIMAN: How much do your character designs change by the time they reach the screen?

KEN ANDERSON: Generally, I'd say that they were pretty much right on. Most of the animators would better, or strengthen, the designs. But nobody ever gave anyone a command to stay right on that same model. We all believed Walt's tenet, which was "Everyone who has an input [into the film] must feel free to keep in-putting anything they can." If some animator made arbitrary changes, they would have to be prepared to defend it, explain why it was better. If they made changes, it was because they were generally stronger.

The thing I would like to impress you all with is this: we didn't have anyone to talk to. We had to learn all of this the hard way. *Nobody knew.*

Animation Preproduction Glossary

action model: a series of poses that show the typical movements and expressions of an animated character. These might be assembled from storyboard drawings to serve as a guide for the final character design.

animatic: digitized storyboards that include simple animation, camera moves, or special effects, edited and precisely timed to a dialogue and/or music track. Animated films are edited in *preproduction* and not *in postproduction* as live-action films are.

animation: an art form that brings life to inanimate objects. See also *Stop Motion, Hybrid Animation,* and *CGI.*

art director: the designer of the production. The art director in an animated film will create settings, color palettes, lighting, character, and prop styles and may also design *layouts.*

atmospheric sketches: experimental color sketches depicting moods or settings that may be used in the film.

barsheet: a printed aid to the director indicating footage and frame counts with space to write music and sound cues beneath. They are still used in commercials to time the film and *slug* dialogue and music tracks. They are nearly identical to the timeline in computer animation programs, which they inspired.

beat: see *Story Beat.*

beat boards: storyboards showing only the main story points and major action of the picture; a visual *outline* of the story.

"Bible": a pictorial guide to all aspects of the characters, props, and backgrounds. Television animation "Bibles" contain final clean model sheets for all characters, props, and backgrounds, brief story outlines, and written descriptions of the characters' personalities and attitudes. Feature "Bibles" may consist of reference and inspirational art assembled as style guides for character designers and layout artists. In television production, a "Bible" is also known as a *model pack.*

blue sky: early stage of development where any idea is acceptable.

board, boarding: drawing storyboards for a film or sequence of a film; used as a verb (e.g., "I'm still *boarding* Sequence 6, then I must *board* Sequence 7"). See also *storyboard.*

boil, boiling: inconsistently applied color that moves independently of character or background motion. A color may *boil* inside a character's outline for an artistic effect in hand-drawn animation.

budget (v.): in *hybrid animation,* the animation component is considered a "special effect" shot. Production managers *budget* the probable cost of producing and compositing the animation with live action in each shot before storyboards are *finaled* (finished).

CGI: computer-generated imagery, commonly referred to as "3D animation," although computer programs are also used for *2D* animation.

cheats, cheating: a technique that allows a stylized or graphic design to appear to move in three-dimensional spaces. Mickey Mouse's ears never turn but are *cheated* as his body moves (e.g., "*Cheat* the hair part as her head turns"). *Cheats* are not meant to be seen by the viewer. See also *Morph.*

clean: see *Tight.*

clean up (v.): the act of standardizing the appearance of an animation drawing or removing extraneous elements from a film image.

cleanups: model sheets, background, layout, or animation drawings that have had their line quality standardized and rough construction details removed.

color keys: copies of panel(s) from the storyboard with characters and backgrounds rendered in color to set the palette, mood, and lighting for each sequence.

color models: standardized color for animated characters and props. Each character may have several color models depicting its appearance at different times of day, changes of outfit or mood, or in changing seasons.

color script: a series of small *color keys* in a timeline showing all changes in the color palettes from the first sequence of the film to the last.

construction model: a simple breakdown of a character design into its component shapes. It enables an artist to move and judge proportions on an imaginary figure in two- or three-dimensional space.

crew: the artists working on an animation production. A *story crew* works on storyboard, character design, and development.

dope sheet: see *Exposure Sheet.*

evolution: in animation, the refinement and simplification of a character design if storyboard or test animation indicates areas for improvement. Hand-drawn and CGI figures may both evolve during preproduction.

exposure sheet: a printed or digital graph depicting each frame of a scene, with specific layers assigned for animation. It also contains action and dialogue columns for timing and track breakdown. They are also known as *dope sheets.*

finaled: finished, approved, or *locked.* In *hybrid animation*, the animation boards will be *finaled* before the live-action shoot starts.

first pass: the initial presentation of the storyboard, characters, or production design ideas to an audience. It is usually experimental and always gets reworked.

flop: to reverse the staging on a storyboard drawing; to mirror the action without making other changes in staging. *Flopping* a drawing is not the same as *turning it over.*

frame: the fixed border of the screen or monitor; a set area where all animated action takes place. Or, an individual photograph from a strip of motion picture film. In storyboarding: synonymous with *Panel*.

handout: a storyboard, animation, or design assignment.

head of story: a lead storyboard artist similar to an assistant director on a live-action picture. He or she will develop the story and *beat boards* with the writers and directors, then assign story *handouts* to the *crew*. The Head of Story answers story questions that arise, keeps track of the continuity and pacing of the film, and reviews the storyboards before they are presented to the directors. Also sometimes known as *Story Head*.

hybrid animation: a combination of live-action and CGI-animated characters in the same movie. Hybrid animation storyboards blend animation and live-action board styles, with fewer cuts and fewer panels than typical for animated films. Scenes will be edited from long takes, live-action style, rather than pretimed as in animation. (See Chris Bailey's description in Chapter 2.)

lay down, laid down: timing dialogue, music, or effects to a soundtrack. See also *Slugging*.

layouts: the animated "stage." Layout develops from storyboard and includes backgrounds, camera angles and apertures, props, overlays, and rough character poses for each scene as a guide for the animators and background painters.

leica reel: a term originating in the Walt Disney Studio, which invented it. Storyboards shot and timed to dialogue and music. This is how animated film is edited. See also *Animatic*.

linetest: see *Pencil Test*.

locked down, locked: finished, without the possibility of further change.

log line: a single sentence that describes the point of the story.

maquette: in French, a model or mock-up. In animation, a three-dimensional sculpture of a character design. They may be *practical* (actual) or digital. Maquettes enable artists to view a design in the round. They are used as drawing aids in hand-drawn animation and as a way to see CGI character designs from all angles before they are modeled in the computer. Maquettes are also constructed for stop motion puppet films. After the modeling and rigging are finished, they are used to design the character lighting in *setups* for CGI and hand-drawn films.

master background: the animated equivalent of a live-action master shot. It establishes the setting, lighting, and scale of a sequence but may not be an actual production background.

model pack: see *"Bible."*

model sheet: a guide for the appearance and construction of an animated character or prop. Model sheets enable different artists to create the illusion of one performance by standardizing the character's appearance and suggesting typical actions. See also *Rough Models, On Model, Off Model, Action Model*, and *Cleanups*.

morph, morphing: a change in attitude or motion that is accomplished by modifying the character's entire design and "growing" it into the next pose. This, unlike a *cheat*, is usually visible to the viewer.

off model: character appearance that does not conform to the *model sheet*. Normal distortion is considered *on model*.

on model: character appearance that conforms to the *model sheet*.

outline: a brief written description of the story in a few paragraphs. Outlines do not include dialogue or scene indications.

panel: an individual storyboard, synonymous with *frame*.

pencil mileage: highly detailed and rendered artwork; or, a difficult design.

pencil test: hand-drawn animation that is shot against *layouts* and used to refine timing and action before coloring and finishing the film. (Also known as *linetest*.)

pickup: a line of dialogue that is recorded after the original session to incorporate script changes; or, a partial retake of a line.

pitch, pitching: the presentation of artwork to an audience in real time, with running commentary by the artist. *Pitching the boards* provides instant feedback on the *readability* of the story and the artwork.

placeholder: a character design that is used for *rough boards* before its final appearance has been standardized. Placeholders (stuffed animals "standing in" for animated characters) are also used in *hybrid animation*.

plus-ing: a creative interpretation or addition that improves the original story or design.

pop, pop It: a graphic shorthand used to turn a character in space without actual three-dimensional movements. If you are asked to *pop* something, the views will change abruptly with no in-between poses. Many characters will *pop* from three-quarter views to full face or profile. Persistence of vision creates the illusion of smooth motion.

pop through: blocking the animation camera and timing in a stop motion film by filming only the big "key poses" without the intermediate frames. It is similar to a *pose test* in hand-drawn or computer animation.

pose test: blocking the animation timing and acting by shooting or digitizing only the main key and breakdown poses without the in-betweens.

post-production: in animation, combining pre-existing visual and audio elements to create a finished picture. Scoring, sound mixing, visual and audio effects, compositing, and final editing are all done *in post* after *production* has finished. Live action and hybrid films are edited in postproduction.

preproduction: the conception, planning, and development of a film's story and characters. In animation, character design, storyboard, rough edit, workbook, art direction, concept art, and production design are all completed in *preproduction*. Preproduction artwork does not appear in the finished film.

presentation boards: highly rendered storyboards with detailed tonal work on characters and backgrounds; finished illustration rather than roughs. They may include a lot of *pencil mileage*.

previsuals, previz: the fourth-dimensional interpretation of a three-dimensional storyboard. *Previz* is done after storyboard and before animation. The previz artist moves the camera through scenes blocking camera moves and character actions in real time using roughly modeled CGI *placeholders*. Previz is a three-dimensional version of *workbook*.

production: creation of artwork that appears in the finished film. This includes CGI models and rigs, dialogue and music, rough and final animation, layouts, backgrounds, and composited color scenes.

push it, pushing: exaggeration of a design, character pose, or story point.

readability: character designs, action, or storyboards that are staged in clear and understandable fashion are said to *read* well. Boards that do not read well are generally *turned over*. Story points and characters that lack *readability* are generally done over.

rough boards: quickly drawn storyboards with basic tonal values designed only to tell the story. They may use *placeholder* characters that are not *on model*.

rough models: *model sheets* that include standardized *construction models, action models,* and comparative sizes for the final design of the characters but do not include *cleanups*. The line quality will vary, and details may not be finalized. Rough model sheets are used by animators to maintain the consistency of the character's construction in hand-drawn film. They also enable a CGI or puppet modeler to accurately reproduce the design in three dimensions.

rough pass: live-action scenes for a *hybrid animation* film that are shot with a stuffed animal or another three-dimensional *placeholder* as a "stand in" for an animated character. The animation is then composited with the actors and the stuffed animal is digitally removed.

roughs: drawings that retain construction lines and contain variable line quality are referred to as roughs. These may be retained in the final project, sometimes in conjunction with *boiling* color. See also *Cleanups*.

scratch track: a soundtrack that is not the final one for the picture. Scratch dialogue and music may be used as *placeholders* to time *story reels* and *animatics*. The composer uses the tempo and mood of the scratch track as a "script" for the final soundtrack.

screen ratio: the proportions of the screen where the finished project will be viewed. Storyboard panels can be designed to specific screen ratios, such as widescreen or Academy standard. *All storyboard panels in a production will have the same screen ratio.*

script: A modular description of action, locations and props, sound effects, and final dialogue for every scene in a film. Character dialogue is labeled by name and written out as *sides*, or sections, so that the actors can record dialogue in small sections and create *pickups* where needed. Animated films can develop from scripts (*Script-driven*) or develop on the storyboard using outlines or treatments (*board-driven*). Settings and action are not described in great detail in animation scripts, since they will be created by the production designer and the storyboard artists before the script is finalized. Animated scripts are often rewritten to incorporate changes made on the storyboard.

sequence: a series of consecutive scenes related by story point. They may or may not take place in the same location. Sequences are like chapters in a film.

setup: a color test in which *color models* and props are placed over a background to check the *readability* and contrast. They may be done in 3D using digital renderings of character art before texturing is completed.

sides: scripted dialogue, labeled by character name and formatted with indentations for easy reference by the actor during a recording session.

slugging: indicating the timing for each storyboard panel prior to creating an *animatic*; also, determining where dialogue and sound effects will appear. Formerly, this was done on *bar sheets* or *exposure sheets*. Slugging is now sometimes done directly in animation programs that create the animatics as the storyboards are drawn.

stop motion: animation created by moving a jointed puppet or other object one frame at a time and photographing the movement in (very slow) real time. It is the only true three-dimensional animation.

story beat: A major change in plot or action; a turning point.

storyboards: (*n*) A visual script for a motion picture. In animation, a storyboard is a guide for character performance, action, editing, and staging for the finished picture. [*Storyboard, Storyboarding, Board, Boarding* (*v.*) The act of storyboarding a motion picture.]

story head: see *Head of Story.*

sweatbox: screening the *animatic* or animation for a critical audience. The Walt Disney Studio was the first to sweatbox pencil tests and story reels, and this is now a common industry practice.

thumbnails: rough drawings or sketches, usually very small in size. [*Thumbnail* (*v.*) Illustrating a story point with small, sketchy drawings to determine staging.]

tied down: see *Tying Down.*

tight: very clean and close to the final model design; the opposite of *rough.*

treatment: a written description of the story in short-story form. It can be several pages long and is more developed than the *outline.* A treatment will include subplots and may include rough dialogue, but does not include scene indications like a *script.*

turnover session: a review session where directors and story artists make changes to the boards and story in real time after a pitch. Panels that are discarded or changed are literally turned over, so that the blank back of the panel faces the audience. Panels may also be *flopped* during the turnover session. Changes can also be drawn on self-stick notes placed over the panels.

tweak: a minor change or improvement to nearly finished work.

two-dimensional (2D) animation: a common term for hand-drawn animation. It will also include various computer-graphic programs, cut-paper, sand animation, painting on glass, and other techniques lacking "three-dimensional" appearance.

tying down: finalizing, finishing, or standardizing a character model, storyboard sequence, or animated scene. After rough art is completed and approved, you will be asked to *tie it down.* See also *Locked Down.*

universe: a consistent design element or technique that relates animated characters to one another and to the props and backgrounds, providing unification for an imaginary world.

up on reels: storyboards assembled and timed on film or digital media with soundtrack. This may be a *scratch track* produced for an *animatic* (e.g., "Sequences 1 through 5 are *up on reels,* and we're still *boarding* Sequence 6"). This term is still used even though we no longer have film or reels!

voice over: 1. The voice of an offscreen narrator accompanying onscreen images. 2. An onscreen character's voice heard without lip synch. Voice over is often used to represent a character's inner thoughts.

wild track (also known as a walla track): sound recorded without a script, such as murmurs, chatter, exclamations, sound effects, or animal noises. These are usually added to the track in postproduction.

workbook: an intermediate stage between *storyboard* and *layout* in which camera moves are designed to work with *rough* feature boards. Workbook drawings are thumbnails for cinematic staging. Camera moves are planned in advance of layout, and cutting is refined.

wrap (n.): the end of the postproduction and completion of the final film. "*It's a Wrap.*"

Index